Land in Libraries

Land in Libraries
Toward a Materialist Conception of Education

Edited by
Lydia Zvyagintseva and Mary Greenshields

Library Juice Press
Sacramento, CA

Copyright 2023

Published in 2023 by Library Juice Press.

Litwin Books
PO Box 188784
Sacramento, CA 95818

http://litwinbooks.com/

This book is printed on acid-free paper.

Publisher's Cataloging in Publication
Names: Zvyagintseva, Lydia, editor. | Greenshields, Mary, editor.
Title: Land in libraries : toward a materialist conception of education / Lydia Zvyagintseva and Mary Greenshields, editors.
Description: Sacramento, CA : Library Juice Press, 2023. | Includes bibliographical references and index.
Identifiers: LCCN 2023938473 | ISBN 9781634001397 (acid-free paper)
Subjects: LCSH: Land tenure. | Social justice and education. | Libraries – History. | Library science – Social aspects. | Library science – Political aspects.
Classification: LCC Z679 L36 2023 | DDC 027--dc23
LC record available at https://lccn.loc.gov/2023938473

To everyone who pursues knowledge and seeks to make a contribution to the LIS and Archives field, even when it is not recognized in your local environment, even when it is challenging, even when you are not certain where the work might take you. You are not alone.

Contents

ix	Acknowledgements
1	**Introduction** *Lydia Zvyagintseva*
13	**Civilizing, Separating, and Organizing** The Geographic Influence on Nineteenth Century Western Libraries *Andrew Weymouth*
37	**Towards a Spirit of Place in Library Architecture** *Gregory Whistance-Smith*
63	**Making Place, Placing Makers** Connecting history, memory, and land by Indigenizing New Hampshire Public Library Local History Collections *Laura Marie Judge and Jedidiah Crook*
95	**Rooting Research** A Critical Examination of Incorporating Land-Based Education in Universities' Research Commons *Courtney S. Nomiyama and Truc Ho*
123	**Bringing the Land into the Library** Land Acknowledgements in an Academic Library *Ashley Edwards, Dr. Julia Lane, Dr. Alix Shield, and Dal Sohal*
143	**Downstream** *Danielle Marie Bitz*
167	**Refusing Growth** Cloud Technology, Climate Change, and the Future of Libraries and Archives *Ariel Hahn*
187	About the Contributors
191	Index

Acknowledgements

This collection would not be possible without the labour of the authors, reviewers, and consultants who helped us steward this knowledge at every step of the way. Our sincerest apologies if we may have missed anyone in the following list:

Alexandra Alisauskas
Holly Arnason
Tanya Ball
Joel Blechinger
Kate Cawthorn
Matthew Davis
Céline Gareau-Brennan
Matt Huculak
Christian Isbister
Laura Koltutsky
Larry Laliberte

Kayla Lar-Son
Kirk MacLeod
Lorisia MacLeod
Amanda Oliver
Bethany Paul
Sarah Polkinghorne
Sam Popowich
Alexander Stewart
Eamon Tewell
Carrie Wade

Some individuals to whom we are indebted took on multiple roles over the course of this project and, for that, we are grateful. Thank you to our friends and families for supporting us. Thank you to colleagues and new collaborators whom we met over the past couple of years, who offered perspective, advice, and patience in challenging times. Thank you as well to Library Juice Press for giving us the freedom to approach this work in our own way.

Introduction

Lydia Zvyagintseva

To talk about land in libraries seems incongruous, even to this day. "Explain, please. What does that mean?" says my doctor, when I casually mention that I am working on this collection as she checks my blood pressure. She's right, of course. What *does* it mean? "Oh, you know," I say, "it's about colonialism and knowledge." Just some light topics, in other words. She nods, half-accepting my answer, probably thinking she's got a weird one on her patient list.

But the question of land persists in my mind as the months pass. It remains from the idea of working on a book, to the collaboration that begins as a stroll along the Oldman River, to the call for chapters, to working with authors and reviewers. From the Morrill Act of 1862 (Sorber, 2018) to the fact that Canadian universities continue to hold a lot of land across the provinces (Bisby, 2019; Bula 2017; CBC News, 2011; University of Guelph, n.d.; University of Toronto, n.d.), the theory feels a little too real in the present moment. History never faded; it is embedded in our learning organizations in North America to this day. Colonialism structures our lives. Its consequences are everywhere. I begin to think about these learning institutions *as* capital, especially as they train, foster, and reward individuals to critique and challenge that very idea. I trust that, even if it feels big and confusing, it must be a sign that there is something there worth investigating.

Urgency and Purpose

We began this book with the assumption that the question of land is largely absent in memory institutions like libraries, archives, and museums. In my professional and academic experience, they appear ahistorical, atheoretical, and landless in their understanding of themselves, their work, and their impact on people. In his chapter, "Towards a Spirit of Place in Library Architecture," Greg Whistance-Smith reminds us that all buildings "are constructed *somewhere*," but that connection to place, and more specifically to the land, as a historical, political, and social meaning, felt marginal in my experience. Perhaps it was me. Maybe I didn't pay enough attention to the history of Scarborough or to the growth of Edmonton as reflected in its public and academic libraries. But where were the Indigenous peoples in that history and operations?

This lack of visible Indigeneity is changing across Canada, as libraries–both public and academic–are increasingly creating Indigenous spaces, including rooms and buildings (Calgary Public Library, n.d.; Canadian Architect, 2022; Dalhousie University, n.d.; University of Toronto Mississauga, n.d.; University of Toronto Scarborough, n.d.). For example, after a multi-year renovation, the central branch of the Edmonton Public Library reopened in 2020. The new Milner Library houses PÎYÊSÎW WÂSKÂHIKAN (Thunderbird House), a dedicated Indigenous space built for ceremony and gatherings (Edmonton Public Library, 2022). Working with local Elders and Knowledge Carriers as well as Indigenous organizations, the library offers programs and services to Indigenous and non-Indigenous peoples in this space. Activities at PÎYÊSÎW WÂSKÂHIKAN include language programming, cultural and land-based teachings, and intergenerational programming. Spaces like these are important in learning organizations like public and academic libraries because they connect the architectural design and the materials used to the land, and most importantly, to the people who teach and learn in them, in order to demonstrate that Indigenous ways of knowing and being are valued.

Thus, with this imperfect effort, we seek to contribute to the growing body of work on libraries, decolonization, and climate change through writing that connects theory and practice. We were interested in both material as well as conceptual perspectives on land in information work. More importantly, we were looking to work with others who centered land as a foundational category underpinning social relations, as a necessity for the function and reproduction of capitalism, and as a place where we work and learn together. Fundamentally, our key assumption was that we all live on the land and how we live in relation to the land matters to how we understand ourselves as individuals and society.

This was perhaps an audacious goal to set, and we knew that some might understand our call while others may be just as confused as my doctor. As we began working with authors and reviewers, we were also keenly aware of the challenge of representation. We knew that Indigenous women librarians and archivists were some of the most over-asked and under-compensated, often precariously employed, professionals. Therefore, soliciting chapters was a delicate matter. We were aware of who has the capacity to write about such topics—that is, employed professionals in the academic environment with benefits, freedom, time, and practice to contribute to such a collection. This is not always the case, as we were thrilled to support the work of early-career librarians. We knew that readers would look critically at the collection as a whole and that we could not always live up to every expectation of the reader.

We were also aware that this collection would be missing the voices of archivists and museum professionals. For various reasons, there is no chapter discussing land in the archives specifically, but we leave that as a goal for subsequent work on this topic. Perhaps the ideas explored here will resonate with you, and you will take up the call to continue this line of inquiry.

Process

Figure 1 Tree trunk cut down by beavers, showing teeth marks.
Image courtesy Lydia Zvyagintseva.

We don't need to tell you that creating anything during the pandemic is difficult. At times, we felt isolated and questioned this entire endeavor, overwhelmed with the chapters coming in at once, following up with already busy reviewers, and clarifying questions with authors. Alternatively, we felt we were behind on our feedback. Our individual lives continued to unfold in their own tragedies, joys, successes, and boredoms. Climate change continued to accelerate, killing thousands in heat waves, landslides, and storms. Magazines like *Briarpatch* and *Funambulist* came out with their land issues (September/October 2020; March/April 2022). This gave us an indication that we were on the right track. Governments changed power, budgets were cut, the so-called Freedom Convoy terrorized Ottawa, and the Russian Federation invaded Ukraine, all while the pandemic continued to rage around the world. We lost friends and colleagues to Covid-19 and fell ill ourselves. Somehow, we continued to work our jobs, serve on committees, and write articles together. What were we thinking?

Ultimately, we thought that this work would be worthwhile to readers and learners in the information field, and we are grateful for the opportunity to work with amazing authors, reviewers, friends, colleagues, and acquaintances. They consulted, reviewed, proofread, suggested, educated, advised, and steered us through this project. We didn't always agree, and we probably didn't do some things as well as we could have. We accept this fact and recognize that this work is a reflection of a moment in time, of our collective learning at this stage. We invite others to build on it, to take it further.

Figure 2 North Saskatchewan River.
Image courtesy Lydia Zvyagintseva.

In 2013, Brian Payton published a book called *The Wind Is Not a River*, but I prefer to think of it the other way around: a river is not the wind, but it is a method. That method has shaped us over the course of working on this project. How does one's understanding of the city change if one travels along the waterway rather than the highway? How does one measure time and distance along the river? By extension, how does one make sense of one's responsibility and positionality when land is central to our work? These are some questions raised by the authors of this collection, and they may have no simple answers.

Themes and Structure

Similarly, like a river through the valley, there are several themes that run through this collection. These include the notions of alienation, recognition, positionality, and relationality. All chapters in this volume grapple with the material aspects of information work. This was important to us as several librarians have emphasized the existing professional gap that exists "between what we say and what we do" (Yousefi, 2017). In other words, we were interested in writing that sought to connect the ideological aspects of LIS and archives with the material, and how much more material can one get than by examining the land?

For example, Weymouth and Bitz challenge the "civilizing influence" of libraries that persists in the professional values and ethos. This ideological aspect of the profession frames libraries as democratizing institutions and librarians as stewards of a certain kind of knowledge. Edwards et al. describe libraries as "perceived gatekeepers of information" that are also "complicit in the attempted assimilation of Indigenous Peoples." Nomiyama and Ho further remind us that libraries, especially academic ones, "uphold principles of Western hegemony and colonialism through their collections, services, and purpose." All authors in this collection approach the topic of libraries as institutions with a critical eye, whether they analyze their design in construction, services, collections, technology, or access models. No aspect of information work is seen as neutral by the authors in this book, and each of their distinct methodologies helps us understand how libraries situate themselves in the process of colonization in North America.

Further, the theme of valuing knowledge runs through this collection, as seen in chapters by Judge and Crook, Nomiyama and Ho, Bitz, and Edwards et al. For example, Judge and Crook draw on Chris Newell's work (2021) to argue that in order to Indigenize (as many learning organizations claim to do these days), "we must value Indigenous Knowledges and lived experience in the same way that we would value colonial degrees and signifiers of authority." The same sentiment is echoed by Bitz in her rejection of the politics of recognition toward an assertion of lived experience as valid knowledge. Thus, she writes, "That I, a Métisse living in the Métis Homeland, must cite texts published in an academic context, in order to make that assertion in this piece of writing and have it respected is evidence of how marginalized Indigenous way of knowing and being are."

Finally, the idea of history as being critical to library and information work is shared by the authors of this volume. We believe this offers a contrast to the way operations in a contemporary library are often framed as being ahistorical, timeless, and seemingly without context. In this sense, the desire to put forward a collection about land supports the belief that time and space are foundational categories of knowledge, and if libraries are more than just information agencies offering access to information resources, then integrating history and the land into our work is part of our professional practice.

Figure 3 Stones in the clay banks of the Mill Creek Ravine, Edmonton, Alberta. *Image courtesy* Lydia Zvyagintseva.

Introduction
Lydia Zvyagintseva

This is not a lengthy book, and as such, it has no sections. Nevertheless, there is a flow of ideas from chapter to chapter. The chapters are organized by methodology, starting with historical research and then presenting several mixed-methods qualitative studies. The final two chapters are about history, the present, and the future as they appear in autoethnographic or grounded theory studies. In arranging the book, we wanted to move from the empirical to the reflective and theoretical, though, of course, all chapters collected here seek to explain and theorize their subject matter. All of them draw on scholarly literature and real-world examples, developing their understanding of the land, particularly in North America, as it shapes learning institutions and which continue to have its political, economic, and social impacts on the land and people who live on it.

In "Civilizing, Separating, and Organizing: The Geographic Influence of Nineteenth Century Western Libraries," Andrew Weymouth traces the history and the emergence of the public library in the United States. The author then connects the service models of these early libraries to the specificity of the land in the western U.S. in order to examine what has changed in their contemporary operations and what aspects of these libraries persist to this day.

In "Toward a Spirit of Place in Library Architecture," Gregory Whistance-Smith explores the relationship between the design of the library building and the notion of place as it exists in specific natural, historical, and material contexts. He uses two theoretical tools to examine how meaning is constructed in library architecture: enactive perception and conceptual metaphors. He then analyzes two recently-constructed buildings of the Edmonton Public Library system to demonstrate to what extent they "ground people in a place, inviting its visitors to become more attentive to local plant and animal life, geological formations, natural materials, and the changing qualities of light over the course of the seasons."

In "Making Place, Placing Makers: Connecting history, memory, and land by Indigenizing New Hampshire Public Library Local History Collections," Laura Marie Judge and Jedidiah Crook turn to local history collections in public libraries across the lands of the Abenaki nation (now referred to as the state of New Hampshire) to answer their research question: what does it mean for a public library to exist on occupied land, and to prioritize exclusionary and harmful white settler colonial narratives? After conducting a comparative analysis and conversing with Abenaki Knowledge Keepers, the authors suggest that local history collections within the boundaries of these lands are problematic but nevertheless important components of American public libraries and American history. They thus urge public library staff to collaborate with Indigenous nations on whose land they work to define local history room policies, missions, as well as access and service models in order to contextualize the knowledge collected and to build meaningful relationships with the Indigenous peoples.

In "Rooting Research: A Critical Examination of Incorporating Land-Based Education in Universities' Research Commons," Courtney S. Nomiyama and Truc Ho conduct a content analysis of 20 research library websites to look for evidence of academic libraries committing to the process of decolonization. The authors begin with the premise that decolonization is distinct but no less crucial than the advances of Diversity, Equity, and Inclusion (DEI) in contemporary academia. Their urgency for this work is reflected in their explanation that, as "cultural and intellectual institutions whose function is to support and sustain academic research, academic libraries are, by extension, implicated in the colonial project." Rather than cast a wide net at all services that make up research librarianship, Nomiyama and Ho look specifically at research commons, as spaces where activities like publishing, digital scholarship, and pedagogy happen in contemporary university libraries. Using this scope of inquiry, therefore, the authors pose two research questions: "How have colonial practices limited the ability of academic libraries to adopt land-based education?" and "How can land-based education challenge colonial practices in academic libraries?"

In "Bringing the Land into the Library: Land Acknowledgements in an Academic Library," Ashley Edwards, Dr. Julia Lane, Dr. Alix Shield, and Dal Sohal engage with Knowledge Keepers and scholarship to examine what crafting and delivering meaningful Land Acknowledgements looks like in the academy. The authors begin by reflecting on the lessons learned in the Positionality and Land Acknowledgement Writing Workshop, which was organized by Simon Fraser University's Decolonizing the Library Interest Group in 2020. The authors then share insights for readers seeking to cultivate a reflective practice, which can guide their work on Land Acknowledgements. Edwards, Lane, Shield, and Sohal's chapter defines Land Acknowledgements, positionality, and the notion of compelling action as they relate to the purpose, function, and the scope of Land Acknowledgements. According to the authors, this work embodies the process of decolonization and reconciliation, to which we must commit with sincerity, heart, and action.

Danielle Marie Bitz's autoethnographic chapter "Downstream" combines the personal, lived, and family experience with the analysis of historical and contemporary documents. It is about Métis history and the history of the Canadian state. It is about resistance that persists, and what the land can teach us "when we form reciprocal relationships." Building on the practice of walking as a method of inquiry (Macpherson, 2016; Middleton, 2011; Pierce & Lawhon, 2015), in "Downstream" Bitz develops paddling as a research method. Drawing on her 2020 journey down the South Saskatchewan River as well as the work of Leanne Betasamosake Simpson, Maria Campbell, and Chelsea Vowel, the author poses key questions, including, How would research change if libraries were to make space for the diversity of knowledges created through reciprocal relationships? How would such a commitment change libraries and librarianship? The personal and the political are intertwined in Bitz's work, as she evocatively demonstrates the role of the land in learning.

Finally, Ariel Hahn's chapter, titled "Refusing Growth: Cloud Technology, Climate Change, and the Future of Libraries and Archives," is a theorization of critical refusal in information work needed to meaningfully address the impacts of climate change, which she argues is "already present and accelerating rapidly." Specifically, the author focuses on the use of cloud-based technologies in libraries and archives and their connection to oil and gas extraction. Drawing on a range of evidence, Hahn sees such service and technology entanglements in information work as actively contributing to climate change. Consequently, Hahn proposes refusal and degrowth as tangible responses to the ongoing climate crisis, which must be taken up collectively by the professions.

This book seeks to offer a perspective on professional practice by bringing into conversation multiple methodological and theoretical perspectives on the topic of land. It builds on the work of many scholars and thinkers cited by the authors, from whom we continue to learn. I write this on Treaty 6 territory and Métis Nation of Alberta Region 4. I do not know how widely this work will find its audience. However, I hope that despite the specificity of the colonial experience in Canada and the United States, the work of making meaning in learning institutions may be shared in places like Australia, New Zealand, Europe, and beyond.

References

Bisby, A. (2019, April 16). Big plan on campus: Canadian universities commercialize their land. *The Globe and Mail.* https://www.theglobeandmail.com/business/industry-news/property-report/article-big-plan-on-campus-canadian-universities-commercialize-their-land/

Bula, F. (2017). Universities as real-estate developers. University Affairs, November 28, 2017. https://www.universityaffairs.ca/features/feature-article/universities-real-estate-developers/

Calgary Public Library. (n.d.). *Indigenous Placemaking | Calgary Public Library.* Retrieved October 2, 2022, from https://calgarylibrary.ca/connect/indigenous-services/indigenous-placemaking/

Canadian Architect. (2022, February 7). Toronto Public Library reveals Indigenous-focused library design. *Canadian Architect.* https://www.canadianarchitect.com/toronto-public-library-reveals-plans-for-first-of-its-kind-library/

CBC News. (2011, December 3). *Hold land for Whitehorse university, says chancellor | CBC News.* CBC. https://www.cbc.ca/news/canada/north/hold-land-for-whitehorse-university-says-chancellor-1.976731

Dalhousie University. (n.d.). *Ko'jua Okuom: Dal's new Indigenous community room offers a space for reflection and celebration.* Dalhousie News. https://www.dal.ca/news/2022/06/27/ko-jua-okuom-indigenous-space-dalhousie.html

Edmonton Public Library. (2022). Milner Thunderbird House. Retrieved August 30, 2022, from https://www.epl.ca/milner-library/thunderbird-house

Macpherson, H. (2016). Walking methods in landscape research: moving bodies, spaces of disclosure and rapport. *Landscape Research, 41*(4), 425-432. DOI: 10.1080/01426397.2016.1156065

Middleton, J. (2011). Walking in the City: The Geographies of Everyday Pedestrian Practices. *Geography Compass, 5*(2), 90–105. https://doi.org/10.1111/j.1749-8198.2010.00409.x

Newell, C. (2021, June, 02). *Re-Indigenizing historical narratives.* [Virtual lecture]. Keynotes of Change, Connecticut. https://www.youtube.com/watch?v=Br4FvqgoL1I

O'Neill, M., & Roberts, B. (2019). *Walking methods: Research on the move.* Routledge.

Payton, B. (2013). *The wind is not a river.* Ecco.

Pierce, J. & Lawhon, M. (2015). Walking as method: Toward methodological forthrightness and comparability in urban geographical research. *The Professional Geographer, 67*(4), 655-662. DOI:10.1080/00330124.2015.1059401

Sorber, N. M. (2018). *Land-Grant colleges and popular revolt: The origins of the Morrill Act and the reform of higher education.* Cornell University Press. https://doi.org/10.7591/9781501709739

University of Guelph. (n.d.). *About Us | Real Estate Division.* Retrieved August 2, 2022, from https://www.uoguelph.ca/realestate/about-us

University of Toronto. (n.d.). *University of Toronto acquires key parcel of land*. University of Toronto News. https://www.utoronto.ca/news/university-toronto-acquires-key-parcel-land

University of Toronto Mississauga. (n.d.). *Maanjiwe nendamowinan: U of T Mississauga's newest building honours the past, looks to the future*. University of Toronto News. https://www.utoronto.ca/news/maanjiwe-nendamowinan-u-t-mississauga-s-newest-building-honours-past-looks-future

University of Toronto Scarborough. (n.d.). *'An inclusive space': U of T Scarborough breaks ground on Indigenous House*. University of Toronto News. https://www.utoronto.ca/news/inclusive-space-u-t-scarborough-breaks-ground-indigenous-house

Yousefi, B. (2017). On the disparity between what we say and what we do in libraries. In S. Lew & B. Yousefi (Eds.), *Feminists Among Us: Resistance and Advocacy in Library Leadership* (pp. 91–106). Litwin Books.

Civilizing, Separating, and Organizing
The Geographic Influence on Nineteenth Century Western Libraries

Andrew Weymouth

> *As you see, with scarcely an exception, the verdict is for closed shelves...The trustees of the Astoria library have only the best interests of the library in view. They make no arbitrary rules.*
>
> – Trustees Astoria P.L., 1894

Thus concludes a somewhat defensive article written on the part of the trustees of the Astoria Public Library. The editorial is a justification of their closed stack system, which required librarians to retrieve materials for patrons rather than allowing the public to browse. The author built their case by inadvertently conducting one of the most comprehensive surveys of libraries across the country up to that point, receiving correspondence from Chicago, New York, Boston and San Francisco, whose institutions also engaged in this now largely unrecognizable public library model.

The survey illustrates three service models of libraries operating during this period. The first is "a public subscription library with free reading room attached," the subscription being membership fees directed towards collection development. The second is "a subscription library established as a money-making enterprise" and cites the Library Association of Portland, which had not yet converted to the third tier, "a free library maintained at the city's expense," the framework most Americans would associate with the modern public library ("The

Library Rules," 1894). Though this financial model was industrialized by Andrew Carnegie, early iterations were tested and developed at a grassroots level throughout the nineteenth century. In fact, Carnegie's standardization efforts may have obfuscated many of the distinct, underlying cultural and environmental traits that initially shaped these institutions (Miner, 1990).

This chapter examines the traits of these pre-Carnegie libraries, how they relate to the geography of the western United States, and how these early, private models of operation can help us gain a more nuanced understanding of our contemporary institutions. Contrary to outwardly "neutral" renderings of the contemporary library, these colonial spaces were often transparent in their intentions to reform patrons. They weren't so much gardens for visitors to pick over, as factories which would rebuild the reader into a more complete and "civilized" reproductive taxpayer, American voter or devoted Christian. These libraries were also active in the sense that they were spaces where their founders could glean information from patrons that would benefit their own interests, whether industrial, religious, or political.

Specifically, I propose that these interests were directly informed by the geography of the western United States. The first substantial private libraries in California ransacked the floundering Spanish missions, just as future financiers were drilling and mining nearby resources (Hurtado, 2010). Temperance groups sought to reform the pioneer communities whom they viewed as the victims of western expansion (Soden, 2021). Grange libraries sought to organize and cultivate the working farmer who didn't have access to urban amenities (Kelley, 1875). Fraternal orders implemented libraries both in order to indoctrinate and to influence, depending on shifting industrial needs ("Knights of Labor", 1890). The founders of the first off-reservation Indian boarding schools weaponized the distance between their institutions and the students' families in order to occupy and develop their land more easily ("Indians of Pitt River," 1901). Chautauquas and lyceums attempted to bridge that same physical space with an itinerant model ("Chautauqua", 1884). The tidal wave of women's clubs which rose across the western United States during the nineteenth century may have been more able to freely organize than was capable in the more rigid social structures in the east (McCammon & Campbell, 2001). While their relationship to the land all influenced these early institutions, libraries are significant because they represent the ideological race that occurred alongside the physical land grab.

In the following examples of early libraries in the western United States, one observes a repeated theme of libraries intended as transformative spaces. These institutions were created variously to empower, subjugate, civilize, proselytize, reform, and entice potential readers, and not always voluntarily. As Suzanne Stauffer notes in *She Speaks as One Having Authority*, "Rather than being the product of a mature and stable society, as in the East, the library was a force in the creation of mature and stable societies in the West through its value as a symbol and sign of that society and its culture" (Stauffer, 2005).

This stabilizing force was also, inherently, a colonizing one. These early institutions also made no attempt at obfuscating their intentions with concepts of neutrality introduced by the American Library Association (ALA) and the advent of "library science" (Wiegand, 1999). To a greater or lesser degree, all of the groups profiled in this chapter had clear objectives to make patrons more closely resemble themselves in ideology, language and appearance. As Mariana Valverde notes in *The Age of Light, Soap, and Water*, "What has been described as imposing values on another class is simultaneously a process of creating and reaffirming one's own" (Valverde, 2008).

Figure 1 Interior of the old Spanish mission, Santa Barbara, California, U.S.A., 1906, Courtesy of the Library of Congress. Retrieved January 16, 2022, from https://www.loc.gov/resource/stereo.1s01716/

The recorded history of libraries in the western United States begins with the Spanish California Missions, which established 21 institutions between San Diego and Sonoma between 1769 and 1823. Library collections were sparse, sometimes containing only five to ten texts, often chained to reading tables by the Franciscan monks who oversaw the collections (Geiger, 1964). Amongst the most notable of these institutions was the Mission Santa Barbara, the longest operating structure perpetually under Franciscan control. The mission was delegated a Franciscan "center of authority" in 1833, following the end of Spanish colonial rule and preceding American annexation. While these institutions survived the nineteenth century, North American interests waned; monks dwindled in numbers as finances receded, mirroring the Spanish colonial reach.

Just as they had sniffed out silver mines and oil fields, industrialists and intellectual elites seized upon the declining missions to create some of the earliest European-owned libraries in the western United States (Salvatore, 2014). H.H. Bancroft, a businessman and historian who amassed some 150,000 volumes through his acumen and diplomatic talent, wrote after one conquest, "Now, I thought, my task is done. I have rifled America of its treasures" (Hurtado, 2010).

Due to the lack of formal banking in the western United States and an unstable gold standard throughout the nineteenth century, books became a dependable form of currency. As Albert L. Hurtado notes in *Professors and Tycoons*, "when money fails, books are fungible" (2010, p. 150). Similar to current practices in fine art collecting, books were sought after as individual cultural artifacts which could endure a spiraling market or, possibly, a failed attempt at nationhood. It's in this environment that the first major library collections began to be developed by European colonists. Some, like Adolph Sutro and Edward L. Doheny amassed fortunes from the silver mines and oil fields before becoming interested in books. Other major figures such as Bancroft approached a private library accumulation as a writer intent on creating the first definitive history of the American West, just as it was in the state of rapid change. As Ricardo D. Salvatore notes, Bancroft's history can be read as "a treatise on the relationship between library accumulation and the creation of regional knowledge" (Salvatore, 2014).

While Bancroft's curation of his library reflected Eurocentric values and shaped narratives around the formation of the American west, Leland Stanford of Stanford University, who would ultimately purchase Bancroft's library, was actively shaping its physical surface. Along with fellow Sacramento merchants Collins P. Huntington, Charles Crocker, and Mark Hopkins, Stanford was a member of the "Big Four," who controlled the Central Pacific and later the Southern Pacific Railroad from 1863 until his death in 1893.

The Big Four's ascendancy owes a great deal to their partnership with the American government, who had passed the Homestead and Pacific Railway Acts a year earlier, and was seeking a transcontinental railroad to populate the west and develop American interests (Congress of the United States, 1862). This arrangement tasked the Central Pacific to haul government property, mail, and even troops westward for the government in return for subsidies and land grants. This arrangement led Stanford to move mountains in at least one instance, when he created faulty geological surveys which displaced the Sierra Nevadas twenty four miles east in order to increase the subsidies per mile rate for difficulty of terrain (Zwagerman, 2006).

By 1887, the Central-Southern Pacific operated 5,500 miles of railroad, blasted 15 tunnels through California's Sierra Nevada mountains, laid ten miles of track in a single day, and delivered 120,000 settlers to the Los Angeles area alone (Heath, 1945). Between 1901 and 1916, the Southern Pacific sold 800,000 "colonist tickets," which were heavily discounted one-way trips to California (Zwagerman, 2006). While Stanford was published in newspapers voicing anti-Chinese views (Ou, 2010), the Central Pacific hired more than 13,000 Chinese workers (Mazhar & Trowbridge, 2021) to help secure a tangled mess of railway lines and real estate plots across California that became known as the "Octopus" (Hurtado, 2010).

Further, Stanford served as the first Republican governor of California during the Civil War, which required regularly working with the federal government to move troops via the Central Pacific (Grenier, 2003). Additionally, Stanford played an active role in organizing the 1st Battalion of California Mountaineers, a militia made up of former Union Army soldiers, empowered to arrest, enslave, and kill Native Americans by the newly-formed state legislature. Stanford assembled the Battalion from "old hunters and mountaineers familiar with the habits of the Indians and accustomed to hunt them" (United States War Department, 1879), ultimately leading to the deaths of between 9,000 and 16,000 Native Americans in California (Rohde, 2016).

This westward land grab and mania for natural resources among the nineteenth century elite created a strained existence for the newly arrived workforce that sustained these interests. Northward, Alfred

Fitzpatrick perceived the conditions of Canadian frontier community life as being not only dangerous to the lives of the men isolated there, but also the nation, as the moral ambiguity of the environment could create citizens "incapable of governing themselves, leading their families, or functioning as rational citizens." Fitzpatrick's solution was to create The Canadian Reading Camp Association, a series of state-sponsored reading rooms located in encampments, purposefully designed to evoke feminine-influenced domesticity in order to inspire "duty to self, family and nation" (Mason, 2015).

Eight years earlier, Lucy Switzer also stated a concern for the moral degradation that frontier interests had imposed on the working class in the west. Switzer observed at the Directory of the Woman's Christian Temperance Unions (WCTU) of Eastern Washington (1893): "The territory… is particularly liable to the ravages of intemperance. The people live under a high state of pressure in their eager rush after wealth, causing often great nervous depression which calls for the dangerous stimulants supplied by intoxicating liquor."

The temperance movement is often traced back to the Women's Crusade, a multi-state phenomena beginning in 1873, where women protested and proselytized outside of saloons, demanding an end of alcohol sales. The formation of the WCTU followed on the East Coast and quickly gained western presence. The organization distinguished itself from the Women's Crusade by not only encouraging laws against intoxicated abusive husbands but also against the parties that contributed to their drunkenness (Pleck, 1983).

As noted in this account from *The Oregonian* in 1881, "The temperance cause is represented by active lodges, and by an… excellent subscription library of over ten thousand volumes, whose purposes have been promoted by a generous endowment from leading citizens" ("An Ethical Estimate", 1881). These subscription libraries were interested not only in providing sober diversions for their club members, but also intended to convert and reform the moral character of the reader. As Dale E. Soden notes in *The Battle for Cultural Control*, "WCTU members sought social reforms on the basis of a biblical version of social justice… banning cigarettes, alcohol and 'impure literature'" (Soden, 2003). In this way, the union was engaged in an ideological equivalent of a land grab. The greater number of libraries they opened, the more dogmatic influence the organization could exert onto the coalescing western populace.

The Young Men's Christian Association (YMCA) was another temperance group generating libraries during this period, which created reading rooms in Portland and Spokane. The organization even proposed a free library model in 1873, when the concept was still in its infancy ("Y.M.C. Association [illegible] Anniversary", 1873). There was also The Dashaway Society, a temperance group created by volunteer firefighters in San Francisco, which quickly established lodges as far north as Vancouver, British Columbia. The Dashaway reading rooms were intended to "attract its members from haunting whisky saloons at night," but unlike the WCTU and YMCA, the organization was secular in nature, hosting events featuring group singing and inspirational speeches, all while keeping alcohol 'dashed away' from their lips (Counter, 2021). While the former groups were structured as missionary efforts of outsiders coming into frontier towns to reform, convert, and expand their flock, The Dashaways more closely resembled a nineteenth century fraternal organization, formed independently to support one another through their struggles with alcoholism.

By 1899, there were at least six hundred active fraternal orders, containing over six million members, which accounted for nearly ten percent of the United States population (Sevens, 1907). David T. Belto defines fraternal organizations' inherent characteristics as "an autonomous system of lodges, a democratic form of internal government, a ritual, and the provision of mutual aid for members and their families" (Beito, 2000).

The membership of fraternal organizations during the 19th century ranged in ethnicity, gender, economic background and religious affiliation, often acting as support systems for immigrant groups, such as the Croatian Fraternal Union of America. and the Italian Cacciatori D' Africa society (Ware, 2016). Tacoma Washington's Gamle Vikingers Forbund, or Ancient Order of Vikings, was formed in 1892 as an extension of The Haabet Literary Society, a Norwegian immigrant club formed as an "english school for newcomers" (no title, 1890). The 350 volume "Viking Library" inherited from the Haabet ("Hope") Literary Society was retained by the Ancient Order of Vikings until the repository was donated in the 1940s ("P.L.C Gets Collection", 1941).

In contrast, Freemasons, the largest fraternal order of the nineteenth century, seemed to inspire consistent trends in many other fraternal organizations of the period. Societies tended to be philosophical rather than religious in nature. Meetings and events contained elements of performance and knowledge was promised to members along with "ancient mysteries" of the arts and sciences "which could be passed on only to specially prepared seekers" (Gross, 2017).

The Grange was one of these organizations which sprung from the mold of Freemasonry, but distinct through their focus on labor organization and cultivation of the agricultural community. Certain elements of the Grange philosophy appeared similar to its parent organization in the use of ceremonial ornaments, detailed seating arrangements, and "processional routes" involved in the opening and closing of grange meetings (Grange, 1915). Crucial elements, like the mixed gender congregations, were distinct from the two orders. Founder Oliver H. Kelly also distinguished the Grange as dispensing "valuable, practical knowledge", stating, "Ours is an operative order. Masonry is merely speculative" (Kelley, 1875).

Figure 2 Group leaving the Willamette Grange Hall, 1925, Courtesy of Oregon Digital. Retrieved January 16, 2022, from https://oregondigital.org/catalog/oregondigital:df70d1786

This practical knowledge extended to creating libraries which could aid in the development of the Grangers, "with books on natural history, agriculture, horticulture, pomology, physiology, rural architecture, landscape gardening, breeding and raising of stock" (Kelley, 1875). As early as 1879, the *Oregonian* notes that a grange library in the Willamette Community and Grange Hall "seems to be a happy success. The books thus far consist mainly of histories, biographies and fiction." With a hint of judgment, the author notes "at present the novels are eagerly read, while the histories and biographies remain on the shelf."

This breaches a contentious debate concerning the intentions of libraries in the western United States: if libraries were the tools which would be used to civilize the west, should anything other than the fortifying vegetables of "religious and instructive" texts be allowed (Dean, 2011)? This dietary metaphor is expanded in an angry letter to the Vancouver B.C. *Daily Chronicle* wherein the author describes novels as "whipped cream or puffed paste" and demanded more "solid food" in the form of 'good books" (Dean, 2011). This emphasis on non-fiction, instructional, and improvement-oriented material also has an indoctrinating effect. In contrast to novels which allow readers to escape into their imaginations and explore ambiguous personal values, nonfiction dictates rather than engages.

It's also possible that fictional work was deemed unsubstantial due to the gender of the writers and readers of the genre. In an article from 1897, the Tacoma Daily News reported that popular author Gertrude Atherton's newest novel had been banned from the San Francisco Mechanics' Institute. The library had deemed the novel "unwholesome," noting, "It is women who write and mostly women who read the decadent literature of the recent years. The revival of a prurient taste for unclean or unwelcome books seems to date in this country to (1888)… All libraries should exclude this immoral or morbid fiction" ("[Gertrude; Atherton; Mechanics; Helen]", 1897).

The Mechanics' Institute represented a branch of trade and labor oriented fraternal organizations, devoted to "elevating the dignity of mechanics, intended to furnish them the place and the opportunity of frequent interchange of views as a means of extending information, and cultivating the literary taste of its members by furnishing… a well stored library of books" ("The Mechanics Institute", 1856). More subtly, the Mechanics' Institute was a nativist organization that held annual "Industrial Expositions" promoting American self-sufficiency and "home production." In the opening ceremony of the twenty ninth exposition, President E.A. Dencke pronounced,

> "Any country which does not possess manufactories must also become poor. That we do possess manufactures of which we have every reason to be proud is proved beyond doubt with this exposition.

The vital question is, therefor, why not patronize them? Thereby keeping for home circulation money now shipped East, the exodus of which is throwing thousands of our citizens out of employment... The gods help him who helps himself!" ("Large Crowds Attend", 1986)

The institution was private, requiring members to purchase shares of the company stock, but didn't actually require members to be mechanics. Similarly, the San Francisco Mercantile Library didn't require its members to be of the merchant class. These institutions both opened in the 1850s and ultimately combined their 160,000 volumes in 1906 into a single collection, destroyed weeks later by the San Francisco earthquake ("Only One Escapes", 1906).

Tacoma, Washington was home to the Labor Library, a reading room created by the Knights of Labor in 1891. This order was, somewhat covertly, the fraternal extension of the Western Central Labor Union (WCLU), based in Seattle. The appointed librarian was a "Master Workman" who made headlines a year earlier for "weeding out of its ranks all anarchically inclined members" and preserving "a body of conservative progressive men who are actuated by humane sentiments... and not aggressive revolutionary action" ("Knights of Labor", 1890). The reading room contained "periodicals and newspapers from all parts of the country" as well as "a library of standard works on economic subjects."

WCLU Secretary W.J. Akers would later divulge in the *Seattle Post-Intelligencer*, that "the Japanese must remain away from this country; that they must be kept out, and that an exclusion not dissimilar to the Chinese exclusion should be enacted for the protection of the American citizen" ("Carnegie Public Library", 1905). Given the administration's racist beliefs and the library's leadership being responsible for "weeding out" progressive members, it seems plausible that the reading room served the purpose of spreading these sentiments, and possibly gathering information to actively suppress labor organization. Just as Bancroft's library was curated to impart a specific version of western history and the WCTU libraries were intended to reform and convert patrons, the WCLU library acted less as a passive patron resource than as an active instrument to promote the interests of its founders.

The Tulalip Reservation school in Washington State began as a Catholic Mission in 1857, and eventually expanded into the first contract

Indian School in America. The designation entailed "an arrangement whereby the government provided annual funds to maintain the buildings while the church furnished books, clothing, housing and medical care" (Marr, n.d.). This concept eventually developed into the Indian Boarding School movement, wherein the U.S. government maintained a total of 367 schools across 27 states between 1860 to 1978 (Love, 2021). While the creation of these schools were often prompted by promises of educational resources in colonial documents, such as the Medicine Creek and Point Elliott treaties, the schools were explicitly designed as a method for cultural domination. Foundational figures Richard Henry Pratt, Edwin Eells, and Melville Cary Wilkinson all had direct experience either capturing or killing Native American people prior to their roles as educators (Collins, 2000).

Reverend Myron Eells, brother of the Cushman Indian School superintendent Edwin Eells, described the purpose of the schools transparently. "As an adopted child it was the duty of the government that he was educated… as there was no way in which we could get rid of them; since we could not kill all of them, nor could we remove them to some good country where they could support themselves" ("Indian Education", 1887). Commissioner of Indian Affairs William Arthur Jones defined the school's purpose more succinctly: "To educate the Indian is to prepare him for the abolishment of tribal relations" ("Give the Indian a White Man's Chance", 1903). Off-reservation Indian boarding schools were the bureaucratic solution to an unwinnable war.

The federal government mandated education for Indian youths in 1893. Parents who refused to send their children up to 100 miles away could be jailed or have their government rations withheld. The great distance between Indigenous communities and the boarding schools was not the result of lack of funding or a bureaucratic oversight, but rather a tactical decision. As the Commissioner of Indian Affairs noted in 1901, "It is better that its location should be some distance away from the parents, the experience of this office demonstrating that such locations are far preferable to those in the immediate vicinity of the Indians" ("Indians of Pitt River", 1901).

It should come as no surprise that the libraries of these institutions reflected the colonial lens of their founders. Myron Eells notes that "Our school books, in this respect, made as they are for white children, often are not suited for Indian children" (Morning Oregonian, 1887) and therefore gave greater emphasis to practical knowledge, which led to these institutions being "limited in text book instruction"("Give the Indian", 1903). Although Eells demonstrated his contempt for Indian reading ability through books donated to the library having "been destroyed or stolen, owing to the fact that no suitable place was had to keep them," ("The Chemawa Indian School", 1889) the Chemawa Indian School eventually did contain a library of over a thousand volumes by 1889. At the Cushman Indian School in Puyallup, Field Matron Lida W. Quimby relayed an accumulated 100 books in 1900, contributing to the "advancement of these people" and their permanent improvement, but noting that "they are not yet self-reliant. They would drift back if left to their own way" ("Indian Schools", 1900).

While the legacy of Indian boarding schools continues to reveal itself as a colonial and genocidal force in North American history, there did appear to be intermittent attempts to reform the institution. Early twentieth century Superintendent Francis E. Leupp recognized the subversion of off-reservation boarding schools and devised means to convert these institutions into specialized higher education centers, a model which remains largely extant. Asked about the off-reservation schools in 1905, Leupp told the *Seattle Post-Intelligencer,* "I wish there were fewer of these, for most of them were located with an eye to the pleasure and profit of some ambitious town rather than of the Indians... I am sorry to say, the methods resorted to for cajoling the parents into parting with their children are sometimes not wholly credible" ("Future of Our Indians as Forecast by Commissioner Leupp", 1905).

While the off-reservation Indian boarding school was developed in part to weaponize the geography of the western United States, the Lyceum and Chautauqua movement was created to counteract its expansiveness and sparse distribution of citizens. The Lyceum movement has its roots in early nineteenth century Scotland, where itinerant librarians would dispense rotating collections of books to rural readers. The program was adopted by Connecticut schoolmaster Josiah Holbrook, who instilled the organization with "associations for mutual instruction in the sciences, and in useful knowledge generally." The target audience for this plan was young men in need of "an economical and practical education," who would come together for lessons in the many "branches of Natural Philosophy" (Gross, 2017).

Lyceums were mixed gender, non-religious organizations, and they intended to reach communities dispersed through westward expansion. Similar to the Labor Library and Fitzgerald's Canadian Reading Camp, there was also a political subtext to the Lyceum's mission. As Joanne E. Passet notes in *Reaching the Rural Reader*, "Librarians also focused on regions with high concentrations of immigrants, hoping that traveling libraries would prevent them from being led by the appeals of future demagogues" (Passet, 1991).

While traveling lyceums did occasionally splinter off into physical libraries such as the Sacramento Lyceum ("Sacramento Lyceum", 1856) and the Walla Walla Lyceum and Library Association (Paulus, 2008), the sibling institution of Chautauquas appears to have always been a traveling lecture model, although they would often work collaboratively with local libraries ("Has Many Books", 1905). The underlying principle of the Chautauquas was "to fill the lives of our young people with earnest employment and innocent recreation; contribute towards fortifying the mind by higher and better principles; giving the heart and mind better impulses; and in all ways up-lifting and up-building; an incentive to higher and better purposes" ("Chautauqua. The People's University or College", 1884). The events took place in parks and fields, with an atmosphere not dissimilar from contemporary outdoor music festivals, providing elements of "a summer outing, combining the freedom of camp life and the general appointments of a social gathering" ("Summer Chautauquas", 1897).

Figure 3 Chautauqua Auditorium at Gladstone, half-open building with domed roof, 1880. Courtesy of Oregon Digital. Retrieved January 16, 2022, from https://oregondigital.org/catalog/oregondigital:df71fr794

The 1900 assembly of the Willamette Valley Chautauqua Association, which took place in Gladstone Park just south of Portland, OR, featured lectures focused on "humane work." Amongst attendees were Hon. R.P. Boise, Worthy Master of the Oregon State Grange, a musical performance by the Chemewa Indian Band and a "physical culture class" hosted by the secretary of the YMCA.

Amongst other lecturers that day, Miss Lena Morrow gave a speech on the "New Factor of Civilization."

> The competitive system, which makes man the sole provider, causes the subjection of women. Inequality is more injurious to man than woman, and the competitive system is wrong, and stands in the way of higher civilization. The time has come when woman is recognized as an individual factor in our civilization.
>
> This is not a sentiment; it is a matter of business for the future preservation of civilization that women be recognized for her individuality. Womanliness and strength are synonymous. Cooperation should be the watchword of our new civilization. ("Crowds Grow Larger Attendance", 1900, p. 5)

The program that day concluded with a performance from the Metropolitan Jubilee singers, a round table by the Ancient Order of the Red Cross, and a reading of Sara Shannon Evans' paper "Oregon's Need of a Free and Uniform Library System."

By 1898, there were 8,410 active women's clubs and at least half a million members. The movement first appears in the historical record in 1852 and arrived on the West Coast in 1883. Unlike the temperance movement, these clubs were not religious, and unlike female-oriented fraternal orders, such as the Daughters of the Nile ("Install Daughters of the Nile", 1914), women's clubs had made no claims on abstract or ancient knowledge. For example, a profile in the *Sunday Oregonian* detailed,

> Women's clubs may be divided into three great classes... self improvement of their own members... practical effort in the furtherance of some cause believed to be good... and the advancement of social conditions in the home and the community.

We find California with a great deal of clubs whose work is political... Women's Parliament of Southern California... In Oregon... social and political questions receive due attention. Washington's clubs are legislative and educational. ("Half A Million Club Women What They Are Doing for", 1989, p. 23)

The article also points out that the three states with the largest number of active, federated women's clubs are Kansas (301), New York (230) and Iowa (194). This is significant because Kansas and Iowa's population combined was roughly half that of New York State when the article was written (United States Bureau Of The Census & Austin, W. L., 1921). Women's club and suffrage group membership rates, as well as early women's voting rights successes in the western United States, may indicate that organization and political mobility was more easily achieved away from the more rigid social structures on the east coast. Some of these successes were immediately connected to the western geography. It's posited that Wyoming became the first state in the nation in order to "lure" women to the majority male region both as morally corrective figures and/or a white vote majority (McCammon, 2001).

Figure 4 A woman believed to be Grace R. Moore and accompanied by a large dog, was photographed while reading in the law offices of her husband, Henry K. Moore, circa 1896. Courtesy of the Tacoma Public Library's Image Archive. General Photograph Collection TPL-4142. Retrieved January 16, 2022, from https://cdm17061.contentdm.oclc.org/digital/collection/p17061coll21/id/21777/rec/1

Whereas suffrage was possibly the third item on the temperance movement's list of priorities behind banning substances and proselytizing, the advancement of women was explicitly stated in purpose of the Women's Club movement, followed by "raising of the standard education in the state" ("Work of the State Federation", 1905). While this unconditional advancement of educational standards is a welcoming sentiment, the early libraries created by women's clubs appeared to be established in order to advocate for women's literacy, when educational opportunities for all but a very small class of women were scarce. Many early libraries didn't allow women, or sequestered them to designated reading rooms (Van Slyck, 1996). When women did have access to library material, female-oriented items were heavily vetted on moral grounds, as in the case of Gertrude Atherton at the San Francisco Mercantile Library, or were otherwise subject to the scrutiny of librarians, as in the Astoria library closed stack system which introduced the chapter.

In contrast to the ornamental and ceremonial aspects of fraternal order libraries, or the industrialized and "scientific" approaches introduced by Melvil Dewey, the Women's Club libraries were straightforward, domestic affairs. For example, the Seattle reading room established by Catherine Maynard in 1875 was simply the library of her home, open to public use (Becker, 2004). Eleven years later, Ms. Grace R. Moore operated a subscription library from her home in Tacoma, Washington–the first public circulating library in the Puget Sound–which would ultimately evolve into a Carnegie Library in 1903 (Smith, 1926).

While the Canadian Reading Camps intended to fabricate the feeling of domesticity across threadbare pioneer mining towns, women's clubs designed their spaces more authentically. The reading room in the Troutdale Woman's Club is described as "a cozy, homelike little place, comfortably furnished and made attractive by a number of good pictures…A capable librarian not only keeps it neat and warm but assists the younger patrons in selecting suitable reading matter" ("Among The Clubwomen Amazing Growth Of Woman's", 1901).

Though these early libraries often didn't last long due to the lack of financial support and the tumultuous nature of social and civic growth in the nineteenth century western United States, these attempts directly influenced the ideological and financial structure of the American public library system. These libraries demonstrated effective methods of fundraising and helped refine and promote the tax-based method for library creation and maintenance. When the Oregon Federation of Women's Clubs organized in 1899, their first successful project was "creating statewide support for levying taxes to establish and maintain public libraries" (Gunselman, 2002). According to president C.B. Wade, every club in the federation had a committee "actively engaged in working for the cause of free libraries" ("Enthusiasm Runs High", 1900).

Due to the volume of organizing during this period, women's clubs have left an indelible print on the modern American models of western academic libraries. Catherine Montgomery, founder of Bellingham, Washington's Progressive, Literary and Fraternal Club (Khan, 2010) also created the New Whatcom State Normal School, which would eventually become Western Washington University, and possessed a library of over 5,000 volumes by 1902 ("At State Normal", 1902). At that same moment, The Seattle Federation of Women's Clubs was "collecting data for a history of the state of Washington... Many personal reminiscences of old pioneers were secured," ("Annual Meeting of Federation", 1902) work very much resembling an academic oral history initiative, taking place 34 years before the Federal Writers' Project would popularize oral history on a national scale (Library of Congress, n.d.).

In addition to pioneering an early financial model for free, public libraries recognizable today, the ideological goals of these early women's clubs are reflected in contemporary American libraries. The Women's Club movement's understanding of the interconnectedness of literacy, culture, and social progress, as well as promoting their advancement to all American citizens, feels distinct from the other organizations discussed in this work. That said, the members of these clubs were primarily White and had the economic means to devote their time to pursuits beyond food and shelter.

This social positionality which undergirds many "progressive" white women's movements has been personified as "Lady Bountiful" by a number of authors critically examining educational power structures. The name derives alternately from an eighteenth century play, a late nineteenth century comic strip, or a twentieth century musical, all involving a benevolent protector of the "little children of the slums" (National Museum of American History, n.d.). In *Dismantling White Privilege*, Helen Harper identifies Lady Bountiful as the utilitarian extension of settler colonization stating that the "ideal of femininity propounded by the British to the colonies became the white woman, the embodiment of chastity and purity who acted as a "civilizing" force" (Harper, 2000).

Examined together, the parties involved in creating early libraries in the western United States provide a unique insight into the mindset of Americans in the nineteenth century. The rush of institutions to reform patron values, appearance, and language was often described as a means of retaining American identity, as it was still clearly being developed.

While we can plainly identify improvements in our modern library institutions in terms of collections, access and efficiency, there is an element of transparency to these models lacking in our contemporary system. There are currently 9,247 American institutions that identify as public libraries for tax purposes (Institute of Museum and Library Services, n.d.). While these libraries fall under one of ten classification systems and varying degrees of privately controlled operations depending on state law, I think it is reasonable to assume that the average patron is not mindful of these distinctions (Owens, 1996). As long as the patron sees the words 'public library' above the door, it is likely they assume a basic, shared ideology similar to the American Library Association's *Bill of Rights*, regarding censorship, discrimination and accessibility. This perception contrasts with the unique industrial, agricultural, and environmental traits which may influence staff, patrons, and donors of each institution, as well as how the community regards the free and equal access to information.

These early institutions were largely transparent about who funded the structures and what values they espoused. For example, one may not have agreed with the goals of Women's Christian Temperance Union or the Grangers, but one knew what to expect when entering their reading rooms. Contrast this with a contemporary American public library, whose principle donors are usually obscured, though they may have the same partisan beliefs and reformative interests as the groups outlined in this writing (Buschman & Warner, 2016).

More direct parallels are drawn between the current search engine and information technology giants occupying the space that these private libraries once held. Today's search engines provide users with a highly curated selection of answers which both benefit the platform economically and glean data from the users, similar to the function of the Labor Library. Like the early private repositories, these platforms are owned by the wealthiest people in the nation, and they have been found to actively shape our perspectives around history, race, and culture algorithmically, much like Bancroft did in crafting his literary narrative of westward expansion through curation of knowledge (Prier, 2020).

Does the return of privatized information services emerge from a vacuum created by a lack of funding for libraries and social programs, or is this an evolutionary progression of institutions being replaced over time by more innovative models that speak to contemporary needs? Or perhaps this return is Darwinian only in relation to the size and means rather than efficiency of information services, where the school of fishes presented in this writing was swallowed up by Carnegie, who, in turn, lost a few appendages via Silicon Valley? If so, efficiency and scalability may be a less effective metric for a library's worth than the greatest accessibility to the most diverse range of materials, selected free of corporate or religious influence.

References

Among The Clubwomen Amazing Growth Of Woman's. (1901, December 16). *Morning Oregonian*, p. 5.

An Ethical Estimate. The Moral and Intellectual Status of the City of Portland. (1881, January 1). *Oregonian*, p. 4.

Annual Meeting of Federation. (1902, April 15). *The Seattle post-intelligencer*, p. 5.

At State Normal. (1902, September 14). *The Seattle post-intelligencer*, p. 13.

Becker, P. (2004, March 3). *Maynard, Catherine Broshears (1816-1906)*. History Link. org. https://www.historylink.org/File/4281

Beito, D. T. (2000). *From mutual aid to the welfare state: Fraternal societies and social services, 1890-1967*. University of North Carolina Press.

Buschman, J., & Warner, D. A. (2016). On community, justice, and libraries. *The Library Quarterly, 86*(1), 10-24. https://www.journals.uchicago.edu/doi/abs/10.1086/684146

Carnegie Public Library as it Looks Today. (1905, March 16). *The Seattle post-intelligencer*, p. 11.

Chautauqua. The People's University or College. (1884, November 16). *The Sunday Oregonian*, p. 6.

Crowds Grow Larger Attendance. (1900, July 17). *Morning Oregonian*, p. 5. https://oregonnews.uoregon.edu/lccn/sn83025138/1900-07-17/ed-1/seq-5/

Collins, C. C. (2000). The broken crucible of assimilation: Forest Grove Indian School and the origins of off-reservation boarding-school education in the west. *Oregon Historical Quarterly, 101*(4), 466-507. https://www.ohs.org/oregon-historical-quarterly/upload/Collins_Broken-Crucible-of-Assimilation_OHQ-Winter-2000.pdf

Congress of the United States. (1862, July 1). *Pacific Railway Act*. National Archives. Retrieved from https://www.archives.gov/milestone-documents/pacific-railway-act

Counter, B. (2021). San Francisco Theatres: Dashaway Hall [Blog post]. San Francisco Theatres. Retrieved from http://sanfranciscotheatres.blogspot.com/2021/07/dashaway-hall.html

Dean, H. (2011). "The persuasion of books": the significance of libraries in colonial British Columbia. *Libraries & the Cultural Record, 46*(1), 50-72. https://muse.jhu.edu/article/420599/pdf

Enthusiasm Runs High For The Free Libraries. (1900, October 4). *Morning Oregonian*, p. 7.

Future of Our Indians as Forecast by Commissioner Leupp. (1905, May 28). *The Seattle post-intelligencer*, p. 56.

Geiger, M. J. (1964). The Story of California's First Libraries. *Southern California Quarterly, 46*(2), 109-124.

[Gertrude; Atherton; Mechanics; Helen]. (1897, May 22). *Tacoma Daily News*, vol. XXIX, no. 51, p. 2.

Give the Indian a White Man's Chance. (1903, November 28). *Tacoma Daily News*, p. 7.

Grange. (1915). *Manual of subordinate granges of the Patrons of Husbandry* (10th ed.). G.S. Ferguson Co.

Grenier, J. A. (2003). "Officialdom": California state government, 1849-1879. *California History, 81*(3/4), 137-168.

Gross, R. A. (2017). Lodges and Lyceums, Freemasonry and Free Grace. *Massachusetts Historical Review, 19*, 1-22. https://www.jstor.org/stable/10.5224/masshistrevi.19.2017.0001

Gunselman, C. (2002). Pioneering Free Library Service for the City, 1864-1902: The Library Association of Portland and the Portland Public Library. *Oregon Historical Quarterly, 103*(3), 320-337.

Half A Million Club Women What They Are Doing for. (1898, May 8). *The Sunday Oregonian*, p. 23.

Has Many Books On India Chautauqua Students May. (1905, October 8). *The Sunday Oregonian*, p. 7.

Heath, E. (1945, December). *Seventy-Five Years of Progress*. Seventy-five years of progress–the southern pacific railroad (1869-1944). Retrieved from http://www.cprr.org/Museum/SP_1869-1944

Hurtado, A. L. (2010). Professors and Tycoons: The Creation of Great Research Libraries in the American West. *Western Historical Quarterly*, 41(2), 149-169. https://doi.org/10.2307/westhistquar.41.2.0149

Indian Education. Festival Suggestions by a Man of. (1887, July 12). *The Morning Oregonian*, p. 3.

Indian Schools. (1900, January 25). *Seattle Daily Times*, p. 6. Retrieved from http://infoweb.newsbank.com/apps/news/document-view?p=WORLDNEWS&docref=image/v2%3A127D718D1E33F961%40WHNPX-1280CF46EDB8A86D%402415045-128012F03B878746%405-128012F03B878746%4

Indians of Pitt River. (1901, February 4). *The Morning Oregonian*, p. 6.

Install Daughters of the Nile. (1914, March 25). *Seattle Daily Times*, p. 13.

Institute of Museum and Library Services. (n.d). Library Search & Compare. Retrieved from https://www.imls.gov/search-compare

Khan, Dean. (2010, March 28). Bellingham woman may be the "mother" of the Pacific Crest Trail. *Bellingham Herald*, p. 2. Retrieved December 27, 2021 from http://infoweb.newsbank.com/apps/news/document-view?p=WORLDNEWS&docref=news/12EAA450DEEE80B8

Kelley, O. H. (1875). *Origin and Progress of the Order of the Patrons of Husbandry in the United States: A History from 1866 to 1873*. JA Wagenseller.

Knights of Labor. (1890, August 16). *Tacoma Daily News*, p. 3. Retrieved from http://infoweb.newsbank.com/apps/news/document-view?p=WORLDNEWS&docref=image/v2%3A10FE6ECC036402F0%40WHNPX-16817E5F-D3941268%402411420-167F758BE1078BE1%407-167F758BE1078BE1%40

Large Crowds Attend. (1896, September 2). *The San Francisco Call*, p. 9. Retrieved from https://www.newspapers.com/image/77946865/

Library of Congress. (n.d.). American Life Histories: Manuscripts from the Federal Writers' Project, 1936 to 1940. Retrieved from https://www.loc.gov/collections/federal-writers-project/about-this-collection/

Love, D.A. (2021, August 10). Residential schools were a key tool in America's long history of Native genocide. *The Washington Post*. https://www.washingtonpost.com/outlook/2021/08/10/residential-schools-were-key-tool-americas-long-history-native-genocide/

Marr, C.J. (n.d.). Assimilation Through Education: Indian Boarding Schools in the Pacific Northwest. American Indians of the Pacific Northwest Collection. University of Washington. Retrieved from https://content.lib.washington.edu/aipnw/marr.html

Mason, J. (2015). Creating a "Home Feeling": The Canadian Reading Camp Association and the Uses of Fiction, 1900–1905. *Labour: Journal of Canadian Labour Studies/Le Travail: revue d'Études Ouvrières Canadiennes*, 76, 109-131.

Mazhar, M., & Trowbridge, C. (2021). Ghost town artifacts reveal home life of Chinese railroad workers. *As It Happens*. broadcast, CBC Radio. Retrieved from https://www.cbc.ca/radio/asithappens/

as-it-happens-the-wednesday-edition-1.6244300/ghost-town-artifacts-reveal-home-life-of-chinese-railroad-workers-1.6244301

McCammon, H. J., & Campbell, K. E. (2001). Winning the vote in the west: The political successes of the women's suffrage movements, 1866-1919. *Gender & Society, 15*(1), 55-82. https://www.jstor.org/stable/3081830

Miner, C. (1990). The "Deserted Parthenon": Class, Culture and the Carnegie Library of Homestead, 1898–1937. *Pennsylvania History: A Journal of Mid-Atlantic Studies, 57*(2), 107–135. http://www.jstor.org/stable/27773366

National Museum of American History. (n.d.) "Lady Bountiful." Retrieved from https://americanhistory.si.edu/collections/search/object/nmah_670868

(no title). (1890, February 21). *Tacoma Daily News*, p. 8.

Only One Escapes San Francisco's Magnificent. (1906, April 29). *The Sunday Oregonian*, p. 12.

Ou, H. Y. (2010). Chinese Ethnicity and the American Heroic Artisan in Henry Grimm's "The Chinese Must Go"(1879). *Comparative Drama 44*(1), 63-84. https://www.jstor.org/stable/23238676

Owens, S. (1996). *Public library structure and organization in the United States*. US Government Printing Office.

Passet, J. E. (1991). Reaching the rural reader: Traveling libraries in America, 1892-1920. *Libraries & Culture*, 100-118.

Paulus, M. (2008). Walla Walla Public Library. Retrieved from https://www.historylink.org/File/8727

P.L.C Gets Collection. (1941, December 19). *The Tacoma News Tribune*, p. 3.

Pleck, E. (1983). Feminist responses to" crimes against women," 1868-1896. *Signs: Journal of Women in Culture and Society, 8*(3), 451-470.

Prier, J. (2020). Commanding the trend: Social media as information warfare. In *Information warfare in the age of cyber conflict*, pp. 88-113. Routledge.

Rohde, J. (2016, October 27). An American Genocide. *North Coast Journal*. Retrieved from *https://www.northcoastjournal.com/humboldt/an-american-genocide/Content?oid=4116592*

Sacramento Lyceum. (1856, November 15). *Daily Democratic State Journal*, p. 2.

Salvatore, R. D. (2014). Progress and Backwardness in Book Accumulation: Bancroft, Basadre, and Their Libraries. *Comparative Studies in Society and History, 56*(4), 995-1026. DOI: https://doi.org/10.1017/S0010417514000474

Smith, C. W. (1926). Early Library Development in Washington. *The Washington Historical Quarterly, 17*(4), 246–258. http://www.jstor.org/stable/40475043

Soden, D. E. (2003). The Woman's Christian Temperance Union in the Pacific Northwest: The Battle for Cultural Control. *The Pacific Northwest Quarterly, 94*(4), 197-207.

Stauffer, S. M. (2005). "She speaks as one having authority": Mary E. Downey's use of libraries as a means to public power. *Libraries & Culture*, 38-62.

Summer Chautauquas. (1897, July 11). *The Sunday Oregonian*, p. 4.

Switzer, L. (1893). "Annual Address". *Directory of the Woman's Christian Temperance Unions of Eastern Washington 1892-93*, Temperance Convention Minutes. 25.

The Chemawa Indian School. It Is In a Prosperous. (1889, June 3). *Morning Oregonian*, p. 4.

The Library Rules. (1894, April 28). *The daily morning Astorian*. https://oregon-news.uoregon.edu/lccn/sn96061150/1894-04-28/ed-1/seq-4/

The Mechanics Institute. (1856, July 5). *The Alta California*, p. 8.

Trustees Astoria P.L. (1984, April 28). *The Daily Morning Astorian* (Astoria, Or.) 1883-1899, Image 4.

United States Bureau Of The Census & Austin, W. L. (1921). Fourteenth census of the United States:... Bulletin. [Washington, Govt. print. off] [Image] Retrieved from the Library of Congress, https://www.loc.gov/item/21026466/

United States War Department. (1897). *The War of the Rebellion: A Compilation of the Official Records of the Union and Confederate Armies*. U.S. Government Printing Office.

Van Slyck, A. A. (1996). The lady and the library loafer: gender and public space in Victorian America. *Winterthur Portfolio*, *31*(4), 221-242.

Valverde, M. (2008). *The age of light, soap, and water: Moral reform in English Canada, 1885-1925*. University of Toronto Press.

Ware, K. (2016). The Historical Cemeteries of Roslyn, Washington by Roslyn Cemeteries. Retrieved from Issuu, https://issuu.com/roslyncemeteries/docs/roslyncemeteries-karen/1

Wiegand, W. A. (1999). Tunnel vision and blind spots: What the past tells us about the present; reflections on the twentieth-century history of American librarianship. *The Library Quarterly*, *69*(1), 1-32.

Work of the State Federation of Washington's Women's Clubs. (1905, December 17). *The Seattle post-intelligencer*, p. 34. Retrieved from http://infoweb.newsbank.com/apps/news/document-view?p=WORLDNEWS&docref=image/v2%3A142FE773BA94746A%40WHNPX-16936B6555B56495%402417197-1693674AE814DC18%4033-1693674A

Y. M. C. Association. [Illegible] Anniversary Of. (1873, July 28). *The Morning Oregonian*, p. 3.

Zwagerman, S. (2006). The View from the Train: The Southern Pacific Railroad and the Construction of the California Landscape. *Interdisciplinary Studies in Literature and Environment*, 65-81.

Towards a Spirit of Place in Library Architecture

Gregory Whistance-Smith

Physical libraries long predate our contemporary conception of "the library" as an institution. At various points in antiquity – and in multiple corners of the globe – people began to collect written texts by a growing number of authors. These collections of scrolls (and earlier clay tablets) had physical requirements for storage, and purpose-built shelving quickly developed in response. For those wealthy and powerful enough to amass a large number of written texts, dedicated rooms lined with shelving to house their collections began to make sense, and the first libraries came into being; Ephesus and Alexandria are two notable examples (Battles, 2003). As physical storage for manuscripts, libraries seem deceptively straightforward; however, in a world of orality there was something bold and radical about placing so many different voices next to each other, ones which told different – and even conflicting – stories about the world (in contrast to more unified oral traditions) (Too, 2010, p. 221). Over the course of their history, libraries moved beyond palace walls into monasteries and places of higher learning. The 19th century saw the arrival of public libraries with a wider social agenda of encouraging mass literacy and ensuring widespread access to books, and recent decades have seen this mandate expand to include countless other media and technologies. As buildings, libraries have evolved alongside these changes, first incorporating dedicated places to read and write texts, and later expanding to include lecture halls, music rooms, and makerspaces. Architectural milestones have included the Bibliothèque Sainte-Geneviève in Paris in 1850, the widespread Anglo-American construction of Carnegie libraries beginning in the 1880s, and the Seattle Central Library in 2004. At its best, the contemporary library exists as a concentrated microcosm of human expression: it holds a collection and gathers a community around it, be that a community of scholars or simply the public as a whole (Whistance-Smith, 2016, 2014). Architecturally, we are invited to ask what sort of space, and what range of aesthetic qualities, are best able to achieve this.

As storehouses of cultural expression, libraries have an inward character that can easily turn away from the geographic places they are built within, a tendency exacerbated by trends in contemporary architecture. All buildings are constructed *somewhere*, and prior to industrialization, most were built out of natural materials found at or near their locations, be it stone quarried nearby, wood from regional forests, or animal skins from local fauna. Buildings had a near-effortless relationship to their land, naturally reflecting the materials at hand and the cultural knowledge of the local peoples constructing them. Yet this all changed with the artificial materials and mass-produced components brought by industrialization: much contemporary architecture is untethered to place, instead being constructed out of elements shipped from all corners of the globe while reflecting transnational trends (Frampton, 1983a). This disconnection from their natural environments can give contemporary buildings an alienating atmosphere: they are standardized enclosures for engaging in various activities, not meaningful anchors that ground us in the surrounding natural world while expressing a local understanding of where we fit within it (Frampton, 1983a; Norberg-Schulz, 1980). This "function" of helping us discover our place in nature, and subsequently feeling at home in it, has been established by some as a foundational purpose of architecture: buildings provide psychological shelter just as much as they provide physical warmth and protection from the rain and snow (Goldhagen, 2017). Grounding us in a particular place is a core way that architecture can become meaningful to us and enrich our lives, especially now that we spend most of them indoors. And for peoples that have inhabited a land for countless generations, new buildings can help reaffirm their history through design motifs that link back to the buildings their ancestors constructed.

Like all other buildings, libraries are free to establish a dialogue with their natural surroundings or to ignore them; a library without a connection to place may indeed serve as a very good storehouse of knowledge for a settler community with roots scattered around the globe. But whether it does – and the larger questions of what a contemporary library should aspire to be and what it should look like – go well beyond our discussion here (for this, see Whistance-Smith [2016] and [2014]). Reflecting arguments in anthropology, architecture, and environmental psychology that buildings can help foster positive attachment to place, I will simply take it as a given that libraries rooted in place are preferable to those that are not (see Gifford, 2014; Goldhagen, 2017; Ingold, 2000). Further, when a library does integrate nature in observable, and perhaps educational ways, this can be understood as a form of local knowledge getting baked into the library's collection, akin to other non-traditional sources of knowledge such as the tools and technologies now held by some libraries.

This chapter will explore how the design of a contemporary library can meaningfully relate to place, responding to the climate and natural context it is built within. I will argue that beyond its collection and programming, the design of a library's building can ground people in a place, inviting its visitors to become more attentive to local plant and animal life, geological formations, natural materials, and the changing qualities of light over the course of the seasons, to name but a few aspects. These elements all contribute to the *genius loci* (spirit of place) of a natural location, and the architectural phenomenologist Christian Norberg-Schulz (1980) has argued that buildings can participate in this broader spirit of place while offering humanity an existential grounding in a world of natural forces. Thus, a building may invite settlers to develop a meaningful relationship to the land for the first time, while for Indigenous visitors it may simply affirm their long coexistence with it (Tuck & Yang, 2012). This chapter will begin by introducing Norberg-Schulz's (1980) theory of *genius loci* as a starting point for the design of place-centered libraries, along with the Critical Regionalist movement that argues for locally-rooted designs while cautiously adopting modern construction techniques. While these offer us a solid foundation for considering place-based library designs, they do not explicitly unpack how we experience buildings *as meaningful* through our bodily experiences of them. For that, I will briefly discuss the theories of enactive perception and conceptual metaphor as tools for analyzing built environments. The chapter will conclude with analyses of two recently constructed libraries in Edmonton, Canada: the Calder and Capilano branches of the Edmonton Public Library. These two buildings are both beautiful, exceptional examples of small libraries, yet one largely turns its back to place while the other creatively embraces it, inviting visitors to develop a meaningful connection to Edmonton's aspen parkland biome.

Before proceeding, it should be noted that "place" is generally used here as a shorthand for "natural place," a geographic location's flora, fauna, geology, topography, and climate. While our experiences of place often include human constructions, this takes on a moral dimension in settler-colonial contexts where construction cultures are brought from other parts of the world, supplanting and repressing Indigenous ones (as the stringent requirements of the National Building Code of Canada surely do). Reflecting this, both libraries discussed here are resolutely settler constructions, ones rooted in the evolution of European architecture and in settler experiences of the Indigenous lands now known as Canada. While an architecture that responds with care to the qualities of a particular place does go against the classic colonial approach of imposing foreign styles, it does not necessarily decolonize or indigenize the space in any meaningful way. It may simply be a European, or Asian, or African building responding sensitively to this land (Tuck & Yang, 2012). While the question of how to decolonize and indigenize library architecture is a valuable one, I respectfully leave it to others to explore.

Genius Loci, Spirit of Place

Humans live between the stability of the earth and the ever-changing presence of the sky. This existential relationship was identified in Heidegger's influential article "Building, Dwelling, Thinking" (2008, pp. 343–363), where he explored how people dwell within nature, making a home for themselves in a world of natural forces. His argument – that we dwell by developing a deep involvement with our unbuilt surroundings, constructing paths, shelters, and other elements within them – has become widely influential among scholarship concerned with how we inhabit places and develop meaningful attachments to them (Ingold, 2000, p. 173). This "dwelling perspective" underscores the importance of feeling at home in the world, and it offers a strong argument for place-based architecture. Norberg-Schulz took this as a starting point for his influential theory of place, and in *Genius Loci: Towards a Phenomenology of Architecture*, he explores the implications, positing two dimensions to our acts of dwelling: "Man dwells when he can orient himself within and identify himself with an environment, or, in short, when he experiences the environment as meaningful" (1980, p.

5). The first aspect, orientation, speaks to how we get our bearings in an environment and learn to successfully navigate it. Elements like mountains, rivers, forests, and lakes, can provide landscapes with a sense of enclosure and directionality, helping us build cognitive maps of them (Tversky, 1993). For instance, a well-trodden path offers some directionality in an otherwise homogenous landscape (such as gently rolling grasslands), and a single mountain on the horizon creates a landmark that orients us (Lynch, 1960). Human settlements that respond to their natural context provide an even stronger sense of order, acting as potent foci that highlight the character of the larger landscape (Norberg-Schulz, 1980, 10). Just imagine looking down a grand boulevard and seeing a single mountain on the horizon to get a sense of this focalizing.

The second aspect of dwelling, identification, speaks to how we come to understand our place within nature, "becom[ing] 'friends' with a particular environment" (Norberg-Schulz, 1980, p. 21). In a passage with strong resonance for Canadians, Norberg-Schulz (1980) notes that "Nordic man has to be friend [sic] with fog, ice and cold winds; he has to enjoy the creaking sound of snow under the feet when he walks around" (p. 21). Architecture plays an important role in this process of learning to love a natural environment, since the design of our buildings can "'explain' the environment and make its character manifest" (Norberg-Schulz, 1980, p. 16). A thunderstorm becomes an enjoyable aesthetic event once we are inside, viewing it from behind the shelter of a pane of glass. And a hill may take on greater beauty if we spy a small lookout built on top, inviting us to make the ascent. Through their form, materials, aesthetic character, and the articulation of openings that mediate inside and out (windows and doors), buildings can establish a meaningful relationship to their natural surroundings. This invites us to dwell in the place, feeling at home in the world instead of in an oppositional relationship with nature. Norberg-Schulz terms this "concretization," where the form of the building embodies our perceptions of nature and our culturally-inflected sense of how we *should* dwell within a certain corner of it (1980, p. 53, 66). I will return to the finer points of how a library's design can invite this identification later in the chapter.

An important dimension to Norberg-Schulz's (1980) theory is that we experience places as cohesive wholes, "totalit[ies] made up of concrete things having material substance, shape, texture and colour" which together form an "environmental character" or "atmosphere" that "is the essence of place" (pp. 7–8). Theorists in other fields have also supported this assertion that we first experience the overall atmosphere of a space before considering its individual elements (Johnson, 2015, p. 46; Tversky, 2003, p. 72), and this underscores why buildings with placeless designs can be experienced as alienating. Instead of resonating with their wider environments and encouraging a cohesive sense of place emerging, these buildings feel arbitrary or attempt to define sterile man-made atmospheres which have little relation to the natural ones around them. We can think here, too, of buildings constructed in one city that evoke styles which are more at home elsewhere, such as the Spanish Colonial-style houses occasionally found in Edmonton. At best these may be interesting and beautiful places, but they cannot offer us a coherent existential foothold in the surrounding natural world.

As noted in the introduction, the placeless character of much contemporary architecture is rooted in industrialization, modern construction processes, and global aesthetic trends. Even when architects or the public desire a return to older ways of building, the realities of industrialized construction – and the huge labour cost of pre-industrial alternatives – become prohibitive (at least in developed nations). This has pushed some architects to grapple with how they can root their buildings in place while working within the constraints of a contemporary context. Responding to what he perceived as a new regional sensitivity emerging in some corners of the profession in the early 1980s, the architectural historian and theorist Kenneth Frampton wrote the twin essays "Towards a Critical Regionalism: Six Points for an Architecture of Resistance" (1983a) and "Prospects for a Critical Regionalism" (1983b). True to the "critical" in the title, Frampton envisions this approach as a form of resistance against the global homogeneity of late capitalism, where the same architectural styles and engineering approaches are universally adopted irrespective of the local context. Giving the example of how buildings receive daylight, Frampton argues that designing a building to embrace a region's unique quality of light "must almost by definition be fundamentally opposed to the optimum use of universal technique" (1983a, p. 26). Critical Regionalism has become something of a rallying cry for the architects that embrace the places they live and work, and as one would suspect, it integrates "passive" (non-mechanical) sustainable approaches where the building form is optimized for its local climatic conditions. The buildings of Alvar and Aino Aalto (Finland), Luis Barragán (Mexico), and

Diébédo Francis Kéré (Burkina Faso) offer suggestions for what Critical Regionalism can look like in diverse ecological and cultural contexts.

Linking placeless universalism with an overvaluing of sight over the other senses, Frampton (1983a) argues for the central importance of our tactile engagement with buildings: our direct, embodied experiences of touching, hearing, and smelling building materials (brick, wood, stone, glass, steel, etc.) "cannot be reduced to mere information, to representation" in the way that an image can (p. 28). In contrast, consider the Kansas City Public Library, designed to look like a giant row of books by having one exterior wall consist of huge graphics of book spines. When we see this building, its billboard-like graphics prime us to consider books, and the materiality of the building itself barely registers. Our architectural experience is mainly tied to our sense of vision and the images that arise in our imagination, not, as in all pre-industrial buildings, to a direct tactile encounter with physical materials (ones which may relate to the natural materials of a geographic locale). If we were speaking of paintings, Frampton would be arguing that painters should create artworks that invite us to pay attention to the brush strokes and the quality of pigment on the canvas, not solely the image depicted by the painting. Offering rich tactile experiences, ones which effortlessly relate to our tactile experiences of nature (the materiality of stone, wood, water, etc.), is one important way in which buildings can root us in place; even if most visitors are not consciously aware of it, they will nonconsciously experience this meaningful tactile connection (Goldhagen, 2017). Equally important is an architectural approach that embraces "the poetics of construction," resulting in buildings where we can see how the elements fit together, in contrast to seamless interiors that make it near-impossible to know how they were built. The first approach emphasizes the materiality of the constructed elements (e.g. a thick wood beam resting on a thin metal column), while the latter de-materializes them, creating an "abstract" interior composed of textured (and often untextured) surfaces (e.g. the beam and column are the same size and the same white material). While this sort of space might make for an interesting piece of installation art, it does nothing to root us in place.

Bringing these concerns into the domain of libraries returns us to the tension identified at the start of this chapter: as buildings, libraries can connect us to where we live, but as containers for collections from around the world, they are easily pulled towards the placelessness of contemporary shopping malls, airports, and hospitals (Augé,

1995). Beyond the more salient reasons of shared financial models, standardized engineering, mass produced parts with global supply chains, and modern construction methods, the placelessness of current buildings also results from an impoverished understanding of "function." Modern architecture brought with it the widely known dictum "form follows function," and when this is conceived in a reductive sense, a building quickly begins to lose a meaningful grounding to place. Someone designing a library may consider the best way to show off its collection, approaches for integrating its diverse areas into a coherent whole, and strategies for keeping noise from a children's area away from quieter places for reading. But they may never consider a connection to place, and "form follows function" will never ask them to, unless they take a wider view that *all* buildings have the function of providing an existential foothold as Norberg-Schulz (1980) has claimed. Whether the library is any good is judged against a placeless universal idea of a "good library," not against the circumstances of a particular library and its natural and social context. Yet approaching buildings in this decontextualized way is not necessary, even within the confines of contemporary engineering, finance, and construction, and Frampton (1983a) affirms that we can still design regionalist buildings in this milieu without having to revert to traditional forms of construction. Returning to the tension noted above, we find a false dichotomy: there is no reason why a library cannot embrace its location while offering a portal to media and culture from all corners of the globe. Arguably it works better when it does this, helping patrons know *where* they stand while engaging with the wider world, instead of offering them a door into a universalized *nowhere*, as shopping malls so frequently do.

Grounding Architectural Meaning

Norberg-Schulz and Frampton clearly formulate the problem of placeless architecture and offer us starting points for overcoming it, but their pieces discussed here do not get into the finer points of *how* we experience buildings as meaningful. For this, we can draw on the insights of architectural phenomenology and the emerging field of embodied cognition. This interdisciplinary area encompasses philosophy, cognitive science, psychology, and linguistics (among others), and it argues that cognitive processes are grounded in our bodily engagement with the world, not abstract symbol processing taking place within the brain (Johnson, 2007; Robbins & Aydede, 2009; Wilson,

2002). Work in this area provides strong justification for an embodied view of architectural meaning: we experience buildings from the position of our bodies, and that experience is necessarily coloured by the abilities and perceptual biases of the human body (Johnson, 2015; Robinson & Pallasmaa, 2015). Consider the sensation of warm sunlight washing over your skin, the visual rhythm of looking down a row of columns, or the tactile experience of grabbing a brass door handle worn smooth from continuous use. Returning to the example of paintings, the beauty of a particular artwork may primarily reside in our direct experience of its vibrant colours and lively brushstrokes instead of in the image that it depicts, and likewise, a great deal of architectural meaning is bound up in our immediate bodily experience of a building. Structures that arise in embodied experience also take on low-level meaning for us, and these include spatial relations like up and down, center and periphery, containment, and linearity among countless others (Johnson, 2007, pp. 136–145). The cardinal directions are another example, arising from the path of the sun and our bodies' distinct front, back, left, and right sides. While the vast majority of humanity shares an understanding of the cardinal directions, they mean different things to different cultures; this is universality at its best. Two embodied cognitive theories are particularly important in how we experience buildings, and they will serve as tools for the analyses that conclude this chapter: enactive perception and conceptual metaphor.

Enactive perception argues that our perception of the world is a form of action, going against the older view that our mind engages in a cycle of perceiving, thinking, and then acting upon the world (Noë, 2004). Gibson (1979) offers an example regarding visual perception: we understand the shapes of objects by walking around them and seeing them from many perspectives. The key idea is that we perceive spaces based on how we can act in relation to them: doors allow us to pass through, stairs and ladders help us move up and down, benches afford sitting, and library shelves afford placing and organizing books (or perhaps putting one's coffee down and subsequently forgetting it). This theory of affordances emphasizes that before we step back and contemplate the form, colour, or materials of things, we immediately assess *what we can do with them*. Recent discoveries in neuroscience have shown that some of the same neurons fire when we think about an action as when we actually complete it, and this lends another dimension to spatial perception: just thinking about sitting on a bench triggers some of the same cognitive response as if we were to actually sit down, and we can simulate the tactile experience of running our hand along a rough wall without actually touching it (Gallese & Gattara, 2015). This is broadly termed embodied simulation, and it means that as we move through buildings, we are constantly simulating interactions with their spaces and materials. The elements of the building *invite* this embodied engagement, and tactile elements are naturally more stimulating than large blank surfaces.

Moving from our direct bodily experiences to associative meaning – the image depicted in the painting instead of the colours and brushstrokes – conceptual metaphor theory argues that human cognition is largely a metaphoric process where we understand unfamiliar and abstract things by relating them back to concrete familiar ones (Lakoff & Johnson, 2003). For example, we understand theories by relating them back to buildings ("the foundation of the theory," "these facts buttress this theory," etc.), and the experience of understanding an idea by relating it to grasping objects ("I grasp that idea") (Lakoff & Johnson, 2003, pp. 52–53; Lakoff & Johnson, 1999, p. 54). Lower-level primary metaphors also charge basic spatial relations: up and down correspond to happy and sad (due to body posture), and we consider affectionate people "warm" and unfriendly ones "cold" (Lakoff & Johnson, 1999, p. 50). This theory initially arose in linguistics, however it has received significant backing in other fields, and this metaphoric process of "understanding one thing in terms of another" has been shown to take place with material objects as well (Lakoff & Johnson, 2003, p. 5; Tilley, 1999). A famous architectural example is the evocative forms of the Sydney Opera House, which invite us to understand them by way of sails, shells, and beaks (Goldhagen, 2017, pp. 255–256). This associative dimension of buildings helps them achieve a certain depth of meaning, and it speaks to how the forms and materials of a piece of architecture can reverberate with a natural context, weaving the built environment into its unbuilt surroundings.

Combining these two theories brings us back to Norberg-Schulz's (1980) discussion of "identification" and a further aspect of it, our propensity to identify with the forms of buildings, mentally stimulating the forces we perceive in the structure (Bloomer et al., 1977, p. 27). As Scott (1914/1980) noted long before recent cognitive explanations: "Weight, pressure, and resistance are part of our habitual body experience, and our unconscious mimetic instinct impels us to identify ourselves with apparent weight, pressure, and resistance exhibited in the forms we see" (pp. 230–231). When we see the Leaning Tower of

Pisa we *feel* its imbalance in a visceral sense, just as the formal balance of many classical buildings invites feelings of stability and repose. This dimension of how we experience buildings provides added justification for designs that show off how their elements are constructed, since we may feel the forces of a heavy wood beam resting on a slender metal column, but we are not likely to feel much at all if the beam and column appear to be made out of the same abstract white material.

Before proceeding on to our analyses, conceptual metaphor theory has some interesting implications for library architecture that are worth discussing. First, patrons' experiences of physical libraries powerfully shape how they conceive of "the library" as an institution in an abstract or ideal sense, since conceptual metaphor theory argues that our abstract reasoning is always grounded in concrete experience. "The Library" will always be a meaningful "where" to patrons as well as a "what." Second, as a concrete place with a particular spatial logic (of storing and organizing media objects and allowing visitors to freely browse and borrow them), "the library" can be used as a source in metaphors to understand other domains. For example, we could coherently say "the city is a library of buildings: its streets are the shelves and its buildings are the books" (Whistance-Smith, 2016, p. 6). And the recent trend of "tool libraries" for borrowing equipment has emerged quite naturally. Thus, innovations in physical library design may suggest new approaches for structuring other domains such as the virtual spaces of digital libraries (an inverse influence is possible, too). Finally, while the character of Carnegie libraries once helped define the public image of this institution in the Anglo-American world, the global shift to Modern architecture has left contemporary libraries without a strong association to a particular architectural style or building form (in contrast with churches, for example). As such, architects and the communities they serve have quite a bit of freedom in determining the aesthetic character of a library. At its worst this can result in bland buildings consisting of little more than a large room of book and media shelving sprinkled with places to sit and read, but at its best, a library can reflect its place and offer a creative response to the diverse needs of patrons, with different areas taking on unique and complementary atmospheres. Discussing this across building types, Norberg-Schulz (1980) notes that "different actions demand places with a different character," and thus a "dwelling has to be 'protective,' an office 'practical,' a ball-room 'festive' and a church 'solemn'" (p. 14). Given the many activities found in the contemporary library, we should desire a certain degree of spatial diversity within the building to best accommodate them (Whistance-Smith, 2016, 2014).

Summing up, we experience buildings as meaningful in two complementary ways: our direct qualitative experience of their materials and form (through touch, sight, smell, and mental simulation), and the associations they trigger for us in our imagination. When these two dimensions have a meaningful link to the natural place a building is located within, it cannot help but root us in that place. Here, the built environment is lovingly woven into the fabric of the unbuilt living world that it rests upon.

Calder and Capilano

Tools in hand, we can now analyze how two contemporary libraries – the Calder and Capilano branches of the Edmonton Public Library – respond to a natural place. Edmonton is located in the northwest corner of the Canadian prairies, within the transitional Aspen Parkland biome where the semi-arid prairies encounter the boreal forest (Hauser, 2021). The northern location and dry climate offer wonderfully crisp daylight, with hours-long sunrises and sunsets in summer and a sun that remains low in the sky during winter. Topographically, Edmonton is defined by the North Saskatchewan River valley which cuts a roughly 60m deep and 650–1000m wide path through the otherwise-flat city. The river valley has many ravines feeding into it, and these add to the natural diversity and spatial richness of the area. The character of the landscape is defined by the flat and gently rolling plains the city is built on, the hills and cliffs of the valley's edge (some with vegetation, others bare), and the intimacy of the densely forested ravines. To respond to this landscape is to interpret the contrast between the gentle grasslands and airy aspen forests, the darkness of the spruce groves, and the dramatic slopes of the valley and ravines. While some of Edmonton's natural areas may appear "wild" or "untouched," all of them are impacted by the history of human settlement in the area.

As a built environment, Edmonton reflects the settler-colonial history of Treaty Six Territory, the forms of construction common in 20th and 21st century North America, and the heavy suburbanization of this continent in the postwar era. As a geographic locale, it remains amiskwaciwâskahikan (beaver hills house), a land inhabited by diverse peoples including the nêhiyaw/Cree, Dené, Anishinaabe/Saulteaux,

Nakota Isga/Nakota Sioux, Niitsitapi/Blackfoot, and Métis, as well as the many Inuit who have made a home here (City of Edmonton, n.d.). This is a good place to dwell, as these peoples know well. Yet as a resolutely settler city, Edmonton's built form does not reflect this land's long history of inhabitation, often actively erasing it. Allowing the interpretive centre for an ancient archaeological site in Strathcona Science Park to fall into disrepair, and eventually be demolished, is but one minor example (Giovannetti, 2015). As noted in the introduction, the two libraries discussed here are unambiguously settler constructions, and this should significantly temper our expectations around how they relate to this land.

The Calder and Capilano branch libraries were selected as case studies for a number of reasons: they both opened in 2018 and are located in postwar suburban neighbourhoods, they have similar floor areas (~10,000 square feet), and they offer visitors a nearly identical set of activity spaces (reading areas, a collection, a program room, a children's area, a quiet study room, etc.). Most importantly, both offer a coherent architectural response to what a 21st century library – envisioned as a gathering place of knowledge and expression – may look like. Thus, we can surmise that Calder and Capilano offer visitors a similar experience in these many dimensions, and the aesthetic character of their architecture becomes a major differentiator. Purely in terms of location, these buildings also have different relations to Edmonton's natural landscape, with Calder located in a flat area far from the river in the northwest, and Capilano located along a ravine in the east. Since our focus will be on how these libraries relate to place, some aspects of the building that usually warrant greater discussion, such as the layout, will take a back seat in favour of a stronger focus on materiality, light, and atmosphere.[1] Finally, since this analysis contrasts a library that lacks a connection to place with one that offers a moderate one, they may too easily be read as 'bad' and 'good' examples respectively. This is unfortunate, since both libraries are compelling buildings, but it is a hard perspective to avoid if we consider a connection to place as a desirable quality.

Beginning with Calder, this library offers an excellent example of contemporary "universalist" architecture, the clean aesthetic of airports

---

[1] The reader is strongly encouraged to visit Calder and Capilano if they reside in Edmonton, and to view more photos of the libraries on their respective architects' websites if they do not.

and shopping malls, exemplified by the seamless minimalism of the Apple Stores found in many of them (fig. 1). As in those spaces, visitors are consumers browsing the products on display. The library was designed as a collaboration between Atelier TAG in Quebec and Marc Boutin Architectural Collaborative (MBAC) in Calgary (Mark Boutin Architectural Collaborative, n.d.), and is located at the southeast corner of a suburban recreational field. The single-storey, flat-roofed library is composed of large sheets of glass and silver metal panels, some of which are perforated to add texture to an otherwise flat facade. It has an irregular asterisk-like floorplan that makes it hard for someone to imagine the overall shape from the outside, but the walls are vertical and have an orderly panelized rhythm, often with glass at the ground level and metal panels above. This floorplan is poorly suited for its northern climate, since it results in a larger surface area of exterior walls (that lose heat in winter) for comparatively little enclosed space. However, this irregular shape works architecturally to define outdoor areas in between the lines of the asterisk, two with local vegetation facing the fields, and one containing the main entrance that opens towards the parking lot. The library's entry is highlighted with pink panels set behind silver perforated metal ones, and the cherry trees planted in this forecourt provide a clever accent when they bloom in the spring. These pink panels are a rare spot where the building exterior invites a clear metaphoric association with nature, since one will often find this shade of pink illuminating the horizon of a winter sunset.

Figure 1 The Calder Library.
Image courtesy of Gregory Whistance-Smith.

Approached from an adjacent arterial road, the library appears as an elegant metal box resting in a field, be it a field of grass or one of wind-swept snow. Here the lack of relation to nature becomes something of a virtue (at least by the building's own logic), since this shiny piece of architecture is the focal point, and its natural and suburban surroundings recede in one's attention. Returning to our discussion of people mentally simulating the forces they perceive in buildings, Calder's form feels quite balanced and lacks any strong gestures towards earth or sky; it simply sits peacefully between them, like a piece of metal suspended in thin-air between two magnets. This sense of rest and balance is somewhat disturbed by the arms of the asterisk plan radiating out from the center. Finally, while one arm of the building does have a berm coming partway up its wall, the artificiality of the silver metal cladding prevents a meaningful relationship to nature arising. Visitors to the library will never encounter a shiny grey material quite like this while spending time in nature (at least not at the scale of a building), and so this metallic library announces its artifice and fundamental separation from nature. It may sit *in* nature, but is not *of* it.

The Calder library is no less contemporary on the inside: the walls, columns, and ceiling are all white, the floor is tones of quietly textured grey, and some accent walls are painted in bright colours with large letters signaling what is to be found near them (fig. 2). Pushing this further, most of the furniture is also white (plastic and metal), including a space-age white fireplace that hangs from the ceiling with lounge chairs set around it. The asterisk-like floor plan has visitors entering the middle of the building, with different wings of the library inviting them to explore different areas, while providing a panoptic view for the centrally-located service desk. Many of the exterior walls are floor-to-ceiling glass out to the field beyond, and during daylight hours the building naturally fades from awareness as one's attention is drawn to the park-like setting beyond, creating a successful spatial link with nature. During long winter nights, however, all of this glass begins to reflect the interior spaces back on themselves and gives the space an ephemeral feeling. The ceiling is a faceted construction that evokes polygonal computer graphics, with lines of bright lights set into this mesh. The extraordinary whiteness and sense of cleanliness and sterility that arises in this library invites the metaphor of "library-as-lab": here people dissect specimens and conduct serious, controlled business. The bright colours provide some contrast, but since

Figure 2 The interior of Calder, looking towards the central service desk from the end of one wing. *Image courtesy* of Gregory Whistance-Smith.

they would not be out of place as accents in a fashionable work environment, they only serve to reinforce this chic ambiance. While some members of the public may enjoy their library feeling like a tech office or upmarket brand store, others may feel somewhat alienated by an atmosphere common in places they are rarely welcome in.

Moving from these overall impressions to the more specific concerns of light and materiality, Calder has an arbitrary response to natural light and a notable lack of tactile surfaces (ones such as rock, concrete, or wood that are stimulating to touch, and which invite our enactive perception when we see them). The asterisk floorplan and floor-to-ceiling glass offer extensive views out to the surrounding field and ample natural light, however these openings and the shape of the building are not *designed around* receiving natural light from the path of the sun. The windows are located where they are because of the layout of the library's areas, and to create views to the outdoor areas between the arms of the asterisk; they are not a direct response to the qualities of Edmonton's natural light. Contrast this with the rooftop light monitors found in Alvar Aalto's Rovaniemi and Seinäjoki libraries in Finland, optimized to take the horizontal light of the low winter sun and diffuse it over their interiors, offering visitors a gentle warm light for reading without the glare of direct sunlight. The light at Calder does receive special treatment at the staff offices by being filtered through perforated metal panels, however one suspects this design element was driven by a desire to offer staff some privacy while they work, as these huge windows face the main entrance.

As noted above, Calder's palette of materials is notable for its artificiality and near-total lack of tactile texture. None of the materials used in the building are natural: the shiny metal and glass of the exterior; the white surfaces of the interior; the greys of the floor, notice boards, anodized aluminum window frames, and some chairs; and the pops of bright colour in the accent walls (and some pieces of furniture). None of these materials have a link to nature, and they are widely used worldwide, giving them an even more universalizing quality. This all-enveloping artificiality, and the sterility that results, gives the library a hermetic feeling that resonates with the "science lab" metaphor noted above. While the spines of books and media offer a colourful, somewhat-tactile surface, these are too localized to alter the wider atmosphere of the space. Thus, the seamlessness of its construction and its untextured materials – the only exceptions are the perforations in some metal panels and the faint textures of the floor – give the library's space an ephemeral quality. Nature is always made up of distinct parts with rich materials that are stimulating to touch, and so to step into a seamless space without texture is to step outside of nature and into somewhere else, perhaps one more akin to the spaces of video games or the flat tones of web pages. This metaphoric link to the spaces of websites is even more salient due to the large text graphics located on the colour accent walls; the letters' large size makes one more aware of their abstract, graphic quality.

Finally, glass boxes have a special allure in Modern and contemporary architecture, and their experiential qualities have pride of place at Calder. Near the entry, visitors are greeted by a fish tank, and the silent study room located in one wing of the library is a floor-to-ceiling glass box with paths around it on both sides. Studying here perversely makes one the specimen on display, and like all glass boxes it brings a strange promise of visual connection and spatial disconnection. This *look-but-don't-touch* quality is most acutely felt in relation to the outdoor gardens located between wings of the library: the floor-to-ceiling glass offers views of these areas, but patrons cannot cross the threshold and wander them without fully leaving the library and awkwardly walking around the building. This is quite unfortunate, as these outdoor spaces were a key element of the design (Mark Boutin Architectural Collaborative, n.d.). One imagines how different this might feel if the glass walls could open up in summer and allow patrons to wander in and out (with the gardens having tall fences to the fields beyond, preventing theft while taking on more of a courtyard quality). The logic of the glass box takes place on three spatial scales at Calder: the fish tank (furniture), the study area (room), and the entire library (building), which is essentially a glass box in a field with metallic casing. This further resonates with the library-as-lab metaphor, since labs require isolation from their surroundings and can be built anywhere. They are the apotheosis of scientific-space, a *nowhere* space where universal laws are uncovered, and where "space" itself is conceived of purely as measurable extension (see Lefebvre, 1991). Criticizing how this conception of space has impacted architecture, Norberg-Schulz laments that "most modern buildings exist ... in a kind of mathematical-technological space which hardly distinguishes between up and down" (1980, p. 190). While against the spirit of this article, it is worth emphasizing that Calder's placeless atmosphere – which can perhaps offer the feeling of wandering through a floating world of information and expression – is a viable and defensible approach to contemporary library architecture.

Moving from a nowhere to a somewhere, the Capilano library offers a compelling response to its particular site along a ravine, and to the wider question of building a library in Edmonton. This library was designed by Patkau Architects in Vancouver in collaboration with Group2 in Edmonton (Patkau Architects, n.d.). No less contemporary than Calder, though with quite a different atmosphere, Capilano sits as a long black monolith between a suburban road and a wall of trees marking the edge of a ravine (fig. 3). Its irregular, jagged form is clad in black metal panels with strips of windows along the tops of the walls, and its main wall facing the street is slanted instead of vertical, taking on a slope akin to the steeper cliffs found in the river valley and metaphorically suggesting landscape forms as a result (be it a cliff face or mound of dirt). Its heavy massing also fits the climate, generally limiting the amount of surface area losing heat (its folded roof notwithstanding). While the metal cladding might suggest an industrial form, the inside of the black monolith is lined in a rhythmic wooden screen that naturalizes it, and light that enters the strip windows is beautifully filtered on the interior. The two ends of the building highlight the evocative shape of the folded roof, which for some visitors seems to suggest half of a maple leaf on its side. The intent is for the library to be overtaken by the ravine's forest, and for the monolithic form to one day be masked by tall prairie grasses and new trees planted between the road and the library: a coherent response to the narrow patch of land the library finds itself on, sandwiched between the suburban

Figure 3 The Capilano Library.
Image courtesy of Gregory Whistance-Smith.

houses and the ravine. This desire to fade into nature, giving visitors the sense of entering a library nestled into the forest, is also realized in one of the building's happier accidents: in conditions of blowing wet snow, the slanted outer wall of the library becomes covered in a thin layer of snow that unites it with the ground, suggesting a metaphor of the library as the interior of a snowy berm.

Visitors approach Capilano's cave-like entrance from a parking lot along the axis of the space, and here the building extends outwards into a long black bench that also includes the sign and a slot to drop off books. It also offers sheltered places to sit outdoors precisely where patrons may want to stop and wait for a friend or for a ride home (the benches and entry at Calder are unprotected). The prominent wood lining gives the building a tactile, natural quality that invites one to go inside, and since it is made of smaller pieces of wood, it also begins to evoke the whole-made-up-of-parts quality found in nature. The wood elements also serve as a strong counterpoint to the monolithic black metal, and their compelling visual rhythm makes this black metal fade from awareness. Further, and in contrast to the silver metal of Calder, this black cladding does have natural counterparts: obsidian, onyx, the coal seams in the nearby river valley cliffs, and the charcoal of burnt logs are all times where one may encounter this sort of blackness in nature.

Entering the library takes one from the cave-like quality of the entrance into the tall wood-lined main room, with the books and computer area below a two-storey ceiling, and seating areas under a low ceiling along a building-length strip window facing the ravine (fig. 4). The service desk greets visitors as they enter (with staff spaces tucked behind), and the library's program room anchors the other end of the building. Natural tones dominate here: a dark red carpet covers the floor, the rhythmic wood lining animates the ceilings, and the occasional walls painted white or black (some with colour accents) fade from awareness. Along with the spines of items in the collection, this space offers ample stimulation for patrons' enactive perception. The library's red carpet is quite bold, but it does relate to the many reds one will find in Edmonton's forests, from leaves in autumn to the bark of dogwoods and bright red mountain ash berries. Capilano's furniture is mostly white, black, and grey, and yet in contrast to Calder, here that becomes a virtue given the strong colour of the floor and ceiling. Its white metal bookshelves are also lined in blue-green glass panels, which evoke the foggy tones of the frozen streams in Edmonton's ravines (this is surely a happy accident, and one that only an active observer might notice). True to a concern with place, the library's interior is designed first-and-foremost around receiving natural light: in the early morning the trees of the ravine filter the East light, and later in the day the West light is filtered through the wooden lining. While the interior and exterior forms of Capilano are very ambiguous, in my experience the warm filtered light, red floor, and orange-browns of the wood metaphorically evoke a sense of being in a forest glade in autumn – a space eons away from the cold sterility

Figure 4 The interior of the Capilano library, looking north towards the service desk. *Image courtesy* of Gregory Whistance-Smith.

of a lab. Unfortunately, the LED lighting set into the wooden screen is quite bright, and the library loses some of its warmth as the sunset fades to night.

The grand central space is flanked by the window to the ravine along the East and the smaller areas of the library along the West (a study room, a printing area, a makerspace, washrooms, and the children's area). The view of the ravine is one of the most prominent ways that Capilano links patrons with nature, letting them watch wildlife pass by as they read. Community video footage of animals near the library is regularly shown on the screens behind the service desk, and on a recent visit I was amused to see a video of a coyote coming right up to the window; Edmontonians share an excitement for wildlife, and here the library facilitates this. While this strip window creates some of the same disconnection found at Calder – there is no easy way to get up from one's seat and quickly be outdoors – the sense in which the building orients itself towards nature is far more prominent here. In contrast to the use of a standardized window system at Calder, with sheets of glass punctuated by silver anodized aluminum frames (the kind found at malls, car dealerships, and highrise towers among countless other buildings), Capilano boldly uses large sheets of glass fastened to each other with a minimal strip of sealant, creating a far more seamless barrier. So seamless, in fact, that these sheets of glass have a grid of dots printed on them to prevent birds from flying right into them. The space of this seating area also gestures towards the ravine by having its glass slanted outwards and its ceiling tilting upwards. This creates a prospect-refuge spatial condition that humans find particularly enjoyable, where one stands protected in a refuge while looking out on a prospect (imagine standing at the mouth of a cave, looking out over a grassland) (Gifford, 2014, p. 61). The area is made even more special by the inclusion of a built-in heated bench along the length of the whole window, allowing one to sit right up against the glass. This sense of protection is also created on the West side of the building, but through different means: here the windows are covered by black metal perforated components, repurposed from their common use as industrial walkways. Peering out at the suburbs through this metal mesh can evoke a sense of peering through vegetation, and one wonders if vines will ever be planted along the building to make the most of this.

Capilano also provides a subtle contrast to the seamlessness of Calder: here some of the construction is visible and expressive, particularly the wood lining. The round black metal columns along the window to the ravine are the same size as the aspen trunks of the neighbouring forest, creating a dimensional relationship between this building component and natural counterparts. And since the ceiling comes down quite low in the reading area to meet these columns, one can easily perceive its construction and see the black fabric lining behind the wooden members, screws and all. While Capilano is far from a "tectonic" building that emphasizes its different parts and how they fit together, it resists the stronger dematerializing tendencies found in much contemporary architecture.

Finally, in discussing Capilano it must be acknowledged that it has two siblings also designed by Patkau Architects: the Audain Art Gallery in Whistler, B.C. (opened in 2016), and the yet-to-be-built Thunder Bay Art Gallery in Ontario. These two buildings somewhat universalize the way in which Capilano relates to nature, as they are also monolithic forms clad in black metal with wood linings. While all three buildings do respond to the particularities of their (semi-) natural sites through different layouts and formal strategies, they are using the same material palette in quite different parts of Canada. In a sense this speaks to the settler roots of these buildings, since all three have been created within the bounds of Canada's design and construction industry, with multiethnic settler Canadians as the primary anticipated visitors. By combining a bold form with a strong sense of interior shelter and connection to nature, they also enter the long line of settler buildings that have adopted this strategy in response to Canada's vast, harsh, and beautiful land (Polo & Ripley, 2014, p. 23).

If Calder offers us the library as a transcendent, place-less lab, then Capilano suggests the library as a man-made place nestled into the woods, one that offers an intriguing ambiguity between nature and artifice. Its bold forms are clearly man-made, and yet the slanted walls, rhythmic wood, and dappled light one will encounter within the library recall fragments of experience one may have in Edmonton's landscape. Here the building's form and materials, the overall atmosphere that results, and the little moments one experiences while dwelling there relate back to the atmospheres and little moments one may have in a particular corner of nature. Returning to Norberg-Schulz (1980), the building orients its patrons along the ravine and invites them to identify with this corner of nature, becoming more aware of its beauty in the process. Capilano is a contemporary building, and it reflects the many disconnections from nature that are inherent in modern construction. Yet this does not prevent the library from having a meaningful connection to the land it is built on, one that animates the space far beyond anything of which artifice is capable.

Conclusion

This chapter began with the assertion that the physical library anchors the broader institution; our experiences in actual libraries shape our understanding of what the library is, and what it can become. While there are countless architectural possibilities for a 21st century library that gathers a community around a collection – one spanning books, films, music, video games, and countless other media and technologies – the formal and material possibilities are quickly reduced when a library also seeks a meaningful relationship to the land it is built on and to the culture(s) of its inhabitants. Towards this end, I introduced Norberg-Schulz's (1980) theory of *genius loci* and Frampton's (1983a, 1983b) formulation of Critical Regionalism, two approaches that affirm the value of place-centered buildings, ones which invite their visitors and occupants to feel at home in a particular corner of the natural world. In an era when so many parts of the built environment begin to approximate a universal "no-place" (Augé, 1995; Norberg-Schulz, 1980, 190), libraries, as key gathering places in their communities, have an important role to play in helping anchor people on the lands they live on.

Taking this as a desirable architectural end, how do we go about achieving it? That formed the core question of this chapter, and I hoped to suggest viable approaches to place-based library design by introducing two theories of architectural meaning – enactive perception and conceptual metaphor – and by contrasting Calder and Capilano. Since these libraries share so many characteristics, and both can be defended as "excellent 21st century libraries," we were able to limit our attention to their differing forms and material palettes, and how these related to place. The colour and tactility of materials, and these materials' relationship to ones found in nature, ended up being the most significant difference between the two libraries, and the deciding factor in their connection to nature. In some sense this is an unfortunate reflection of contemporary architecture and construction: neither building made use of historic construction techniques with ties to the land (settler or Indigenous), neither used "raw" local materials such as river rocks or unmilled trees, neither was constructed by the community that uses it, and neither was designed with elements that could teach visitors about the local environment (one could imagine, for instance, a concrete wall panel with impressions of local leaves cast into it). These are all important ways that a library could relate to place, but many of them are hard to achieve in Canada's contemporary building industry, and one can only hope for an industry-wide shift away from globalized mass production to localized mass specialization. Until then, we will have to do what we can with the tools at hand.

To conclude: a library building achieves a meaningful connection to place when it responds to its natural context, orienting visitors within it, and when its atmosphere and tactile materials invites them to identify with the larger landscape they call home: its changing qualities of light and abundant materiality. While there is a certain cold beauty in Calder's lab-like interior, it is the warmth of light and texture in Capilano that leaves one feeling truly at home in Edmonton, drifting off into fictions on the page as a deer strolls by.

References

Augé, M. (1995). *Non-Places: Introduction to an anthropology of supermodernity* (J. Howe, Trans.). Verso. (Original work published 1992)

Battles, M. (2003). *Library: An unquiet history*. W.W. Norton & Company.

Bloomer, K. C., Moore, C. W., & Yudell, R. J. (1977). *Body, memory, and architecture*. Yale University Press.

City of Edmonton. (n.d.). *Land Acknowledgement*. City of Edmonton. https://www.edmonton.ca/city_government/indigenous-relations-office/land-acknowledgement

Frampton, K. (1983a). Towards a critical regionalism: Six points for an architecture of resistance. In H. Foster (Ed.), *The anti-aesthetic: Essays on postmodern culture* (pp. 16–30). Bay Press.

Frampton, K. (1983b). Prospects for a critical regionalism. *Perspecta 20*, 147–162.

Gallese, V., & Gattara, A. (2015). Embodied simulation, aesthetics, and architecture. In S. Robinson & J. Pallasmaa (Eds.), *Mind in architecture: Neuroscience, embodiment, and the future of design* (pp. 161–179). MIT Press.

Gibson, J.J. (1979). *The ecological approach to visual perception*. Houghton Mifflin.

Giovannetti, J. (2015, October 18). Once celebrated science park becomes shuttered casualty in Alberta. *The Globe and Mail*. https://www.theglobeandmail.com/news/alberta/once-celebrated-science-park-becomes-shuttered-casualty-in-alberta/article26866498/

Goldhagen, S. W. (2017). *Welcome to your world: How the built environment shapes our lives*. Harper Collins.

Hauser, S. (2021). North Saskatchewan spiritual: Reconnecting with nature in the Edmonton river valley [Master's thesis, Dalhousie University]. DalSpace Institutional Repository.

Heidegger, M. (2008). Building Dwelling Thinking. In D. F. Krell (Ed.), *Basic Writings* (pp. 343–363). Harper Collins.

Ingold, T. (2000). *The perception of the environment: Essays on livelihood, dwelling, and skill*. Routledge.

Johnson, M. (2007). *The meaning of the body: Aesthetics of human understanding*. University of Chicago Press.

Johnson, M. (2015). The embodied meaning of architecture. In S. Robinson & J. Pallasmaa (Eds.), *Mind in architecture: Neuroscience, embodiment, and the future of design* (pp. 33–50). MIT Press.

Lakoff, G., & Johnson, M. (1999). *Philosophy in the flesh: The embodied mind and its challenge to western thought*. Basic Books.

Lakoff, G., & Johnson, M. (2003). *Metaphors we live by*. University of Chicago Press.

Lefebvre, H. (1991). *The production of space*. Blackwell.

Lynch, K. (1960). *The image of the city*. MIT Press.

Mark Boutin Architectural Collaborative. (n.d.). *Calder Community Branch Library*. MBAC. http://www.the-mbac.ca/#/portfolio/cultural/calder-community-branch-library

Noë, A. (2004). *Action in perception*. MIT Press.

Norberg-Schulz, C. (1980). *Genius loci: Towards a phenomenology of architecture*. Academy Editions.

Patkau Architects. (n.d.). *Capilano Library*. Patkau Architects. https://patkau.ca/projects/capilano-library/

Polo, M., & Ripley, C. (2014). *Architecture and national identity: The centennial projects 50 years on*. Dalhousie Architectural Press.

Robbins, P., & Aydede, M. (2009). A short primer on situated cognition. In P. Robbins & M. Aydede (Eds.), *The Cambridge handbook of situated cognition* (pp. 3–10). Cambridge University Press.

Robinson, S., & Pallasmaa, M. (Eds.). (2015). *Mind in architecture: Neuroscience, embodiment, and the future of design*. MIT Press.

Scott, G. (1980). *The architecture of humanism: A study in the history of taste*. The Architectural Press. (Original work published 1914)

Tilley, C. (1999). *Metaphor and material culture*. Blackwell.

Too, Y. L. (2010). *The idea of the library in the ancient world*. Oxford University Press.

Tuck, E., & Yang, K.W. 2012. Decolonization is not a metaphor. *Decolonization: Indigeneity, Education & Society* 1(1), 1–40. https://jps.library.utoronto.ca/index.php/des/article/view/18630

Tversky, B. (1993). Cognitive maps, cognitive collages, and spatial mental models. In A. U. Frank & I. Campari (Eds.), *Spatial information theory: A theoretical basis for GIS* (pp. 14–24). Springer-Verlag.

Tversky, B. (2003). Structures of mental spaces. *Environment and Behaviour* 35(1), 66–80.

Whistance-Smith, G. (2014). Reframing the Branch Library: Enhancing Communication for the Public Good [Master's thesis, Dalhousie University]. DalSpace Institutional Repository.

Whistance-Smith, G. (2016). Reframing Library Architecture. https://www.gregws.ca/wp-content/uploads/2016/09/ReframingLibraryArch_v1.00.pdf

Wilson, M. (2002). Six views of embodied cognition. *Psychonomic bulletin & review* 9 (4), 625–636.

Making Place, Placing Makers
Connecting history, memory, and land by Indigenizing New Hampshire Public Library Local History Collections

Laura Marie Judge and Jedidiah Crook

> Everything in U.S. history is about the land—who oversaw and cultivated it, fished its waters, maintained its wildlife; who invaded and stole it.
>
> – Dunbar-Ortiz, 2014, p. 1

Land Acknowledgement

We are a white settler educator and a white settler librarian, meaning we are non-Indigenous peoples living in the United States who are part of "the European-descended sociopolitical majority" (Thomas, 2019). We honor and offer deep gratitude to the Abenaki people on whose land this chapter was written. We recognize that N'dakinna, which includes the land now known as New Hampshire, is the unceded territory of the Abenaki people, and that their land exceeds the now imagined boundaries of this state. We recognize that they have cared for and lived on this land for thousands of years, and that they continue to do so to this day. We acknowledge the history of violence and mass genocide that led to our present occupation of these lands.

As settlers working and living on the occupied land of the Abenaki peoples, we believe in the work of reconciliation, indigenization, and rematriation within our communities as a necessary step towards decolonization. We write this with profound appreciation for the Abenaki peoples without whom this chapter would not have been possible.

It is important to recognize that the effects of colonialism are visible and present still today, and that one of these effects is the fracturing and destruction of Abenaki nationhood, identity, and sovereignty. Colonial borders and genocide deeply fragmented Abenaki homelands (Obomsawin, M., 2020). For this reason, we worked with both self-identified Abenaki peoples within the state, as well as with Abenaki members of the First Nations reserve at Odanak. It is necessary to point out that these groups see themselves as separate, and do not work in tandem. Despite controversies of recognition, we sought to work with groups who are in current partnerships with New Hampshire public libraries, and who are active shapers of Indigenous Knowledges within the state. In doing so we recognize the plurality of these knowledges within and between Indigenous nations and communities (Jacob et al. 2018).

Introduction

Narratives of settler colonialism permeate the collective national identity of the United States of America. Settler colonialism is distinguished from extractive, or franchise, colonialism in that Indigenous land is the resource desired for its new settler population (Sturm, 2017, p. 4). Settlers colonize Indigenous land "with the intention of making a new home on the land, a homemaking that insists on settler sovereignty…and the disruption of Indigenous relationships to land" (Tuck and Yang, 2012, p. 5). In this way, settler colonialism relies on the destruction of Indigenous peoples, their communities, knowledge systems, culture, and claims to their land. The presumptions that underlie settler narratives have had paramount impacts across N'dakinna, now known as New England, marking it as a locus of colonial myth and genocidal erasure, particularly because it is the mythologized site of the 'first landing' of the Mayflower at Plymouth Rock (Bradford, 1899). These narratives, regardless of accuracy, impact all institutions—from their names, to their influence on community understanding of local place and history. Public education institutions, namely libraries and schools, have historically worked to normalize the fabricated conception of the settler colonial 'new world'; their active perpetuation of this untruth further divorces the communities they serve from the land on which they live and on which these spaces are located.

A tandem fallacy is that of library neutrality, and many in the profession have outlined how libraries are not currently, and have never been, socially or politically neutral spaces (Bertot et al., 2013; Carlton, 2018; Gohr, 2017; Leung & López-McKnight, 2021). Libraries are often upheld—particularly by those of historical and economic privilege—as major symbols of impartial access and knowledge in the national misconception of free and equal education (Borell et al., 2018). Yet historically, they can be understood as collaborators in genocidal efforts of assimilation, erasure, and destruction of Indigenous cultural practices, all in the name of manufacturing an 'American' identity fueled by white supremacy[2] (Genovese, 2016; Smith, 1999). In prioritizing the written word, the English language, and the white male cisgendered able-bodied perspective, libraries are complicit in the delegitimization and devaluation of Indigenous Knowledges (Schlesselman-Tarango, 2017). Centering Indigenous Knowledges is an essential part of decolonization in libraries, which we understand as the prioritization of Indigenous voices, practices, and lived experiences while "*decentering* whiteness" (Cooke, 2020, para. 5). This shift is also a core element of indigenization, "a process of naturalizing Indigenous Knowledge systems and making them evident to transform spaces, places, and hearts" (Antoine et al., 2018, p. 6). The practice of privileging whiteness and unquestioning the culture of white supremacy is deeply embedded in librarianship and the information science field in the United States (Chiu et al., 2021). This must be addressed. As Sofia Y. Leung and Jorge R. López-McKnight put it, "we must upend the relationship between library and information studies (LIS) and White Supremacy" (2021, p. 318). As settlers, as white people, we cannot dismantle the effects of white supremacy in libraries without collaborating with and (re)empowering those who have systematically been oppressed, erased, and disparaged.

We want to be clear that when we use the plural pronoun 'we' throughout this chapter we use it in reference to ourselves as settlers as well as in reference to non-Indigenous people more broadly, though we

---

[2] When we refer to white supremacy, we are employing Frances Lee Ansley's definition (1989, p. 1024).

are primarily speaking as and to white people. When we refer to the first people of what is now known as the United States we use the terms Indigenous, American Indian, Native American, and Native interchangeably to mirror the language used in the various sources referenced throughout this chapter. We recognise the problematic nature of these collectivizing terms that group together vastly different and unique nations and their distinct experiences with settler colonialism (Smith, 1999, p. 6).

As residents of what is now known as New Hampshire, we focused our studies on the libraries within its boundaries and their collections' narration of its individual history but recognize that these state borders continue the imagined borders of a colonized land. The public libraries in what is now called New Hampshire are undeniably part of the colonial project—the very names of a multitude of towns and public libraries mark the appropriation of Indigenous language (ex. Merrimack Public Library, Penacook Branch Library, Nashua Public Library, Contoocook, Hooksett, Ossipee). Peterborough, New Hampshire is the site of the first free public library supported entirely by taxation in the United States, and famed Dartmouth College in Hanover, New Hampshire was originally founded for the "education and instruction of Youth of the Indian Tribes in this Land" (Rubin & Rubin, 2020; Wright, 1995, para. 6). Yet, New Hampshire public library local history collections often lack recognition or accurate representation of local Indigenous histories. A close examination of the historical works most prevalent in New Hampshire public library local history collections exemplifies that Indigenous peoples are consistently relegated to a distant past, and harmfully depicted as 'savage' by a majority colonial white authorship, casting indigeneity in the light of myth and folklore.

Great violence and loss took place on this land, and to this day, New Hampshire differs from its neighboring New England states (ME, VT, MA, NY, RI) in that it does not have any federally or state recognized tribal land (Bureau of Indian Affairs, 2016; Vermont Land Trust, 2012). The forced removal and genocide of Abenaki peoples from this land is rarely mentioned as such in New Hampshire library local history collections or narratives. Thus, this chapter focuses on the libraries and local history collections within the boundaries of the lands of the Wabanaki Confederacy, and specifically of the Abenaki nation, which are now referred to as New Hampshire. We aim to investigate the relationship between New Hampshire public library local history collections, lived local histories, and shared understandings of land. We are specifically interested in local history collections, as "we first have to determine what is taught to us that originates from White Supremacy and then consciously unlearn it" (Leung et al., 2021, p. 20-21).

Research Framework

Research Aims and Questions

We have worked and lived in New Hampshire, a state without federally recognized tribal nations or ceded lands, for twenty plus years, and we were problematically accustomed to the lack of visibility, recognition, and education about Abenaki peoples and nationhood. Despite the ever-present appropriation of Indigenous languages, place names, and images throughout the state, public awareness is rarely ever drawn to the peoples who were displaced and murdered for the colonial settlement of this land, and even less so to their current lived experiences. This national trend of intentional erasure of Indigenous histories and peoples is deeply harrowing given that there are 6.9 million American Indian and Alaska Natives (either alone or mixed race) according to a 2021 U.S. Census Bureau report. Furthermore, U.S. census questionnaires and results have strategically mis- and underrepresented Indigenous populations since the first census taken in 1790 which exacerbates erasure (Deerinwater, 2019).

As educators, public service professionals, and environmentalists, we believe in the necessity of acknowledging difficult truths, of allowing what should be unsettling to rightly unsettle. As settlers, we feel an ethical responsibility to reckon with the harmful historical narratives that we and our communities create and perpetuate. To repair and reconnect with the land and the people who have suffered from settler colonial genocide and its foundational methodologies of resource exploitation and overconsumption, we must make an intentional cultural and epistemological shift toward uplifting Indigenous Knowledges and recognizing colonial responsibility. Following Indigenous scholars Shauneen Pete (Cree), Chris Newell (Passamaquoddy), and Spencer Lilley (New Zealander and Māori), we refer to this process as indigenization. Pete refers to the work of Ghanaian scholar Akwasi Asabere-Ameyaw in her explanation of indigenization, stating that "indigenizing works hand in hand with decolonizing. It's not enough to challenge both 'colonial and colonizing curricula [or in this case collections],' we must also recognize that it's about 'affirming the relevance of Indigenous [K]nowledge[s]'" (2013, p. 103). Newell argues that, to indigenize libraries, we must "incorporate Indigenous [K]nowledge[s] of sustainable lifeways that existed here for 12,000 years" into our collections, policies, and daily practices (2021, 16:14-16:20). Lilley writes that indigenization "gives libraries and information management agencies an opportunity to incorporate and integrate Indigenous Knowledge systems, values and practices into existing institutions and tailor these to meet the needs of their Indigenous community" (2021, p. 308)

Thus, in our investigations, we are primarily interested in prioritizing and affirming Abenaki knowledge and truths. To this end, we also employ Tribal Critical Race Theory (TribalCrit) as defined and developed by Bryan McKinley Jones Brayboy, and work specifically with three of its main tenets: "colonization is endemic to society"; "the concepts of culture, knowledge, and power take on new meaning when examined through an Indigenous lens"; and, "[t]heory and practice are connected in deep and explicit ways such that scholars must work towards social change" (2005, pp. 429-430). Using a theoretical lens informed by TribalCrit and ongoing practices of indigenizing historical narratives, we asked ourselves and New Hampshire public library staff to reflect on the relationship between their library's local history collections, local Abenaki nations, and our shared land. With Deloria et al., "[w]e can imagine a future when the United States and its citizens commit to grappling with fundamental questions: What does it mean to live on Indian land? What does it mean that Indian people are still here?" (2018, p.15). In this chapter, we endeavor to further these questions by asking: for settlers and non-Indigenous library staff, what does it mean for a public library to exist on occupied land, and to prioritize exclusionary and harmful white settler colonial narratives?

We recognize that our process of addressing shared narratives of colonial history is one that, although working towards the goals of Indigenous sovereignty and representation, is focused on white settler enlightenment and the unlearning of colonial ideologies. The history that has been erased by and from colonial systems, and settler colonial shared knowledge is not unknown to Abenaki peoples, nor is it singular to this one state or this one Indigenous nation. The findings presented in this chapter may be unsettling to some, but we encourage non-Indigenous library staff to sit with that discomfort as "solidarity is an uneasy, reserved, and unsettled matter that neither reconciles present grievances nor forecloses future conflict" (Tuck &

Yang, 2012, p. 3). We did not work to seek *an* answer, but to develop a deeper understanding and to find new methods and potential ways of engaging with New Hampshire history, memory, and land. This is a shared work, and it is rooted in ongoing partnerships, continual commitments, and a perpetual openness. As this work is shared, we invite and encourage anyone reading this to contact us and participate—to expand, question, and sustain our collective efforts.

Research Design

We conducted a comparative analysis of how New Hampshire public libraries function as keepers of a selective and exclusive past, curated to tell a specific settler colonial history. To gain a broader understanding of the inaccurate and harmful representations prevalent throughout the state, we digitally surveyed New Hampshire public libraries (n=36) to analyze the depth of local history collections, and their inclusion of Indigenous voices and histories. Suzie O'Bomsawin (Abénakis d'Odanak), Director of the Ndakinna Office and member of the Grand Council of the Waban-Aki and Daniel G. Nolett (Abénakis d'Odanak), Kin8dokawawinno/General Director of the Counsel of Abenaki at Odanak were instrumental contributors throughout our research process. Paul and Denise Pouliot, the Sag8mo/Head Male Speaker/Grand Chief and Sag8moskwa/Head Female Speaker of the Cowasuck Band of the Pennacook-Abenaki People, also provided us with insight into their experiences with New Hampshire libraries. With the perspective and input of local Indigenous peoples we have been given great guidance—not only on which questions are most important to ask ourselves as settler researchers, but on how New Hampshire library staff can take steps towards indigenizing New Hampshire public library local history collections.

Our survey consisted of three parts and a total of 18 questions. The first part determined general demographics and geography, the second asked library staff to analyze their library's local history collections, and the last asked library staff to reflect on their library's programming and collection development partnerships with Abenaki groups and nations over the past ten years. The section regarding local history collections asked respondents to gauge collection size, usage, discoverability, and policies in congruence with Reference and User Services Association (RUSA) guidelines for establishing local history collections. The section regarding partnerships with local Indigenous groups asked whether their institutions had made efforts to work with Indigenous groups through collection development, deaccession, and/or programming. The survey questions were informed by our conversations with Abenaki peoples in order to center their preferences and concerns. A total of 213 New Hampshire public libraries were identified, based on the annual Institute of Museum and Library Services (IMLS) supported Public Library Statistics data logs, which are maintained by the New Hampshire State Library. Of these 213 libraries, staff from 36 libraries anonymously completed the digital survey which was delivered via email through a combination of direct message, phone calls, and the New Hampshire Automated Information System (NHAIS) listserv. There was representation from six of the eight counties in the state, with Coos and Belknap left unrepresented, despite efforts to encourage their participation. In total, the survey results made for a response rate of 17%.

Additionally, we hosted a focus group in which librarians from across the state participated in a dialogue about their own library's local history collections, cataloging, and possible solutions to the issue of Indigenous erasure in New Hampshire public library local history collections. Finally, we also worked with Leigh Ann Hamel (Anishinaabe), co-liaison of the New Hampshire Library Association's Equity, Diversity, and Inclusion Committee, and met with the Committee as a whole to share our findings and seek out interest for collaboration.

We have seen the work that some New Hampshire librarians are doing to reckon with our past and move toward a more socially just future, such as Portsmouth Public Library's Indigenous Stories program series or Cooke Memorial Library's Wabanaki History, Ecology, & Experiences program series (Portsmouth Public Library, n.d.; Chocorua Lake Conservancy, n.d.). We believe this to be a shared work, but that labor must be put in by non-Indigenous librarians and educators. So, we sought out, listened to, and elevated the perspective of local Indigenous peoples. As a result, we set a framework, asked questions of New Hampshire library staff members, analyzed the intersections between memory, local history collections, and land within the state, had conversations, and collectively brainstormed possible solutions.

Throughout this research, we worked with local Abenaki nations and individuals to understand how we could best serve and effect positive change for their communities. We are deeply grateful to those who have offered us necessary guidance and education in this endeavor. This work would not be possible without their input and support.

Findings

On 'Firsting and Lasting' in New Hampshire Settler Colonial Narratives

When people go to a New Hampshire public library seeking information about a town or city's history, they are often directed to local history collections. When surveyed about the presence and usage of these collections, 62% of responding libraries say they have a dedicated local history room, and, on average, these rooms are accessed by the public more than 5 times a month. Furthermore, 14% of respondents state that their collection is accessed by the public more than 10 times a month. These collections give context and perspective that link the present to the past, marking the public library as "a logical place for residents to gather information about their community, its residents, and its history" (Bijali & Khan, 2018, p. 96). Nearly a quarter of respondents estimated the size of their local history collection to be 1,000 items or more. The median New Hampshire public library collection size for all print materials is 17,140 items (NHSL, 2020). These statistics point to the importance of local history collections in terms of place and sensemaking and mark the significance of a collection audit and analysis.

Titles that appear most frequently in local history collections throughout the state of New Hampshire include Edwin Charlton's *New Hampshire As It Is* (1856), Jeremy Belknap's *The History of New Hampshire* (1831), Francis Chase's *Gathered sketches from the early history of New Hampshire and Vermont* (1856), John McClintock's *History of New Hampshire* (1888), Everett Stackpole's *History of New Hampshire* (1916), Coolidge and Mansfield's *A History and Description of New England* (1859), and George Barstow's *The History of New Hampshire* (1842) (see Appendix A). These historical accounts all rely on the myth that colonizers were the first to discover the land now known as New Hampshire.

According to Jean O'Brien, an Ojibwe scholar and author of *Firsting and Lasting: Writing Indians Out of Existence in New England* (2010), the act of 'firsting' is the intentional depiction of settlers as the 'first' to discover, name, develop, and cultivate culture in a place. The notion of 'firsting' is not only based upon but requires the othering of the Indigenous peoples already on this continent. 'Firsting' is problematically instrumental to a majority of New Hampshire history books housed in New Hampshire public library local history collections.

Barstow's *The History of New Hampshire* describes the colonization of Abenaki land as the establishment of a "new world—a world conquered from barbarians" (1842, p. 5). Charlton writes in *New Hampshire As It Is* that "the discovery of America in 1492 by Christopher Columbus was one of the most remarkable events in the history of the world" (1856, p. 9). Charlton's inaccurate 'firsting' credits Christopher Columbus with 'discovering' an already occupied North America when it is well documented that he never set foot on North American soil (Dunbar-Ortiz, 2021). In a similar act of 'firsting,' Belknap's chapter titled "Remarks on the Tempers and Manners of the Indians" begins with "at the time of the first discovery" (1831, p. 100). Barstow frequently refers to the English colonizers as "the *first* settlers of New Hampshire" and accordingly, to England as "the first that discovered the continent of America" (1842, p. 6 & p. 9). Stackpole describes "the first discoverer" of the New Hampshire region as Captain Martin Pring highlighting the importance of European fishermen and seafarers to the settlement of the area (1916, p.4) McKintock does acknowledge that "before the advent of the first white settlers, there were living within the present limits of New Hampshire a powerful tribe of Indians" which he later identifies as the Pennacook tribe (1889, p. 21). Yet he still refers to the land now known as New England as the "new world", and to settlers as "first comers" throughout his book (1889, p. 23 & p. 79). This process of 'firsting' employed by New Hampshire historians acts principally to dehumanize Indigenous peoples, mark their land as uninhabited, and thus excuse the genocidal acts committed upon them in the name of colonial expansion.

The 'new world' construct "implicitly argues that Indian peoples never participated in social, cultural, or political practices worthy of note" (O'Brien, 2010, p. 6). The devaluing of Indigenous practices is imperative to settler colonization and the colonial understanding of land. Many Indigenous peoples of what is now called New England live in subsistence communities that hold deep generational, relational, and scientific understandings of the various habitats in which they live (Obrien, 2010; Portalewska, 2014; Strobel, 2020). The colonial 'new world' construct disparages these relations and divorces settlers from the land which they were/are newly inhabiting. Early American historian, Peter S. Leavenworth, observes the frequent reference to usufructuary rights to hunt, fowl, fish, plant, and harvest in New England deeds of Indigenous land transactions from the 1630s to the 1690s. Leavenworth states specifically that colonists' reliance on "usufruct rights was, therefore, a critical condition of Indian dispossession," as the ability for Indigenous peoples to continue to be in relationship with their land was used as a coercive tactic by the settlers who already possessed legal and political dominance in land exchange (Leavenworth, 1999, p. 282). Even Stackpole—though problematically—acknowledges that "the Indians were cheated in trades and in purchase of lands as the ignorant are generally cheated by those who have superior power" (1916, p. 89).

In "Re-evaluating Tribal Land Use Customs," John C. Hoelle maintains Leavenworth's findings stating, "in tribal societies, individual or clan ownership of land was often based exclusively on use" (2011, pp. 552). Hoelle further states that settler colonial "[a]ssimilationist pressures also severely altered traditional forms of tribal land tenure… to the point that tribal customary land rights have been almost totally supplanted by Anglo-American concepts of unqualified private ownership" (2011, pp. 552-553). Indigenous dispossession and colonial expansion, therefore, relied upon devaluing acts of 'firsting' that degrade Indigenous peoples and their traditional practices to that of an untamable 'wild' that is irrevocably of the land while physically being uprooted from it.

As colonial settlers continued to lay claim to Indigenous land, Indigenous belief systems and cultures, traditional ecological knowledge sources, and ceremonial practices were proscribed under such acts as the Code of Indian Offenses in 1883.[3] As O'Brien states, "the modernity New Englanders claimed as their hallmark depended upon breaking with an Indian world they interpreted as rooted in nature" (2010, pg. 4). To dehumanize Indigenous people meant a complete turning away from valuing the natural world, and the embracing of capitalist exploitation of all resources. This othering—and concomitant destructive processes—is effected and perpetuated throughout New Hampshire libraries' local history rooms, in accounts which lay the foundation of New Hampshire historical memory.

---

3 This legislation classified traditional dancing as well as ceremonial and medicinal practices as "Indian offenses," and permitted authorities to use force, imprisonment, and the reduction of rations with the aim of having "the evil practices…. ultimately abolished" (Rules Governing the Court of Indian Offenses § 4, 1883). See R.N. Clinton (2008) for further explanation of the Code, how it has been amended, and why it is so difficult to locate the original document on government web sources.

Processes of dehumanization are evident in the terminology used to describe Indigenous peoples in New Hampshire history books housed in local history collections. Charlton, Stackpole, and Barstow all refer to Indigenous peoples as "savage," "savage tribes," and "savage men of the wilderness" (1856, pp. 42-65; 1916, p. 91; 1842, p. 437). McClintock writes that Indigenous peoples are "generally addicted [. . . to] drunkenness", and states "the white man was their superior" (1889, p. 80 & p. 120). Though critical of how many English historians refer to Indigenous peoples as "dogs, caitiffs, miscreants, and hellhounds," Belknap still uses "savages" and "unhappy creatures" to refer to Indigenous peoples throughout his volumes (1831, pp. 102-103). Stackpole asserts that "it is foolish to contend that the scanty tribes of Indians owned the soil and forests of all New England" (1916, p. 90). Barstow puts the validity of Indigenous peoples' existence into question when he refers to them as "the red race, of doubtful origin" (1842, p. 5). These colonial narratives effectively synonymize Native with 'wild,' 'savage' and 'uncivilized', marking Indigenous peoples as inherently tied to the land and nature so as to make them indistinguishable from it.

Chris Newell explains in his lecture Re-Indigenizing Historical Narratives that "by classifying the human beings that they [English colonizers] were seeing here in the Americas as part of the wilderness rather than part of their own idea of civilization... they [Indigenous peoples] were somehow less than human. By being less than human... land was ripe for discovery because it was technically–under European standards–unoccupied" (2021, 40:10-40:41). The settler colonial understanding of Indigenous peoples as tantamount to the land and in opposition to European civility marked both Indigenous peoples and their land as rightly exploitable. Anthropologist Taylor Genovese (2016) draws the disturbing conclusion that not only does this dehumanization provide justification for acts of colonial genocide and exploitation, but it also provides "early archival institutions with the justification to house items [cultural artifacts and expressions] that were—particularly in the late 19th century—stolen from Indigenous land" (p. 34).

The dehumanization of Indigenous peoples in New Hampshire colonial historical narratives is furthered to that of 'extinction' in some of the titles regarding New Hampshire history. Mansfield and Coolidge address New England history, and in their introductory chapter on the state of Maine, write "now the whole of that once noble [Abenaki] nation is extinct" (1859, p. 20). In their chapter on Indigenous tribes of

New Hampshire, these authors assert that "the aboriginal inhabitants, who held the land of New Hampshire as their own, have been swept away" (Coolidge & Mansfield, p. 404). In Belknap's questioning of how historians have "generally represented Indians in a most odious light," he resolves that "providence has now put an end to the controversy by their almost total extirpation" (1831, p. 103). These are examples of 'lasting,' which O'Brien describes as "the narrative construct of Indian extinction" that work to further justify present day settler colonial occupation (2010, p. xxiv). O'Brien contends that "the collective project of local [New England] narrations cast Indian peoples as teetering on the brink of extinction if they [do] not relegate them explicitly to the past by declaring them extinct" (2010, p. 4).

There are explicit examples of how these narratives affect Abenaki peoples to this day such as the Vermont Supreme Court's specific reliance on "the increasing weight of history" in *State v. Elliott* (1992) which asserted that the Abenaki nation in New England "no longer held aboriginal title to their ancestral homeland" within the state of Vermont (Gilio-Whitaker, 2019, p. 37). The court based its denial of Abenaki rights on the unsubstantiated claim that extinguishment of "aboriginal rights...may be established by the increasing weight of history" (State v. Elliott, 1992). The court ultimately argued that "the Abenakis (as we shall refer to them for purposes of this opinion) are no longer a tribe, and, even if they are, any aboriginal title to the land was extinguished by governmental action long ago" (State v. Elliott, 1992).

Suzie O'Bomsawin and Daniel G. Nolett also both acknowledge the intersections of dispossession and the lack of accurate Abenaki history or perspective in the libraries situated upon occupied Abenaki land. Still, O'Bomsawin points out that although the accounts of Abenaki history in canonized settler colonial written texts are often racist and problematic, they are still important. She says, "There are some words that are not being used [anymore], because they would be hurtful, but the information is still valid and still helping us understand the [Abenaki] nation better. So, it's not always...black and white in the analysis as well" (personal communication, June 8, 2021). Nolett and O'Bomsawin both speak to the ways in which the Abenaki Council of Odanak use colonial documents for historical reconstruction while at the same time acknowledging these texts' harmful inaccuracies.

In 'firsting' colonial settlers and 'lasting' Indigenous peoples—in labelling Abenaki peoples and their neighboring nations as 'savage' and 'of the wild,' and then promptly disappearing them—early New Hampshire historians shaped the canon of New Hampshire history with the tools of genocide. In the name of assimilation, civilization, and modernity, colonizers attempted to eradicate Indigenous peoples and their knowledge systems, so as to distance themselves from the reality of their atrocities. Thus, the shunning of all things Indigenous meant a turning away from a reciprocal relationship with the land, and from the vast ecological knowledge of its caretakers. Edwin Charlton's *New Hampshire As It Is* (1856), Jeremy Belknap's *The History of New Hampshire* (1831), Francis Chase's *Gathered sketches from the early history of New Hampshire and Vermont* (1856), John McClintock's *History of New Hampshire* (1888), Everett Stackpole's *History of New Hampshire* (1916), Coolidge and Mansfield's *A History and Description of New England* (1859), and George Barstow's *The History of New Hampshire* (1842) all engage in the incredibly harmful acts of firsting and lasting. Their inaccuracies detach present day readers from the harrowing truths of the state's history and encourage the complicit occupation of unceded lands. Still, a title search in the NHAIS catalog reveals these are the titles that New Hampshire public libraries uphold as canonical to the collective understanding of New Hampshire history (see Appendix A).

Analyzing Contemporary Representation

Addressing the harmful settler colonial canon should occur in parallel to an analysis of titles published in the last twenty years which work to inform New Hampshire communities about Abenaki present and future, as well as about Indigenous peoples in the region more broadly. Decolonization and indigenization should not just be about historical reconstruction. Indigenous peoples "should not be viewed in terms of the past, but through the lens of futurity" (Deloria et al., 2018, p. 9). Circulating library collections should include titles authored and/or contributed to by Abenaki peoples such as *Dawnland Voices: An Anthology of Indigenous Writing from New England* by Siobhan Senier (2014), *Woven Through the Sweetgrass* (2021) by Claudia Chicklas, or *The Visual Language of Wabanaki Art* by Jeanne Morningstar Kent (2014), which uplift Indigenous voices and invite readers to engage with and support the work of contemporary Indigenous makers in literature, film, and craft. Maori scholar Linda Tuhiwai Smith, explains how "decolonization must offer a language of possibility, a way out of colonialism" (Smith, 1999, p. 204). This language of possibility cannot rest on the biased perspectives of a colonial past. However, according to the NHAIS

ILL System, fewer than ten libraries have *Dawnland Voices*, and fewer than five have *Woven Through the Sweetgrass* and *The Visual Language of Wabanaki Art* in their collections. The titles most prevalent in New Hampshire public libraries published in the last twenty years that relate specifically to Abenaki people have a majority non-Indigenous male authorship and historicize an Abenaki past more than they outline Abenaki futurity. These titles are listed below in order of their quantity throughout the state.

Held by more than 70 New Hampshire libraries:

- Atkinson, J. (2015). *Massacre on the Merrimack: Hannah Duston's captivity and revenge in colonial America.* Rowman & Littlefield Publishers, Inc.

Held by more than 50 New Hampshire libraries:

- Caduto, M. (2003). *A time before New Hampshire: The story of a land and Native Peoples.* University Press of New England.

- Heald, B. D. (2014). *A history of the New Hampshire Abenaki.* The History Press, Charleston, S.C.

- Piotrowski, T. (2002). *The Indian heritage of New Hampshire and northern New England.* McFarland.

We shared this list of titles to Suzie O'Bomsawin, Director of the Ndakinna Office and member of the Grand Council of the Waban-Aki, Daniel G. Nolett, Kin8dokawawinno/General Director of the Counsel of Abenaki at Odanak, and David Bernard, a member of the Waban-Aki Research Coordination Committee for the Grand Council of the Waban-Aki Nation; all three were unfamiliar with these publications (D. Nolett & S. O'Bomsawin, personal communication, June 8, 2021; D. Bernard, personal communication, July 12, 2021). These titles are offered by New Hampshire public libraries as supposed authoritative resources and yet they are unknown to the peoples who are the very subjects of these accounts.[4] All four authors of these titles are or were faculty members or lecturers at colleges and universities throughout New England and Nolett and O'Bomsawin expressed concerns about

---

4 It should be noted that Heald's publication has a forward by Rejean Obomsawin (Abénakis d'Odanak), and an address by Chief Donald Stevens (Nulhegan Band of the Coosuk-Abenaki Nation). Still, the majority of the information Heald provides throughout the book is without citation or source and a multitude of photographs and drawings of Abenaki peoples as well as mappings of Indigenous lands are marked "courtesy of author."

non-Indigenous scholars inaccurately writing or rewriting Abenaki history. In reflecting on his and O'Bomsawin's involvement with our research process for this chapter Nolett explained their aim is "to make sure that the information [we] collect at least from [their] side is accurate" (personal communication, June 8, 2021). He states that the Abenaki at Odanak "are trying to fight against so-called historians and experts on [their Abenaki] culture and history" (personal communication, June 8, 2021). As Chris Newell (2021) reminds us, to indigenize we must value Indigenous Knowledges and lived experience in the same way that we would value colonial degrees and signifiers of authority.

We are currently working with David Bernard on verifying the accuracy and examining the cultural sensitivity and historiography of the titles listed above. This project is ongoing and findings from this investigation will be published elsewhere with the support of the New Hampshire Library Association's Equity, Diversity, and Inclusion Committee.

'Right to Know': Addressing Discoverability and Deaccession within Local History Collections

The U.S. Department of Interior lists libraries as one of the first places tribal members should go in order to research their ancestry stating, "visiting the local library is a good starting point for gathering facts about Indians and Indian tribes. A wealth of information exists concerning the history of Indian tribes, tribal cultures, the historic tribal territories, and the migration patterns" (n.d., para. 7). The National Indian Law Library also recommends local libraries as a "helpful source of information" on their Tracing Native American Family Roots resource guide (n.d., para. 3). This means that libraries are not only understood as keepers of settler colonial history, but that of the colonized as well.

In "Right to Know" (1978) a paper prepared for the White House Pre-Conference on Indian Library and Information Services on or Near Reservations, Standing Rock Sioux activist and scholar Vine Deloria Jr., calls for "the implementation of specific services and practical solutions for Native American archives, cultural heritage, and traditional knowledge held in public repositories" (O'Neal, 2015, p. 2). Deloria asserts that part of the federal government's treaty responsibilities to Indigenous communities is to provide them with the information that they "need to know; to know the past, to know the traditional alternatives advocated by their ancestors, to know the specific experiences of their communities, and to know about the world that surrounds them" (O'Neal, 2015, p.2). As the U.S. Department of Interior points out, and Vine Deloria Jr. advocates for, libraries *should* be providing patrons, Indigenous and settler, with the history, culture, and experiences of Indigenous nations and their peoples. The responsibility of a public library to collect, preserve, catalog, and circulate information and histories of Abenaki peoples is being neglected by New Hampshire public libraries.

Our survey findings show that 62% of responding New Hampshire libraries have items that are not cataloged or keyed in their local history collection and 64% have materials in their local history collection that are not discoverable through an Online Public Access Catalog. This data corroborates the experiences of Abenaki peoples who struggle to uncover what New Hampshire library history collections contain. Paul and Denise Pouliot, the Sag8mo/Head Male Speaker/Grand Chief and Sag8moskwa/Head Female Speaker of the Cowasuck Band of the Pennacook-Abenaki People spoke to the biggest barrier they face with New Hampshire's local history collections: "We just don't know what they have" (P. Pouliot, personal communication, March 29, 2021). The Pouliots described that one of the difficulties of shaping and understanding their Pennacook-Abenaki cultural history lies in how many historical records are unknown and inaccessible to them. Suzie O'Bomsawin, Director of the Ndakinna Office and member of the Grand Council of the Waban-Aki, says "it's not only about archives or pictures it's also about artifacts…they are kept in basements of libraries or museums, and we don't really know about them" (personal communication, June 8, 2021).

Local history collections should seek to "provide user access to materials and collections" but uncatalogued and undiscoverable local history collections hinder both Indigenous and non-Indigenous peoples alike from engaging with their shared, complex, and unique histories (Philips, 2017, p. 96). Our survey results found that 77% of responding libraries do not have a policy statement for their local history collection or room. Ideally, a local history policy would contain information on collection development, scope, physical location, access, and fiscal considerations (RUSA, 2012). When developing a local history room policy, library staff should consider exactly who that "policy will serve, and if patrons will expect your institution — not another in their community — to meet these needs" (Marquis & Waggener, 2011, p. 44). The creation and maintenance of an effective local history collection policy statement can help library staff focus their collections, which provides the opportunity for closer analysis and the potential of a collection audit. Furthermore, some items held in local history collections may not coincide with the policy statement, the mission of the library, or the scope of the library's ability to preserve. These items can be relocated or returned to Indigenous nations. Intentional deaccession is a necessary part of an effective collection development policy (Philips, 2017; RUSA, 2012, 3.8). The opportunity exists to create a more accessible transfer of both knowledge and physical collections between public libraries and Indigenous peoples at the state level. This is where the New Hampshire Library Association and the Equity Diversity and Inclusion Committee can take the lead in establishing a statewide initiative.

This existence of an inaccessible and undiscoverable past is fundamental in the continuance of colonial mythologies and the erasure of Abenaki perspectives past, present and future. Both the Pouliots and O'Bomsawin point out the potential that libraries hold for Indigenous peoples in their ability to provide historical context, primary and secondary source evidence, and to act as a platform for education and Indigenous representation. All participants in this research, both settler and Indigenous, see libraries as an indispensable resource for bringing Abenaki culture, history, and knowledge back to these communities but also to the patrons whom these libraries serve on occupied Abenaki land.

Further Opportunities for Change and Collaboration

This chapter began out of an effort to reckon with colonial historical memory, and our problematic and incomplete understanding of the history of the land now known as New Hampshire. Close analysis reveals that New Hampshire public library local history collections often lack accurate representation of local Indigenous histories, and that these collections instead pedestal and canonize settler colonial narratives thus continuing the use of libraries as an instrument of colonization. There is no doubt that one major challenge to advancing Indigenous priorities in library and archival sectors is the incongruities between Indigenous and Western methods of managing information, archives, and knowledge. This leads to the necessary solution of creating holistic and decolonial learning environments, and to creating employment opportunities within the field of library and information science alongside "the recruitment of Indigenous individuals into higher education information science programs" (Genovese, 2016, p. 39).

According to the American Library Association's most recent Diversity Counts findings, Native Americans represent less than 1% of credentialed librarians in the United States (2012, Table A-1). New Hampshire library staff and the New Hampshire Library Association can address this harmful lack of representation through paid internships for Indigenous people curious about or already in the field, the intentional hiring and retention of Indigenous staff into leadership positions, as well as through the creation of New Hampshire Library Association scholarships specifically for Indigenous staff interested in pursuing an MLIS. It is important to note that diversity initiatives in L.I.S. such as those that we suggest here do not always work as intended since often, "they are themselves coded to promote whiteness as the norm in the profession and unduly burden those individuals they are most intended to help" (Hathcock, 2015, para. 2). Librarian, blogger, and 2018 Library Journal Mover and Shaker, April Hathcock, thus contends that programs aimed at aiding people from underrepresented groups to enter and remain in librarianship should be carried out alongside a "critical study of whiteness and its effects on L.I.S." (Hathcock, 2015, para. 27).

Additionally, "many archivists deny the fact that they have significant influence, power, and authority over what records will be preserved" in local history rooms (Genovese, 2016, p. 41). Yet they are precisely the people who should be vying for the decolonization of archival practices and the rematriation of Indigenous cultural property. There is a power differential between library staff, administrators, professionals and paraprofessionals and that hierarchy can either encourage or hinder this work. Still, indigenizing historical collections should be part of the labor of *all* library staff regardless of stature. In this way, The First Archivists Circle, a group of 19 Native American and non-Indigenous American librarians, historians, and archivists gathered in 2006 to identify best practices for the culturally responsive preservation and use of Indigenous materials. The gathering resulted in the publication of "Protocols for Native American Archival Materials" (Underhill, 2006) and the establishment of a resource guide under the same name (First Archivists Circle, 2007). These protocols are an invaluable resource to the work of all knowledge keepers on colonized lands. The First Archivists Circle calls for an increase in collaboration between Indigenous peoples and information centers, and points to the success of Indigenous-run archival institutions such as the National Museum of the American Indian and the Association of Tribal Libraries, Archives, and Museums (Genovese, 2016). The protocols speak specifically to the importance of providing context to patrons, asserting that

> "[a] primary task for libraries and archives is to organize and describe information resources for efficient and effective retrieval. Collecting institutions also wish to share as much context as possible[...]the use of outdated, inaccurate, derogatory, or Eurocentric language impedes access" (First Archivists Circle, 2007, para. 70)

The protocols further advise collecting institutions to acquire contemporary scholarship by Indigenous peoples. Archivists and library staff in New Hampshire public libraries can refer to these protocols if they have specific questions around deaccession, policy development, and accessibility of materials.

Acknowledging the importance of intentional and accessible historical collections in New Hampshire public libraries positions library staff to collaborate with the Indigenous nations on whose land they work and learn. The creation of a local history room policy that defines mission, scope, deaccession, and community engagement is just one way that archivists and librarians can employ the power they have to indigenize local history rooms. This need not be done in isolation. Library staff can consult the "Protocols for Native American Archival Materials," seek support from New Hampshire Library Association's Equity Diversity and Inclusion Committee, and should work in partnership with local Indigenous groups to create meaningful and effective policies.

When we exclude Indigenous peoples from the policy creation processes, we participate in their erasure. Daniel Nolett expressed that First Nations peoples are some of the most researched peoples, but they are rarely given access to the content written about them that is often protected and preserved in museums, archives, and libraries (personal communication, June 8, 2021). The Pouliots also say "we know [libraries] have collections that they don't understand, but they won't ask" (personal communication, March 29, 2021). This points to Genovese's assertion that "[r]esearch and colonialism are explicitly connected within Indigenous collective memory," which is precisely why "Indigenous populations should take on an active role within archival methodology" and historical research (Genovese, 2016, p. 33). Collaboration is foundational to building relationships between libraries and Indigenous nations.

Our conversations with Abenaki peoples in the region and abroad revealed that early Abenaki language dictionaries and grammar guides are frequently used in their respective work to halt the loss of their native language. According to the World Atlas of Language Structures, Abenaki is a critically endangered language (Dryer & Haspelmath, 2013). Revitalization efforts are ongoing across Abenaki bands, nations and working groups.[5] New Hampshire public libraries can support these efforts by preserving historically significant titles on the language, as well as by adding reprints of those titles to their circulating collections (See Appendix B for a list of suggested titles). Though not all, multiple New Hampshire public libraries catalog books about Abenaki language as 970.03–History and Geography–North America–Special Tribes or 970.04–History and Geography–North America–Ethnic and National Groups. We encourage Abenaki language books be cataloged in the 400s alongside other living languages as 497.34, in accordance with the Dewey Decimal Classification system path 400–Languages → 497–North American Languages → 497.3–Algic and Muskogean Languages → 497.34 Eastern Algonquian Languages (Dewey & Kyrios, 2021).

The call to preserve and re-incorporate culturally significant Abenaki titles does not mean that we also have to entirely remove the problematic canonical titles such as Jeremy Belknap's *The History of New Hampshire* (1831) and Everett Stackpole's *History of New Hampshire* (1916). The questions arise: what should be done with these historical accounts? What purpose do they serve? The Awikhiganigamikok Library on the Abenaki nation's reserve at Odanak in Quebec, Canada works to answer these questions with cultural sensitivity and context. The Awikhiganigamikok Library primarily serves the Abenaki nation but is also a part of a larger consortium of libraries in Quebec. The Abenaki at Odanak work to keep both the perspectives of their own people and the derogatory and reductive accounts created by colonial authors. O'Bomsawin says, "If we erase any books that we think are judgmental...we also forget that at some point our relationship between each other was not good" (personal communication, June

---

5 See www.westernabenaki.com or the Abenaki language class offerings by The Abenaki Council of Odanak for active examples of Abenaki language revitalization (Rancourt, 2021).

8, 2021). So, the Awikhiganigamikok Library labels these various settler colonial history books with a content warning to forewarn readers that the book contains pejorative words and accounts of Abenaki peoples. O'Bomsawin and Nolett both spoke to the necessity of retaining these books despite their cultural and racial biases (personal communication, June 8, 2021). To remove these titles from history collections would be to remove the historical accounts of systemic genocidal violence. For O'Bomsawin and Nolett, it is equally as important to not romanticize the relations between Abenaki peoples and colonizers as it is to reclaim Indigenous truth. This praxis used at Odanak is an example of how one nation and locale is confronting biased historical narratives, however this may not correspond to all contexts. United States colonization is not monolithic and the historical accounts and authorship of the country's creation and parallel destruction of Indigenous nations is vast. Thus the local history and colonial narratives held within New Hampshire state's libraries are parts necessary as well as tragic. The context of New Hampshire and much of New England is unique and collection management should be addressed as such in direct partnership with local Indigenous peoples and each library's staff and community.

Incentivizing and supporting information science education in Indigenous communities, preserving culturally significant titles in local history rooms, contextualizing harmful historical accounts, and returning Indigenous land and property are only some of the ways that we can work to indigenize New Hampshire Public Libraries. Chris Newell makes excellent suggestions for how to work collaboratively and respectfully with Indigenous peoples, stating specifically that "to engage with [Indigenous communities] you have to build meaningful relationships and that requires sometimes the giving up of some power on the hand of your institution" (2021, 55:34-55:41). We paraphrase and summarize his recommendations here:

Commit yourself to the continual process of coming to know and the inherent discomfort of that process. This means unlearning, relearning, and changing. Understand that acceptable terminology will change as we continue to build meaningful connections with one another. Be flexible and willing to work in Indigenous spaces and communities, rather than asking Indigenous people to continually come to colonial institutions. As much as possible, work cooperatively and collaboratively rather than bringing completed projects, such as land acknowledgements, for 'approval.' Value Indigenous Knowledges and experience in the same way that you would value colonial knowledge and offer equivalent compensation to Indigenous peoples for their time and expertise. Understand that no single individual or voice can speak for an entire Nation, Community, or collection of communities, and instead aim for a collaboration of voices. Respect the differences in perspectives and opinions within Indigenous communities. Be flexible with timelines and expectations.

The pervasive narrative of the United States of America and its mythical origins is a foundation that is not easily dismantled. Indigenous nations and intertribal groups across North America have been working towards the inclusion of truth in the American origin story. We encourage New Hampshire library staff to join them as allies and collaborators. Intentional representation is something that all New Hampshire libraries could endeavor towards to bring their patrons into a deeper relationship with the land on which they live. To find more information on contacting local and regional Abenaki bands and nations, hosting professional trainings led by Indigenous peoples, auditing library collections, and more, visit https://sites.google.com/view/nhlandlibraries, which leads to our resource guide collaboratively compiled throughout our research process.

Conclusion

Libraries, like many institutions on the land of what is now called the United States of America, have historically served to validate its occupation. Thus, libraries are also in the unique position to challenge their own servitude to colonial myths, to affirm and uplift Indigenous truths, to indigenize their collections, and to decolonize their structures and policies. Public library local history collections perform a distinctive service in that they actively construct and collect a community's shared historical memory. However, these collections often lack an integral voice: that of the Indigenous nations that have existed on these lands for thousands of years and continue to do so to this day. The fact that Indigenous peoples are here and have always been is thwarted by the overbearing presence of the shared U.S. American idea that "Indians," a fantasized homogenous colonial grouping, have vanished or disappeared into a vague and mythological past. The living Abenaki peoples are inherently at odds with the harmful narrative of the New England origin story upheld in New Hampshire public library local history collections.

The problems presented throughout this chapter can be addressed in a myriad of ways, and though we cannot offer a universal prescriptive praxis, we can share our belief that the practice of indigenization and the input of Indigenous people are at the root of every potential solution. More than 73% of survey respondents agree that their library would like to be in relationship with Abenaki nations and would like to better support Indigenous-led organizations yet less than 5% had partnered with tribal nations or organizations in the past ten years. The necessity of and interest in collaborative efforts between New Hampshire public libraries and Abenaki peoples is deeply prevalent, however, not fully realized.

It has been proven in many cities, states, and communities that indigenization "does not just benefit Native peoples by re-inserting [them] into the narratives of history" but it benefits institutions and the non-Indigenous people that engage with them (Newell, 2021, 61:44-61:44). Naomi Bishop, who served as President of the American Indian Library Association (AILA) from 2017-2018, directed us to libraries such as The Seattle Public Library and the Los Angeles County Library whose Indigenous Sovereignty Programs and American Indian Resource Center respectively are great examples of how public libraries can engage in the work of indigenization and have seen paramount impact in their communities (personal communication, May 14, 2021). These libraries can be referenced as guides and models, but New Hampshire needs to reckon with its distinct history and the ways in which its public libraries have perpetuated colonialism.

The efforts and conversations described throughout this chapter mark the beginning of that process. We did not set out to find answers or immediate solutions; rather we intended this research to be an opening and unveiling for ourselves as a settler educator and settler librarian, for the New Hampshire Library Association, and for non-Indigenous library staff and New Hampshire residents. It may be troubling for settlers who are focused on the goal of reconciliation and healing to acknowledge that the work of indigenization and truth seeking is an active and ongoing process that cannot be rushed—that the pace should be set by Indigenous peoples. We cannot dismiss the long-lasting effects of colonial genocide here in New Hampshire, nor can we pretend that they have no ramifications, and that there is nothing to be done about them. We must move beyond settler colonial selective memory.

To return to Deloria et al., we repeat: "[w]e can imagine a future when the United States and its citizens commit to grappling with fundamental questions: What does it mean to live on Indian land? What does it mean that Indian people are still here?" (2018, p.15). We must imagine and work toward a future when New Hampshire and its public libraries and citizens 'commit to grappling' with what it means to live on Abenaki land, what it means that Abenaki people have been and still are here. It is necessary in order to further cultivate the relationships between non-Indigenous New Hampshire residents, New Hampshire public libraries, Abenaki peoples, and the true history of the land on which we all live, work, and learn.

References

American Library Association. (2012). *Diversity counts 2012 tables*. ALA Office for Research & Statistics, ALA Office for Diversity, Literacy and Outreach Services and Decision Demographics. http://www.ala.org/aboutala/offices/diversity/diversitycounts/divcounts

Ansley, F. L. (1989). "Stirring the ashes: Race class and the future of civil rights scholarship." *Cornell Law Review* 74(6): 994–1077. https://scholarship.law.cornell.edu/clr/vol74/iss6/1/

Antoine, A., Mason, R., Mason, R., Palahicky, S. & Rodriguez de France, C. (2018). Pulling Together: A Guide for Curriculum Developers. https://opentextbc.ca/indigenizationcurriculumdevelopers/

Barstow, G. (1842). *The history of New Hampshire: From its discovery, in 1614, to the passage of the Toleration Act, in 1819*. I.S. Boyd.

Belknap, J. (1831). *The History of New Hampshire*. S. C. Stevens and Ela & Wadleigh.

Berger, B. (2009). Red: Racism and the American Indian. *UCLA Law Review, 56*, 591–656. https://opencommons.uconn.edu/law_papers/26

Bertot, J., Gorham, U., Jaeger, P. & Sarin, L. (2013). Democracy, neutrality, and value demonstration in the age of austerity. *The Library Quarterly, 83*(4), 368–382. https://doi.org/10.1086/671910

Bijali, A. & Khan, S.C. (2018). Marketing of local history collection of public libraries in the age of IT. *International Journal of Information Dissemination and Technology, 8*(2), 96–98.

Borell, B., Moewaka Barnes, H., & McCreanor, T. (2018). Conceptualising historical privilege: the flip side of historical trauma, a brief examination. *AlterNative: An International Journal of Indigenous Peoples, 14*(1), 25–34. https://doi.org/10.1177/1177180117742202

Bradford, W. (1899). *Bradford's history "Of Plimoth Plantation": From the original manuscript: With a report of the proceedings incident to the return of the manuscript to Massachusetts.* Wright & Potter Print. Co., State printers.

Brayboy, B. M. K. J. (2005). Toward a Tribal Critical Race Theory in education. *Urban Review, 37*(5), 425–446. https://doi.org/10.1007/s11256-005-0018-y

Bureau of Indian Affairs. (2016). *Indian lands of federally recognized tribes of the United States* [map]. (ca. 1:4, 250,000.) United States Department of the Interior. https://www.bia.gov/sites/bia.gov/files/assets/public/webteam/pdf/idc1-028635.pdf

Carlton, A. (2018, March 21). Are libraries neutral? *American Libraries Magazine.* https://americanlibrariesmagazine.org/blogs/the-scoop/are-libraries-neutral/

Charlton, E. A. (1856). *New Hampshire as it is.* Tracy, Kenney & Co.

Chase, F. (1856). *Gathered sketches from the early history of New Hampshire and Vermont: Containing vivid and interesting accounts of a great variety of the adventures of our forefathers, and of other incidents of olden times; original and selected.* Tracy, Kenney & Co.

Chocorua Lake Conservancy. (n.d.) Wabanaki History, Ecology, & Experiences. https://www.chocorualake.org/wabanaki-history

Chiu, A., Ettarh, F., & Ferretti, J. (2021). Not the shark, but the water: How neutrality and vocational awe intertwine to uphold white supremacy. In S. Y. Leung & J. R. López-McKnight (Eds.), *Knowledge justice: Disrupting library and information studies through Critical Race Theory* (pp. 49-71). The MIT Press. https://doi.org/10.7551/mitpress/11969.001.0001

Clinton, R. (2008, February 24). *Code of Indian offenses.* Office of Robert N. Clinton RSS. http://robert-clinton.com/?page_id=289

Cooke, N. (2020, December 14). What it means to decolonize the library. *Publishers Weekly.* https://www.publishersweekly.com/pw/by-topic/industry-news/libraries/article/85127-what-it-means-to-decolonize-the-library.html

Coolidge, A. J. & Mansfield, J. B. (1859). *A History and description of New England, general and local: Maine, New Hampshire, and Vermont.* A.J. Coolidge.

Deerinwater, J. (2019, December 9). *Paper genocide: The erasure of native people in census counts.* Rewire News Group. https://rewirenewsgroup.com/article/2019/12/09/paper-genocide-the-erasure-of-native-people-in-census-counts/

Deloria, P. J., Lomawaima, K. T., Brayboy, B. M. K. J., Trahant, M. N., Ghiglione, L., Medin, D., & Blackhawk, N. (2018). Unfolding futures: Indigenous ways of knowing for the twenty-First Century. *Daedalus, 147*(2), 6–16. https://doi.org/10.1162/daed_a_00485

Dewey, M., & Kyrios, A. (2021). *Dewey Decimal Classification.* OCLC, Inc.

Dryer, Matthew S. & Haspelmath, Martin (eds.) 2013. *The world atlas of language structures online.* Max Planck Institute for Evolutionary Anthropology. http://wals.info

Dunbar-Ortiz, R. (2014). *An indigenous peoples' history of the United States*. Beacon Press.

Dunbar-Ortiz, R. (2021). *Not "A nation of immigrants": Settler colonialism, White Supremacy, and a history of erasure and exclusion*. Beacon Press.

First Archivist Circle. (2007, April 9). *Protocols for Native American Archival Materials*. http://www2.nau.edu/libnap-p/protocols.html.

Genovese, T. R. (2016). Decolonizing archival methodology: Combating hegemony and moving towards a collaborative archival environment. *AlterNative: An International Journal of Indigenous Peoples*, 12(1), 32–42. https://doi.org/10.20507/AlterNative.2016.12.1.3

Gilio-Whitaker, D. (2019). *As long as grass grows: The indigenous fight for environmental justice, from colonization to Standing Rock*. Beacon Press.

Gohr, M. (2017). Ethnic and racial diversity in libraries: How white allies can support arguments for decolonization. *Journal of Radical Librarianship*, 3, 42–58. https://journal.radicallibrarianship.org/index.php/journal/article/view/5

Hathcock, A. (2015). White librarianship in blackface: Diversity initiatives in LIS. *In the Library with the Lead Pipe*. http://www.inthelibrarywiththeleadpipe.org/2015/lis-diversity/

Hoelle, J. C. (2011). Re-Evaluating tribal customs of land use rights. *University of Colorado Law Review*, 82(2). https://ssrn.com/abstract=1995119

Jacob, M. M., Sabzalian, L., Jansen, J., Tobin, T. J., Vincent, C. G., & LaChance, K. M. (2018). The gift of education: How Indigenous Knowledges can transform the future of public education. *International Journal of Multicultural Education*, 20(1), 157–185. https://doi.org/10.18251/ijme.v20i1.1534

Kent, J. M. (2014). *The visual language of Wabanaki art*. The History Press.

Leavenworth, P. S. (1999). "The best title that Indians can claim": Native agency and consent in the transferal of Penacook-Pawtucket land in the seventeenth century. *The New England Quarterly*, 72(2), 275–300.

Lee, D. (2011). Indigenous knowledge organization: A study of concepts, terminology, structure and (mostly) Indigenous voices. *Partnership: The Canadian Journal of Library and Information Practice and Research*, 6(1), 2–33. https://doi.org/10.21083/partnership.v6i1.1427

Leung, S. Y., & López-McKnight J. R. (2021). *Knowledge justice: Disrupting library and information studies through critical race theory*. The MIT Press.

Lilley, S. (2021). Transformation of library and information management: Decolonization or Indigenization? *IFLA Journal*, 47(3), 305–312. https://doi.org/10.1177/03400352211023071

Marquis, K., & Waggener, L. C. (2011). Historical collections: Is adding one right for your public library? *Public Libraries*, 50(2), 42–48.

McClintock, J. N. (1888). *Colony, Province, State 1623-1888: History of New Hampshire*. B.B. Russell.

National Indian Law Library. (n.d.) *Tracing Native American family roots.* https://narf.org/nill/resources/roots.html

New Hampshire State Library. (2020) *2020 complete library statistics.* https://www.nh.gov/nhsl/lds/public_library_stats.html

New Hampshire State Library. (n.d.). *Researching Your NH Family History Online from Home.* https://www.nh.gov/nhsl/services/public/research-inggen.html

Newell, C. (2021, June, 02). *Re-Indigenizing historical narratives.* [Virtual lecture]. Keynotes of Change, Connecticut. https://www.youtube.com/watch?v=Br4FvqgoL1I

Obomsawin, M. (2020, September 15). The myth of Native American extinction harms everyone. *The Boston Globe.* https://www.bostonglobe.com/2020/09/15/magazine/myth-native-american-extinction-harms-everyone/.

O'Brien, J. (2010). *Firsting and Lasting: Writing Indians out of Existence in New England.* University of Minnesota Press.

O'Neal, J.R. (2015). "The right to know": Decolonizing Native American archives, *Journal of Western Archives,* 6(1), 1–17. https://doi.org/10.26077/fc99-b022

Pete, S., Schneider, B., & O'Reilly, K. (2013). Decolonizing Our Practice–Indigenizing Our Teaching. *First Nations Perspectives,* 5(1), 99–115.

Phillips, F. (2017). *Creating a local history archive at your public library.* ALA Editions, an imprint of the American Library Association.

Portalewska, A. (Ed.). (2014). Tribes in New England stand their ground [Special issue]. *Cultural Survival Quarterly, 38*(2).

Portsmouth Public Library. (n.d.). *Indigenous Stories Resources.* https://www.cityofportsmouth.com/library/indigenous-stories-resources

Rancourt, J. (2021, September 14). Virtual Abenaki language classes. *Conseil des Abénakis d'Odanak.* https://caodanak.com/en/virtual-abenaki-language-classes/

Reference and User Services Association. "RUSA guidelines for establishing local history collections." (2012, May). American Library Association. http://www.ala.org/rusa/resources/guidelines/guidelinesestablishing

Rubin, R. & Rubin, R. G. (2020). *Foundations of library and information science.* ALA Neal-Schuman.

Rules Governing the Court of Indian Offenses. (1883). Department of the Interior, Office of Indian Affairs.

Schlesselman-Tarango, G., ed. (2017.) *Topographies of whiteness: Mapping whiteness in library and information science.* Library Juice Press.

Smith, L. T. (1999). *Decolonizing methodologies: Research and indigenous peoples.* Zed.

Stackpole, E. S. (1916). *History of New Hampshire.* New York: American Historical Society.

State v. Elliott, 616 A.2d 210, 218 (VT. 1992).

Stolen identities: The impact of racist stereotypes on Indigenous people, Hearing before the Committee on Indian Affairs and the United States Senate, 112th cong. (2011). https://www.govinfo.gov/content/pkg/CHRG-112shrg66994/html/CHRG-112shrg66994.htm

Strobel, C. (2020). *Native Americans of New England*. Praeger.

Sturm, C. (2017). Reflections on the anthropology of sovereignty and settler colonialism: Lessons from Native North America. *Cultural Anthropology, 32*(3), 340–348. https://doi.org/10.14506/ca32.3.03

Thomas, A.-R. (2019, February 15). *Who is a settler, according to indigenous and black scholars*. Vice. https://www.vice.com/en/article/gyajj4/who-is-a-settler-according-to-indigenous-and-black-scholars

Tuck, E. & Yang, K. (2012). Decolonization is not a metaphor. *Decolonization: Indigeneity, Education & Society, 1*(1), 1–40. https://jps.library.utoronto.ca/index.php/des/article/view/18630

Underhill, K. (2006). Protocols for Native American archival materials. *RBM: A Journal of Rare Books, Manuscripts, and Cultural Heritage, 7*(2), 134–145. https://doi.org/10.5860/rbm.7.2.267

U.S. Census Bureau (2021). *Facts for features: American Indian and Alaska Native Heritage Month: November 2020*. https://www.census.gov/data/tables/time-series/demo/popest/2010s-national-detail.html.

U.S. Department of the Interior. (n.d.) *Tracing American Indian and Alaska Native (AI/AN) ancestry*. https://www.bia.gov/guide/tracing-american-indian-and-alaska-native-aian-ancestry

Vermont Land Trust. (2012, December 18). *Nulhegan Abenaki attain first tribal forestland in more than 200 years* [Press release]. https://vtdigger.org/2012/12/18/nulhegan-abenaki-attain-first-tribal-forestland-in-more-than-200-years/

Wright, B. (1995). The broken covenant: American Indian missions in the colonial colleges. *Tribal College Journal of American Indian Higher Education, 7*(1), 26–33. https://tribalcollegejournal.org/broken-covenant-american-indian-missions-colonial-colleges/

Appendix A

Holdings of Settler Colonial Narratives in New Hampshire Public Libraries

(compiled June 2021)

Book Details	Number of New Hampshire Libraries Holding Title According to NHAIS
Barstow, G. (1842). *The history of New Hampshire: From its discovery, in 1614, to the passage of the Toleration Act, in 1819*. I.S. Boyd.	20
Belknap, J. (1831). *The History of New Hampshire*. S. C. Stevens and Ela & Wadleigh.	139
Charlton, E. A. (1856) *New Hampshire as it is*. Tracy, Kenney & Co.	40
Chase, F. (1856). *Gathered sketches from the early history of New Hampshire and Vermont: Containing vivid and interesting accounts of a great variety of the adventures of our forefathers, and of other incidents of olden times; original and selected*. Tracy, Kenney & Co.	91
McClintock, J. N. (1888). *Colony, Province, State 1623-1888: History of New Hampshire*. B.B. Russell.	41
Stackpole, E. S. (1916). *History of New Hampshire*. New York: American Historical Society.	103

Table 1

It is also worth noting that the New Hampshire State Library website hosts an annotated compilation of online resources for researching your New Hampshire family history online and recommends Stackpole's and Belknap's works as good sources of information on the general history of New Hampshire (New Hampshire State Library, n.d.).

Appendix B

The titles listed below are culturally significant texts regarding Abenaki history, culture, and language (Nolett & O'Bomsawin, personal communication, June 8, 2021). If you live or work in New Hampshire or better yet are a New Hampshire public library staff member we urge you to make the case at your local library that these items be preserved. Thus, if any of the titles listed below are 1st edition and in your library's circulating collection, we recommend they be relocated to the local history collection for preservation.

- Day, G.M. (1963). *The tree nomenclature of the Saint Francis Indians*. Canada, Dept. of
- Northern Affairs and National Resources.
- Day, G.M. & J.A. Brink. (1990). *Alnôbaôdwa!: a Western Abenaki language guide*. Swanton, Vt.: The Authors
- Day, G.M. (1994). *Western Abenaki dictionary*. Vol. 1&2, Hull, Quebec: Canadian Museum of Civilization.
- Laurent. J. (1884). *New familiar Abenakis and English dialogues, the first ever published on the grammatical system*. Printed by L. Brousseau. It should be noted that Applewood Books, a publishing company which specializes in reissuing original versions of historical books, republished this historically significant text in 2007.
- Masta, H.L. (1932). *Abenaki Indian legends, grammar, and place names*. Victoriaville, P. Q., La Voix des boisfrancs. It should be noted that there are multiple republications of this title ranging from that of 2007 to the most recent reprint in 2021.

Rooting Research
A Critical Examination of Incorporating Land-Based Education in Universities' Research Commons

Courtney S. Nomiyama and Truc Ho

Introduction

The University of Washington Libraries (UW Libraries) have recently placed greater emphasis on Indigenous peoples in its diversity, equity, and inclusion efforts. This is most evident in organizational land acknowledgments, which aim to highlight on whose land UW operates (*Land Acknowledgement — UW Libraries*, n.d.). However, recognition is simply that – these statements stop short of addressing relationships with Indigenous peoples as well as the role of land in settler-colonial relations. In particular, the Libraries' Research Commons, which is a space for research services like publishing and digital scholarship, fails to incorporate land-based education into its services, staffing, and programming (*What Is the Research Commons? — UW Libraries*, n.d.). For example, Indigenous perspectives are notably absent in programming with most events focused on supporting Western research methods. UW Libraries is not the only academic library that lacks resources and support for other ways of knowing. This raises important questions about the role of land-based education or land education in publicly funded academic libraries. Notably, we ask: how have colonial practices limited the ability of academic libraries to adopt land-based education, and how can land-based education challenge colonial practices in academic libraries?

By design, academic libraries uphold principles of Western hegemony and colonialism through their collections, services, and purpose. By this, we refer to Western knowledge systems, whiteness, and proximity to them (Fanon, 1968; Fanon, 2008; Mignolo & Walsh, 2018). Furthermore, libraries are often praised for upholding democracy, liberty, and other liberal values tied to the Enlightenment; however, this "liberal discourse" ultimately "support[s] and reproduce[s] capitalist structures of domination and oppression" rather than challenging them (Popowich, 2019, p. 90). Academic libraries also occupy a curious position—they are figuratively attached to and affiliated with a specific higher education institution, meaning they are in service to a specific college or university, including their curriculum and research (Roundtable on Technology and Change in Academic Libraries, 2007).

Historically, United States higher education institutions have embodied colonial practices through their prioritization of specific types of knowledge over others (de jesus, 2014; Stein, 2018). For one, higher education institutions have focused on universalist and positivist types of knowledge, which tend to discount the importance of relationships and place-specific knowledge (Akena, 2012; Pack, 2019). Second, the Morrill Acts of 1862 and 1890 established land-grant universities by designating federal public lands–lands stolen from Indigenous peoples–in each state to create universities focused on teaching agriculture, science, and mechanical arts (Sorber, 2018; Nash, 2019). In particular, land-grant universities gave credence and further rise to scholarship and specialization "premised on mechanization and scientific principles" to further support American industrialization and nation-building (Sorber, 2018, p. 5). Land-grant universities thus embodied and furthered settler colonialism as the designated recipients of the government's systematic dispossession of Indigenous lands (Nash, 2019; Stein, 2020). As cultural and intellectual institutions whose function is to support and sustain academic research, academic libraries are, by extension, implicated in the colonial project. Additionally, because libraries are integral to knowledge production, they play a central role in perpetuating colonial structures. We argue that land-based education is essential to the decolonization of academic libraries, yet academic libraries frequently fail to recognize this in their efforts to challenge colonial structures (la paperson, 2017).

To ground this discussion, we rely on the following terms and definitions. Library research commons are dedicated physical or virtual spaces that offer research services, or services that support scholarly activity, in one place or a one-stop shop (Blummer & Kenton, 2017; Gould, 2011; Somerville & Harlan, 2008; Steiner & Holley, 2009). Land-based or land education is a learning approach that centers Indigenous epistemologies, ontologies, and knowledges regarding land, "including Indigenous understandings of land, Indigenous language in relation to land, and Indigenous critiques of settler colonialism" (Tuck et al., 2014, p. 13). Indigenous epistemologies, ontologies, and knowledges refer to the ways in which Indigenous peoples define, relate, and explain their lives, society, and the world (Drummond, 2020; Jacob et al., 2018; Thomas, 2022). Land-based education is significant in decolonization as it envisions Native futures with realized Indigenous agency, land rights, and stories (Tuck et al., 2014; Wildcat et al., 2014).

Finally, we acknowledge that decolonization is multi-faceted. One, decolonization is *not* an "abstract universal" (Mignolo, 2018b, p. 108) but rather contextual (Tuck & Yang, 2012). Second, decolonization is not a philosophical approach, a figure of speech, or a stand-in for social justice initiatives (Tuck & Yang, 2012). Most importantly, decolonization is a process that must center Indigenous perspectives; repatriate land; and fundamentally change settler-Indigenous relationships (Tuck & Yang, 2012; Wildcat et al., 2014). Decolonization cannot fall on the shoulders of the Indigenous community alone; rather, everyone is implicated and involved in it (Bouvier, 2013). Furthermore, decolonization does not mean eliminating all forms of Western knowledge (Smith, 2021).

Land-based education in libraries' research commons thus far is not widely implemented, but we theorize this could take on several forms. For one, research commons should explicitly acknowledge its library's settler colonial history and the role of the land on which the library operates in advancing settler colonial interests, whether they are carried out through exhibits, events, or services (Calderon, 2014). This "self-reckoning" and self-reflection are key to transforming Indigenous and settler relationships (Irlbacher-Fox, 2014; Wildcat et al., 2014). While land acknowledgments in their current popularity may recognize the historical and modern existences of Indigenous peoples, rarely do they uphold the role in which libraries have played in settler colonialism, nor do they reflect any self-reckoning or intended future actions regarding Indigenous lands. We contend that land acknowledgments should also acknowledge the ways in which individual libraries and more generally, academic institutions, have marginalized Indigenous peoples and stolen Indigenous land through settler colonialism.

Second, research commons should create space for Indigenous ontologies and epistemologies as they relate to land in their events, services, and staff complement. For example, while not a library-specific event, Earth Partnership at the University of Wisconsin-Madison hosted an Indigenous-led event about culturally responsive research relationships (*Culturally Responsive Research Relationships*, 2020). A more recent example is boundary work, as articulated by Zurba et al. (2019; 2022), which allows for "knowledge sharing, the co-creation of knowledge, and translation of research outcomes into direct benefits for communities" (p. 10). While this specific practice took place in Canada and through an academic department rather than the library, it offers a model framework in which Indigenous and settler communities can collaborate on land-based education programming. Nonetheless, we acknowledge that decolonization does not happen overnight and that the scholarship on decolonization in academic libraries continues to evolve.

However, we note that many academic libraries focus on diversity, equity, and inclusion initiatives rather than land-based education or decolonization efforts. For example, while the University of North Carolina at Chapel Hill began a "Reckoning Initiative," there are no references to land and its role in settler colonialism, nor about either's impacts on Indigenous communities past or present (*University Libraries' Reckoning Initiative Framework – UNC-Chapel Hill Libraries*, 2021). We argue that diversity, equity, and inclusion efforts are not the same as land-based education or decolonization efforts, which must also be prioritized by academic institutions.

In the first section, we review existing literature on land-based education and current decolonization efforts in academic libraries. We also establish a framework to guide our analysis. Next, we outline our methodology in assessing U.S. academic libraries' research spaces for evidence of land-based education and decolonial efforts. We then examine the current landscape of research commons in academic libraries. Finally, we discuss the importance of land-based education in decolonization efforts, the conditions in which it must take place, and its implications for the field.

Literature Review

To ground our research, we focus on several scholarly areas: land-based education or land education and decolonization efforts in libraries. Existing literature on land-based education contends that this type of education is critical to decolonization. Because land-based education fosters connections with land, culture, and community (Corntassel & Hardbarger, 2019), it has the power and potential to challenge colonial structures by recentering land and our relationships to it as "sources of knowledge and strength" and "a mode of education" (Wildcat et al., 2014, p. II). Similarly, Tuck et al. (2014) posit that land education is key to research because this approach envisions a future built on Indigenous perspectives and acknowledges the structural aspects of settler colonialism. Land education, however, is not simply adopting Indigenous methods and knowledge. Morgenson (2010) clarifies that this adoption is merely settler emplacement, which displaces and erases Indigenous knowledges, people, and land. Therefore, land-based education is important to decolonization because it centers Indigenous epistemologies.

Decolonization is not new to academic libraries. Most academic libraries' decolonization efforts have largely focused on collections, classification, and library programs' curriculums. Blume and Roylance (2020), for example, established the "Authentic Authorship Workflow," which incorporates intentionality into creating inclusive collections by building relationships with communities to find authors of diverse backgrounds. Duarte and Belarde (2015), on the other hand, focus on cataloging, arguing that information systems must imagine and incorporate a wealth of Indigenous epistemologies and perspectives in order to truly decolonize information systems used in libraries. Although specific to Canada, Edwards (2019) notes that LIS curriculums should offer Indigenous librarianship tracks as a way to decolonize and prepare graduates for working with Indigenous patrons and resources. While these scholars all discuss decolonization in librarianship, they do not address research commons, nor any land-specific initiatives. We point to these examples to illustrate that the growth of decolonization efforts in librarianship has yet to address research spaces specifically.

Another attempt to decolonize academia has been through requiring Indigenous content in colleges (i.e. "Indigenous Content Requirements" or "ICR"). In 2017, Canadian higher education institutions began debating the idea of ICR in college courses as a way to transform relationships with Indigenous peoples and communities (Gaudry & Lorenz, 2018). In order for such transformation to happen, Stockdill and Danico (2012) emphasize that such efforts must be rooted in anti-oppression. However, "indigenizing" academic programs presents a challenge: ICR's transformative success is dependent on overcoming "internalized racism and victim-blaming of Canadian societal discourse," which may not be possible within present academic structures (Gaudry & Lorenz, 2018, p. 170). In practice, this often means that non-Indigenous perspectives and concerns are privileged over Indigenous ones in the classroom (Gaudry & Lorenz, 2018). While envisioned as an attempt to transform academia's relationship with Indigenous peoples, Gaudry and Lorenz (2018) note that these efforts run the risk of "exposing Indigenous students and instructors to intensified colonialism" by expecting Indigenous faculty and students to lead these conversations (p. 171). These scholars have illustrated that the transformation of academic spaces cannot happen with a singular requirement or with cursory inclusion of Indigenous faculty and students; rather, transformation must be solidly anti-oppressive and requires structural change.

Additionally, some scholars have addressed the importance of community to library spaces. In particular, Halperin (2020) transforms the idea of library commons into ones based on community but does not explicitly address the question of land in decolonizing these spaces. All scholars cited above point to relationship-building and Indigenous epistemologies as being essential to the decolonization process. We build on the work of these scholars by acknowledging the role and impact of research commons in entrenching colonialism and articulate land-based education as a concrete way of decolonizing these spaces.

Our research aims to understand the prevalence (or lack thereof) of land-based education in research commons. Specifically, we draw on Tuck et al. (2014) and Gruenewald (2003) to develop our understanding of what constitutes land-based education. Unlike place-based education, land-based education centers Indigenous epistemologies in decolonization (Tuck et al., 2014). In practice, for example, land-based education incorporates Indigenous naming conventions, terminology, and history into the library space, services, and programming. As we demonstrate, however, such land-based education practices are largely absent from many research commons in academic libraries.

Methodology

Sample Selection

In order to answer our research question, we examined research commons of the top twenty public institutions according to Association of Research Libraries (ARL) data as of April 2021 (*Peer Libraries*, 2021). We define research commons as a dedicated physical or virtual site that encompasses and provides research services, or services that support scholarly activity (Blummer & Kenton, 2017; Gould, 2011; Somerville & Harlan, 2008; Steiner & Holley, 2009). Annually, ARL collects academic research library statistics from 98 libraries, 68 of which are public institutions (University of Washington Libraries, 2018). The rankings among them are decided based on total library expenditures, collections expenditures, and staffing; these rankings can change annually depending on these expenditures.

We selected the top twenty universities to record how the top public universities in library expenditures across the U.S. are dedicating library resources within the research commons' spaces (*Peer Libraries*, 2021). The universities we selected depend on public resources and are nominally committed to the public interest, which underscores the need to apply greater scrutiny to those universities. Beyond the philosophical justification for our focus on public universities, there is also an important practical reason for our choice: as state institutions, public universities often share similar characteristics and fill analogous roles in their geopolitical communities, making them more accessible for comparison. A complete list of the universities reviewed in this study can be found in Appendix A.

Methods

Following the study sample selection, we conducted a content analysis of the universities' research commons through the criteria outlined in Table 1. We devised these criteria based on publicly available information on library websites. Each of the areas we focused on constitutes a component of a research space. Each researcher reviewed ten universities. For each university, the researchers looked at libraries' websites, any dedicated research commons' websites, and the libraries' social media accounts for information regarding the university's research commons' space, services, and organizational strategic plan.

To review and analyze the research commons' spaces, we looked at the physical location of the library to record whether it was historically or contemporarily located on Indigenous land(s). Next, we looked at whether the library acknowledges the relationship of the research commons' physical location to the land. Additionally, we analyzed staff directories to assess who manages these spaces in order to document their expertise and background. In comparing the various services and programs, the research team also derived an evaluation of the theories and frameworks in which the services and programs were grounded. Lastly, we compared each library's strategic plan and stated values with the library's execution of said goals through their annual reports and similar statements. We thus analyzed multiple data sources in order to make conclusions about the libraries' priorities and whether the libraries have implemented land-based education initiatives in the recent year. To determine whether or not these libraries were executing their strategic plans, we assessed libraries' blog posts and press releases and cross-referenced them with statements about specific, concrete changes that the libraries made in their strategic plans.

Criteria	Subcriteria	Description
Spaces	Location	Where is the research commons physically located–is it on Indigenous land? What Indigenous communities historically and contemporarily reside on this land? Does the university acknowledge the Indigenous communities' relation to the land? If yes, how do they acknowledge this relationship?
	Experts/Staff	Individuals who run, manage, and provide services at the research commons. Note background, expertise, subject areas
Services/ Programming	Theory/Framework	What theories and frameworks are services and programming grounded in? • Is there a land acknowledgement? • History of place? • What names are used (Indigenous vs. Settler vs. Immigrant)? • What geographical boundaries? • How are knowledge and expertise defined?
Strategic plan/mission	Values	How does the library define its priorities? Is DEI or decolonization part of these goals? How is DEI/decolonization valued in practice? In what aspects?
	Practice	In practice, how does the library execute its strategic plan? What steps have the library or the research commons taken to achieve those goals? Are there any land-based education initiatives that have been implemented in the recent year?

Table 1

Findings

In this section, we highlight general findings of how research commons spaces are utilized in the twenty universities observed. Definitions of each conceptual framework can be found in Appendix B. The first four theories and frameworks are derived from concepts from existing land education literature. When reviewing the data, we found that these existing terms did not fully capture most of the language used by academic libraries. We then developed the terms "Western context of knowledge" and "Data Driven" to capture commonly used phrases in our data sample.

Theory or Framework	Number of Universities
Land Education	0
History of Place	0
Indigenous Science	0
Land experts	0
Western context of knowledge	20
Data Driven	16

Figure 1 The frameworks or theories grounding academic library programming and services

Figure 1 above illustrates the frameworks–or lack thereof–observed through examination of the spaces, programming, and services offered by the universities. Overall, the universities' research commons lacked land acknowledgments and general acknowledgment of the Indigenous peoples whose land the libraries occupy. In our analysis, none of the programs or services studied included land education, history of place, or Indigenous science. Examination of the staff directories also showed that none of the research commons we studied have staff who identified as land experts. We define land experts as self-identified "cultural knowledge holders" whose knowledge is tied to the land and based on Indigenous ways of knowing (Bang et al., 2014; Zurba et al., 2022). For example, while there weren't any institutions in this study that had any cultural knowledge holders on staff, we

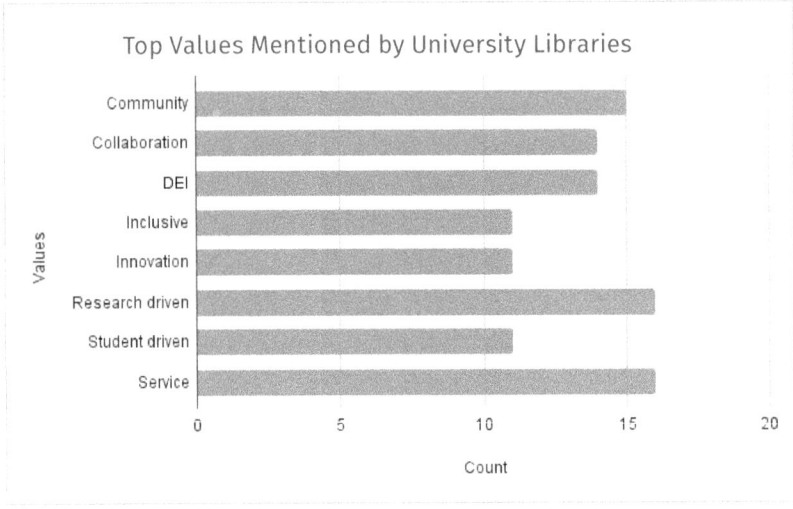

Figure 2 Top organizational values expressed by the study population

note that Zurba et al. (2022) partnered with an Indigenous Elder from Wabaseemoong Independent Nations as part of a land-based education pilot project. The research commons primarily focused offerings on programming and services grounded in Western knowledge. Additionally, most universities placed a heavy emphasis on technology and data driven approaches to research services.

Our examination of the values presented within the university libraries show common values across libraries. These were calculated by adding the total count of each value presented for the various universities and selecting the top eight values that were mentioned by ten or more universities. For example, Figure 2 shows that the top two values were "research driven" and "service," which 80% of the libraries included as their core values. "Community" was the next most frequent value, which 75% of the libraries included in their strategic plans, mission statements, or diversity statements. Values such as "collaboration" and "DEI" were included by 70% of libraries. Lastly, "inclusive," "innovation," and "student driven" were included by 55% of libraries. Although these results show that community was stated as being important to many libraries, the meaning of community in this context relates to institutional affiliation. That is, community refers to students, staff, and faculty at the university, rather than the larger community in which the institution is located.

Discussion

Through our assessment, it is evident that academic libraries' research commons have not integrated land-based education into their spaces, services, staffing complements, mission statements, or expressions of values. In analyzing research commons spaces, it is evident that many research commons lack any acknowledgement of Indigenous peoples and communities as well as their relations to the land on which the libraries operate, much less including a self-reckoning of the role that the libraries have played in furthering settler colonialism in North America. For example, the University of Illinois Urbana-Champaign library's research commons lacks a land acknowledgement or any reference to Indigenous peoples on whose land the university sits (*Scholarly Commons*, n.d.). Likewise, the University of California, Los Angeles (UCLA) library's research commons does not recognize any Indigenous peoples or lands on its public-facing website or social media (UCLA Library, n.d.). Furthermore, UCLA's research commons does not offer any self-reflection about its role in Western knowledge production (*Research Commons*, n.d.).

Rather, research commons focus on technology and data without contextualizing their role in the broader community or culture. To the extent that research commons referred to community, they focused almost exclusively on the campus community, rather than the surrounding geopolitical, social, and economic community where the library was located. In assessing the most recent complete academic year of research commons' services, including workshops, we found that most focused on developing skills like GIS, data management, digital scholarship, and computer programming. In particular, most research commons arranged their services around technological how-to topics using particular software, such as creating data management plans or creating story maps with ArcGIS ESRI. For example, the University of Pittsburgh's Digital Scholarship Commons encompasses research data services, geospatial data and analysis, and coding and computational support (*Digital Scholarship Commons*, n.d.). In addition to appointments and drop-in hours, the Commons offers regular workshops that span specific skills and tools from exhibit building in Omeka to data visualization basics. Florida State University's R&D Commons takes a similar lead, hosting regular skill-building events related to Tableau and Python, for example (Florida State University Libraries, n.d.). Based on the institutions assessed, research commons are intended to primarily support STEM, data, and digital scholarship.

While land-based education is not independent of scholarly and research activities, the lack of services and programming relating to this concept suggests that it is outside the scope of most research commons' services. Consequently, land-based education plays a minor, if not absent role, in research commons' services.

In addition to services, experts who staff research commons lack expertise in land-based education. Most research commons are staffed by librarians, data specialists, graduate and undergraduate students, and professors. While it is possible that research commons' experts have backgrounds in or knowledge of land-based education, we found no public-facing references to this domain on their websites. Rather, staff members' specializations are described in terms of their titles, degrees, academic areas of scholarship, and professional affiliations. For example, Rutgers University's Digital Learning Commons frames its staff team's background in terms of degrees, research interests, and technological expertise (Rutgers University Libraries, n.d.). Similarly, the Learning Commons at Indiana University Bloomington details the backgrounds of their staff in terms of prior work experience and degrees (Indiana University Bloomington Libraries, 2013). Land-based education does not feature prominently in research commons staff backgrounds. At least publicly, research commons' staff lack the expertise and interest in land-based education.

A library's overarching strategic plan, mission, and values guide research commons services and experts. Many academic libraries included in our study have incorporated elements of diversity, equity, and inclusion (DEI) as part of their strategic plan, missions, and values; however, none of these statements reference decolonization, nor do they acknowledge the ways in which DEI is limited in its ability to adequately address colonial structures and whiteness, as well as envision a future that centers Indigenous ways of knowing. Furthermore, we found zero references to land and its relationship to Indigenous communities in our content analysis of this aspect of academic library websites. For example, the University of Illinois Urbana-Champaign Library's strategic plan strives for inclusion in its values; however, there are no explicit, public references to the history and present-day status of Indigenous land (*Strategic Planning – Staff Website*, n.d.). Likewise, University of Pittsburgh's mission statement outlines goals such as a commitment to diversity and inclusion but lacks any concrete examples or steps to land-based education, much less decolonization (University of Pittsburgh University Library System, n.d.). In fact, these statements lack any reference to Indigenous peoples or any accountability to them or their land. Furthermore, neither university library website lists any concrete actions related to Indigenous peoples and communities. While libraries may see DEI strategies as a way to radically change libraries, these efforts are largely superficial as they do not alter or change colonial structures, much less relationships with Indigenous peoples.

In examining a range of American public research universities' libraries across regions, specialties, and sizes, it is clear that the lack of land-based education is not specific to a particular area or a type of library, but is rather a consistent, institutional pattern. Furthermore, research commons, and university libraries more broadly, are focused on diversity, equity, and inclusion, rather than decolonization. The lack of land-based education strategies and decolonization initiatives in these spaces illustrate the complexity of decolonizing academic libraries. In order for land-based education to take root, several conditions must exist.

First, land-based education and decolonization cannot fall on the shoulders of the Indigenous communities alone. As Bouvier reminds us, the Indigenous communities are integral to the process, but everyone has a role to play in decolonization, including the non-Indigenous community (2013). Specifically, within higher education, scholars must move from "analysis toward action" and also be cautious of superseding Indigenous scholarship and perspectives (Davis et al., 2017, p. 393). Furthermore, non-Indigenous scholars should not depend on Indigenous scholars and the larger Indigenous community for direction in the larger movement of decolonization (Davis et al., 2017). Rather, all researchers have a responsibility to take active roles in working towards a decolonized academy (Thambinathan & Kinsella, 2021), such as building relationships with the Indigenous community based on trust, accountability, and respect (Wallace, 2011).

Second, decolonization is distinct from diversity, equity, and inclusion. While DEI efforts introduce and highlight alternative narratives, such as those about BIPOC, they fail to address structural inequities and systems of oppression (Ettarh, 2014). DEI cannot be the stand-in or the substitute for decolonization based on the following reasons.

Unlike decolonization, DEI continues to center whiteness and imagines a future based on existing colonial structures (Makhubela, 2018; Samudzi, 2018). DEI does not explicitly name or engage whiteness or colonialism as structural problems to address, shifting the conversation away from addressing structures and institutions (Walcott, 2019). This shift often renders whiteness and colonialism invisible, allowing these institutions to escape critique and reckoning, while making it seem like "progress" or "real change" has been made in addressing past injustices (Walcott, 2019). Moreover, diversity is often described as a "problem to be solved rather than...reflective work to dismantle institutional bias" (Galvan, 2015). In fact, DEI in its current manifestations do not necessarily amount to "real change," as they do not fundamentally change institutions or the structures that govern them (Ahmed, 2012; Yousefi, 2017). Often, "doing diversity" means simply adding the term "diversity" to mission statements, publicly signifying commitment to diversity, or performing audits without any accountability (Ahmed, 2012).

This is evident in the recent proliferation of diversity statements and frameworks in academic libraries. While these statements and frameworks vaguely gesture at realizing DEI in the libraries examined in our study, they do not reference past injustices, nor do they attempt to rectify them, resulting in little change. For example, the University of Washington Libraries seek to "hold [them]selves accountable for inclusive and institutional change by routinely seeking feedback from campus and community partners" (*Equity, Diversity, Inclusion and Anti-Racism — UW Libraries*, n.d.). However, there is no self-reckoning regarding the land which the libraries occupy, nor are local Indigenous peoples considered "community partners" beyond their presence in land acknowledgments (University of Washington Libraries, n.d.; 2021). Additionally, in sharing their DEI accomplishments, UW Libraries list a slew of working groups and additional related diversity statements with little evidence of or connection to structural change. The highlighted accomplishments of an EDI committee, working group, and racial equity program focuses on raising awareness and understanding of racial equity for employees, which shifts the responsibility of confronting the university's maintenance of systematic oppression to the individual employees and makes the reckoning an individual responsibility, rather than a structural one.

Similarly, the University of Wisconsin-Madison released a statement reaffirming their commitment to diversity and inclusion (*Our Commitment to Diversity and Inclusion*, n.d.). While the libraries reiterate their dedication to "end[ing] the many forms of discrimination," there are no concrete examples that demonstrate how structural changes have been made to address this (*Our Commitment to Diversity and Inclusion*, n.d.; *Diversity, Equity & Inclusion*, n.d.). Their public-facing website page dedicated to DEI lacks any updates since March 2020 (*Diversity, Equity & Inclusion*, n.d.).

This "progress" or "real change" also often manifests itself as celebrations of multiculturalism. This framing posits that multiculturalism alone is enough to celebrate, even though structural inequities persist (Gohr, 2017). In libraries, DEI has become the preferred strategy in anti-racism efforts; however, DEI equates addressing racism through inclusion without rectifying power or influence (Hudson, 2017). Hiring individuals of diverse backgrounds in libraries, for example, does not radically change the institution unless existing power structures are also changed. In these settings, "diversity hire[s]" are often subject to gatekeeping and marginalization, while library systems of oppressions, including colonialism, remain intact without scrutiny (Galvan, 2015). Furthermore, diverse individuals may find themselves "inhabiting whiteness" in order to survive in these spaces (Ahmed, 2012). Notably, 12 of the 20 institutions we researched participated in the Association of College and Research Libraries (ACRL) Diversity Alliance Librarian program, which aims to diversify librarianship by hiring diverse individuals for temporary appointments, in 2020 and 2021 (*ACRL Diversity Alliance 2020 Members*, n.d.; *ACRL Diversity Alliance 2021 Members*, n.d.). However, while these efforts do lead to the brief, albeit temporary, employment of diverse individuals, it has little impact on diversifying the field, much less challenging whiteness (Galvan, 2015; Garrison, 2020) in the long term.

Furthermore, library practices do not necessarily align with library values (Yousefi, 2017). Despite signaling their values, libraries are often unwilling to acknowledge that change will not look like anything they've done before, resulting in a continuation of the status quo (Yousefi, 2017). DEI efforts may attempt to transform academia, including libraries, but they will not adequately address nor remove structural barriers (Ahmed, 2012). Thus, diversity, equity, and inclusion should not be confused with or substituted for decolonization, as these concepts fail to adequately address colonialism.

There were exceptions in our study, however, that point to promising developments regarding land-based education. Some universities, for instance, included resources for researchers seeking to work closely with the community in which the institution was located. For example, while not a library-sponsored event, the University of Wisconsin-Madison's College of Agricultural and Life Sciences offered a workshop on "Cultural responsiveness in working with Wisconsin Native Nations" in November 2020 (*Workshop: Cultural Responsiveness in Working with Wisconsin Native Nations*, 2020). Although not affiliated with the university libraries, this workshop offers ideas on what kinds of resources and programming the library could offer to move towards repairing relationships with Indigenous peoples and communities.

Similarly, while place-based education is not sufficient for enacting decolonization within university libraries, its limitations may point to valuable strategies for decolonization. For example, the University of Texas at Austin hosted "Data & Donuts: Texas Land History in GIS" which combined local land history with learning GIS tools (University of Texas Libraries, 2020). While this event did feature area history, it did not frame local land history in terms of Indigenous knowledges, much less advance the stories and ways of knowing of Indigenous peoples. Therefore, examples of place-based education offer lessons by highlighting ineffective strategies to decolonize research spaces.

Conclusion

While we have not assessed research commons in all US academic libraries, based on the study of the top 20 publicly-funded postsecondary institutions, we observe a clear lack of commitment to incorporate land education within spaces, programming, or services in most research libraries. Our research highlights the importance of incorporating land-centered concepts and practices within university libraries. Our work also seeks to underscore the ways in which DEI efforts that conclude at "racial awareness training" and "DEI committees" fail to address coloniality that structure academic institutions today. As discussed, the strategy of diversity by universities often offers a defanged interpretation of decolonization where knowledge and experiences of marginalized groups "are rarely valued, except perhaps through tokenistic 'recognitions' of cultural diversity that make the institution appear to be welcoming, but otherwise do not threaten the status-quo of their operations" (de Oliveira Andreotti et al., 2015). Furthermore, the term "decolonization" should not be plastered on social justice initiatives as an addendum, as this continues to imagine a settler future without accountability towards Indigenous communities (Tuck & Yang, 2012; Tuck et al., 2014).

This suggests that key to breaking away from these marginal attempts at decolonization is to decolonize practices and structures of the academy. However, the process of decolonization is complex. Paraphrasing Fanon, Prinsloo (2016) explains that "decolonization is a process of remaking—a violent phenomenon that has as its goal the creation of a new humanity" (p. 165). Makhubela (2018) contextualizes this definition within the decolonization of the university, stating "Decolonisation, in our instance, will then call for a distance from the 'Given' and perhaps also only mean a refusal to participate in the structures of our subjugation" (p. 17). Application of these frameworks to academic libraries provides a similar conclusion: the call of liberatory practice that forces institutions to come to terms with their complicity in colonial practices.

But what does decolonization of the academic libraries as institutions truly entail? Fanon's framework for decolonial efforts forces us to reckon with the fact that academic libraries may be irreparable, and would therefore call for the undoing of academic libraries as we know them. In building on Maldonado-Torres' (2007) argument, Makhubela offers a perspective on this struggle: "A consistent assault on coloniality, the lasting impact of colonialism, and all its manifestations should embark on a process of decolonial justice and repel the favour for the settler" (p. 16). Most importantly, we should not limit our conceptualizations of decolonization simply because we cannot imagine them in our current ontology (Stein, 2019). Mignolo (2018a) writes that decoloniality is an option of intervention to the system of knowledge (field of knowledge), system of beliefs (religions) and systems of ideas (such as liberalism). And thus, one of decoloniality's major tasks is to "delink from modern/colonial praxis of living and knowing, and to walk toward re-existing in the borderland and the borderlines in decolonial praxis of living, knowing, sensing, and of loving" (Mignolo, 2018a, p. 223). For academic libraries, this calls for the confrontation with the three stated spheres that shaped the "biological and cultural praxis of living" (Mignolo, 2018a, p. 223). Additionally, it requires academic libraries to reimagine goals and principles grounded in Indigenous knowledges and ways of knowing.

Research commons are unique sites to embark upon the process of decolonial justice because they are locations of scholarly knowledge production, as well as places where library workers provide programs and services. As discussed, research commons focus primarily on production of Western science scholarship, especially within STEM disciplines, which rarely acknowledges the way in which Western science disciplines perpetuate colonized practices and beliefs due to their position as "ideologically neutral" (Schwartz-DuPre & Parmett, 2018). In regard to exploitation and displacement of Indigenous communities for economic profit "scientists have participated in this in various ways often not in the best interest of Native nations" (Spang & Bang, 2015). By focusing material and financial resources on only Western knowledge production, programming, and services, academic libraries have "legitimized a set of practices with problematic relationships to land and to Indigenous sovereignty" (Tuck & Yang, 2012, p. 28). Because of this, learning the relationship, history, and politics of the land on which the library resides from the perspective of Indigenous community is crucial to understanding the socio-political conditions that have shaped research services within academic libraries, as well as the missing perspectives. Most importantly, to make material differences in the structure of academic libraries, funding should be directed toward engaging land experts in implementing more programming and services grounded in land education.

This research intends to build the foundation for future conversations on the importance of land education within academic libraries' decolonization efforts. Importantly, academic libraries should take more active roles in challenging research structures. For example, our research suggests that diversity, equity, and inclusion efforts, while prevalent, do little to implement land-based education and often serve as a distraction from more concrete efforts. The focus on DEI efforts has prevented libraries from looking at other areas in the academy that are actively implementing land-based education initiatives. For example, Zurba et al. (2022)'s boundary work provides a model, collaborative framework for land-based education in an academic setting. Sato et al. (2014) have also proposed participatory social maps as a form of land education to chart local groups' identities, histories, and conflicts over land and water. However, discussion of these applications is nowhere to be found in academic library discourse. Our research emphasizes that libraries must take the initiative to implement extensive changes to existing research support infrastructure.

As articulated, solutions offered from the diversity, equity, and inclusion frameworks have shown to not be a propitious method of addressing the coloniality situated within academic libraries. Academic institutions have an impact on the community and the environment in which they are located, yet none of the universities we examined pushed beyond the modern colonial ideas and institutionalization to engage the unique bioregions on which the universities reside through their programming or services. Thus, right now, it is critical for academic libraries to see decoloniality as imperative, rather than another framework to form racial awareness training. Decoloniality allows for a reimagination of how to engage with biological and cultural interrelated spheres beyond the Western canon. Furthermore, it cannot be engaged in the abstract. To decolonize, the libraries must answer to the call for the praxis of living that reject colonial modernity and build toward a decolonial path of knowing and interacting with the cultural and biological experience of being.

References

Ahmed, S. (2012). *On being included: Racism and diversity in institutional life*. Duke University Press.

Akena, F. A. (2012). Critical analysis of the production of western knowledge and its implications for Indigenous knowledge and decolonization. *Journal of Black Studies*, 43(6), 599–619. https://doi.org/10.1177/0021934712440448

Association of College & Research Libraries (ACRL). (n.d.). *ACRL Diversity Alliance 2020 members*. https://www.ala.org/acrl/issues/diversityalliance/2020roster

Association of College & Research Libraries (ACRL). (n.d.). *ACRL Diversity Alliance 2021 members*. https://www.ala.org/acrl/issues/diversityalliance/2021roster

Bang, M., Curley, L., Kessel, A., Marin, A., Suzukovich, E. S., & Strack, G. (2014). Muskrat theories, tobacco in the streets, and living Chicago as Indigenous land. *Environmental Education Research*, 20(1), 37–55. https://doi.org/10.1080/13504622.2013.865113

Blume, R., & Roylance, A. (2020). Decolonization in collection development: Developing an authentic authorship workflow. *The Journal of Academic Librarianship*, 46(5), 102175. https://doi.org/10.1016/j.acalib.2020.102175

Blummer, B., & Kenton, J. M. (2017). Learning commons in academic libraries: Discussing themes in the literature from 2001 to the present. *New Review of Academic Librarianship*, 23(4), 329–352. https://doi.org/10.1080/13614533.2017.1366925

Bouvier, R. and Battiste, M. (2013). Foreword. In *Decolonizing education: Nourishing the learning spirit* (pp. 8–12). UBC Press.

Calderon, D. (2014). Speaking back to Manifest Destinies: A land education-based approach to critical curriculum inquiry. *Environmental Education Research, 20*(1), 24–36. https://doi.org/10.1080/13504622.2013.865114

Corntassel, J., & Hardbarger, T. (2019). Educate to perpetuate: Land-based pedagogies and community resurgence. *International Review of Education, 65* (1), 87–116.

Culturally responsive research relationships. (2020). UW–Madison Events Calendar. https://today.wisc.edu/events/view/153508

Davis, L., Denis, J., & Sinclair, R. (2017). Pathways of settler decolonization. *Settler Colonial Studies, 7*(4), 393–397. https://doi-org.offcampus.lib.washington.edu/10.1080/2201473X.2016.1243085

de jesus, nina. (2014). Locating the library in institutional oppression. *In The Library With The Lead Pipe.* https://www.inthelibrarywiththeleadpipe.org/2014/locating-the-library-in-institutional-oppression/

de Oliveira Andreotti, V., Stein, S., Ahenakew, C., & Hunt, D. (2015). Mapping interpretations of decolonization in the context of higher education. *Decolonization: Indigeneity, Education & Society, 4*(1), Article 1. https://jps.library.utoronto.ca/index.php/des/article/view/22168

Duarte, M. E., & Belarde-Lewis, M. (2015). Imagining: Creating spaces for Indigenous ontologies. *Cataloging & Classification Quarterly, 53*(5–6), 677–702. https://doi.org/10.1080/01639374.2015.1018396

Drummond, A. (2020). Embodied Indigenous knowledges protecting and privileging Indigenous peoples' ways of knowing, being and doing in undergraduate nursing education. *The Australian Journal of Indigenous Education, 49* (2), 127–134. https://doi.org/10.1017/jie.2020.16

Edwards, A. (2019). Unsettling the future by uncovering the Past: Decolonizing academic libraries and librarianship. *Partnership: The Canadian Journal of Library and Information Practice and Research, 14*(1), Article 1. https://doi.org/10.21083/partnership.v14i1.5161

Ettarh, F. (2014). Making a new table: Intersectional librarianship. *In The Library With The Lead Pipe.* https://www.inthelibrarywiththeleadpipe.org/2014/making-a-new-table-intersectional-librarianship-3/

Fanon, F. (1968). *The wretched of the earth* (First Evergreen Black Cat Edition.). Grove Press, Inc.

Fanon, F. (2008). *Black skin, white masks* (Revised edition). Pluto Press.

Florida State University Libraries. (n.d.). *Introducing the R&D Commons.* Florida State University Libraries. Retrieved May 8, 2022, from https://www.lib.fsu.edu/news/introducing-rd-commons

Galvan, A. (2015). Soliciting performance, hiding bias: Whiteness and librarianship. *In the Library with the Lead Pipe.* https://www.inthelibrarywiththeleadpipe.org/2015/soliciting-performance-hiding-bias-whiteness-and-librarianship/

Garrison, J. (2020). Academic library residency programs and diversity. *Portal: Libraries and the Academy, 20*(3), 405–409. https://doi.org/10.1353/pla.2020.0020

Gaudry, A., & Lorenz, D. E. (2018). Decolonization for the masses?: Grappling with Indigenous content requirements in the changing Canadian post-secondary environment. In L. T. Smith, E. Tuck, & K. W. Yang (Eds.), *Indigenous and Decolonizing Studies in Education*. Routledge.

Gohr, M. (2017). Ethnic and racial diversity in libraries: How white allies can support arguments for decolonization. *Journal of Radical Librarianship, 3*, 42–58.

Gould, T. H. P. (2011). *Creating the Academic Commons: Guidelines for Learning, Teaching, and Research*. Scarecrow Press. http://ebookcentral.proquest.com/lib/washington/detail.action?docID=709477

Gruenewald, D. A. (2003). The best of both worlds: A critical pedagogy of place. *Educational Researcher, 32*(4), 3–12.

Halperin, J. R. (2020). The library commons: An imagination and an invocation. *In the Library with the Lead Pipe*. https://www.inthelibrarywiththeleadpipe.org/2020/the-library-commons/

Hudson, D. J. (2017). On "diversity" as anti-racism in library and information studies: A critique. *Journal of Critical Library and Information Studies, 1*(1), 1–36.

Indiana University Bloomington Libraries. (2013, December 6). *Learning commons*. https://libraries.indiana.edu/learning-commons

Irlbacher-Fox, S. (2014). Traditional knowledge, co-existence and co-resistance. *Decolonization: Indigeneity, Education & Society, 3*(3), Article 3. https://jps.library.utoronto.ca/index.php/des/article/view/22236

Jacob, M. M., Sabzalian, L., Jansen, J., Tobin, T. J., Vincent, C. G., & LaChance, K. M. (2018). The gift of education: How Indigenous Knowledges can transform the future of public education. *International Journal of Multicultural Education, 20*(1), 157–185. https://doi.org/10.18251/ijme.v20i1.1534

la paperson. (2017). *A third university is possible*. University of Minnesota Press.

Land acknowledgement—UW Libraries. (n.d.). Retrieved January 8, 2022, from https://www.lib.washington.edu/gmm/constitution/land-acknowledgement

Libraries–University of Wisconsin-Madison. (n.d.). *Diversity, equity & inclusion*. Retrieved May 5, 2022, from https://www.library.wisc.edu/diversity/

Makhubela, M. (2018). "Decolonise, Don't Diversify": Discounting diversity in the outh African academe as a tool for ideological pacification." *Education as Change, 22*(1). https://doi.org/10.25159/1947-9417/2965

Maldonado-Torres. (2007). On the coloniality of being: Contributions to the development of a concept. *Cultural Studies (London, England), 21*(2-3), 240–270. https://doi.org/10.1080/09502380601162548

Mignolo, W. D. (2018a). Decoloniality is an option, not a mission. In W. D. Mignolo & C. E. Walsh (Eds.), *On Decoloniality: Concepts, Analytics, Praxis* (pp. 211-226). https://doi-org/10.1215/9780822371779-012

Mignolo, W. D. (2018b). What does it mean to decolonize? In W. D. Mignolo & C. E. Walsh (Eds.), *On Decoloniality: Concepts, Analytics, Praxis* (pp. 105–134). Duke University Press. https://doi.org/10.1215/9780822371779-007

Morgensen, S. L. (2010). Un-Settling settler desires. In *Unsettling Ourselves: Reflections and Resources for Deconstructing Colonial Mentality* (pp. 157–158). https://unsettlingminnesota.files.wordpress.com/2009/11/um_sourcebook_jan10_revision.pdf

Nash, M. A. (2019). Entangled pasts: Land-Grant colleges and American Indian dispossession. *History of Education Quarterly, 59*(4), 437–467. https://doi.org/10.1017/heq.2019.31

Pack, J. (2019). The need for an ethics of sustainable knowledge production. *Metaphilosophy, 50*(4), 551–562. https://doi.org/10.1111/meta.12378

Peer libraries. (2021). Retrieved December 1st, 2021, from https://staff.lib.uw.edu/operations/cas/for-all-staff/management/peer-libraries

Popowich, S. (2019). *Confronting the democratic discourse of librarianship: A Marxist approach*. Library Juice Press.

Prinsloo, E. H. (2016). The role of the Humanities in decolonising the academy. *Arts and Humanities in Higher Education, 15*(1), 164–168. https://doi.org/10.1177/1474022215613608

Roundtable on Technology and Change in Academic Libraries. (2007, February 13). *Changing roles of academic and research libraries*. Association of College & Research Libraries. https://www.ala.org/acrl/issues/value/changingroles

Rutgers University Libraries. (n.d.). *Digital learning commons*. Rutgers University Libraries. Retrieved May 8, 2022, from https://www.libraries.rutgers.edu/new-brunswick/visit-study/locations/alexander-library/digital-learning-commons

Samudzi, Z. (2018, March 11). *We need a decolonized, not a "diverse", education*. Harlot Media.

Sato, M., Silva, R., & Jaber, M. (2014). Between the remnants of colonialism and the insurgence of self-narrative in constructing participatory social maps: Towards a land education methodology. *Environmental Education Research, 20*(1), 102–114. https://doi.org/10.1080/13504622.2013.852654

Schwartz-DuPre, & Parmett, H. M. (2018). Curious about George: Postcolonial science and technology studies, STEM education policy, and colonial iconicity. *Textual Practice, 32*(4), 707–725. https://doi.org/10.1080/0950236X.2016.1267038

Smith, L. T. (2021). *Decolonizing methodologies: Research and Indigenous peoples*. Bloomsbury Academic & Professional.

Somerville, M. M., & Harlan, S. (2008). From information commons to learning commons and learning spaces: An evolutionary context. In B. Schader (Ed.), *Learning commons: Evolution and collaborative essentials* (pp. 1–36). Chandos Publishing.

Sorber, N. M. (2018). *Land-Grant colleges and popular revolt: The origins of the Morrill Act and the reform of higher education.* Cornell University Press. http://muse.jhu.edu/book/62998

Spang, M. & Bang, M. (2015). *Teaching STEM In ways that respect and build upon Indigenous peoples' rights.* STEM Teaching Tools. http://stemteachingtools.org/brief/10

Stein, S. (2018). Confronting the racial-colonial foundations of US higher education. *Journal for the Study of Postsecondary and Tertiary Education, 3*, 077–096. https://doi.org/10.28945/4105

Stein, S. (2019). Beyond higher education as we know it: Gesturing towards decolonial horizons of possibility. *Studies in Philosophy and Education, 38*(2), 143–161. https://doi.org/10.1007/s11217-018-9622-7

Stein, S. (2020). A colonial history of the higher education present: Rethinking land-grant institutions through processes of accumulation and relations of conquest. *Critical Studies in Education, 61*(2), 212–228. https://doi.org/10.1080/17508487.2017.1409646

Steiner, H. M., & Holley, R. P. (2009). The past, present, and possibilities of commons in the academic library. *The Reference Librarian, 50*(4), 309–332. https://doi.org/10.1080/02763870903103645

Stockdill, B. C., & Danico, M. Y. (2012). The ivory tower paradox: Higher education as a site of oppression and resistance. In *Transforming the Ivory Tower* (pp. 1–30). University of Hawaii Press.

Strategic planning – staff website. (n.d.). University of Illinois Library. Retrieved May 8, 2022, from https://www.library.illinois.edu/staff/administration/strategicplanning/

Thambinathan, V., & Kinsella, E. A. (2021). Decolonizing methodologies in qualitative research: Creating spaces for transformative praxis. *International Journal of Qualitative Methods, 20*, 16094069211014766. https://doi.org/10.1177/16094069211014766

Thomas, H. (2022, January 13). *Indigenous knowledge is often overlooked in education. But it has a lot to teach us.* EdSurge. https://www.edsurge.com/amp/news/2022-01-13-indigenous-knowledge-is-often-overlooked-in-education-but-it-has-a-lot-to-teach-us

Tuck, E., McKenzie, M., & McCoy, K. (2014). Land education: Indigenous, post-colonial, and decolonizing perspectives on place and environmental education research. *Environmental Education Research, 20*(1), 1–23. https://doi.org/10.1080/13504622.2013.877708

Tuck, E., & Yang, K. W. (2012). Decolonization is not a metaphor. *Decolonization: Indigeneity, Education & Society, 1*(1), Article 1. https://jps.library.utoronto.ca/index.php/des/article/view/18630

University of California Los Angeles Library. (n.d.). *Research commons*. Retrieved May 8, 2022, from https://www.library.ucla.edu/destination/research-commons

UNC-Chapel Hill Libraries. (2021, April). University Libraries' Reckoning Initiative framework. *The Reckoning Initiative at the University Libraries*. https://library.unc.edu/reckoning/framework/

University of Illinois Library. (n.d.). *Diversity, equity, inclusion and accessibility at the University Library – general information – U of I Library*. Retrieved May 8, 2022, from https://www.library.illinois.edu/geninfo/deia/

University of Illinois Library. (n.d.). *Scholarly commons*. Retrieved May 8, 2022, from https://www.library.illinois.edu/sc/

University of Pittsburgh Library System. (n.d.). *Digital scholarship commons*. Retrieved May 8, 2022, from https://www.library.pitt.edu/digital-scholarship-commons

University of Texas Libraries. (2020, October 23). *Data & donuts: Texas land history in GIS*. University of Texas at Austin. https://www.lib.utexas.edu/events/399

University of Washington Libraries. (n.d.). *Community Engagement — UW Libraries*. University of Washington Libraries. Retrieved May 5, 2022, from https://www.lib.washington.edu/about/edi/community-engagement

University of Washington Libraries. (n.d.). *Equity, diversity, inclusion and anti-racism: Libraries Position Statement*. Retrieved May 5, 2022, from https://www.lib.washington.edu/about/edi

University of Washington Libraries. (2021, May 27). *One year later: George Floyd, Black Lives Matter and systemic change— UW Libraries*. University of Washington Libraries. https://www.lib.washington.edu/about/news/announcements/one-year-later-george-floyd-black-lives-matter-and-systemic-change

University of Washington Libraries. (2018). *UW Libraries peer comparisons*. University of Washington Libraries. https://www.lib.wasington.edu/assessment/statistics/uwashington-libraries-arl-peer-comparisons-2018

University of Wisconsin-Madison Libraries. (n.d.). *Our Commitment to Diversity and Inclusion*. Retrieved May 5, 2022, from https://www.library.wisc.edu/about/administration/commitment-to-diversity-and-inclusion/

Walcott, R. (2019). The end of diversity. *Public Culture, 31*(2), 393–408. https://doi.org/10.1215/08992363-7286885

Wallace, R. (2011). Power, practice and a critical pedagogy for Non-Indigenous allies. *The Canadian Journal of Native Studies, 31*(2), 155-172.

What is the research commons? —UW Libraries. (n.d.). University Libraries University of Washington. Retrieved April 17, 2022, from https://www.lib.washington.edu/commons/about/what

Wildcat, M., McDonald, M., Irlbacher-Fox, S., & Coulthard, G. (2014). Learning from the land: Indigenous land based pedagogy and decolonization. *Decolonization: Indigeneity, Education & Society*, *3*(3), I–XV.

Workshop: Cultural responsiveness in working with Wisconsin Native Nations. (2020, October 15). University of Wisconsin-Madison. https://ecals.cals.wisc.edu/2020/10/15/workshop-cultural-responsiveness-in-working-with-wisconsin-native-nations/

Yousefi, B. (2017). On the disparity between what we say and what we do in libraries. In S. Lew & B. Yousefi (Eds.), *Feminists Among Us: Resistance and Advocacy in Library Leadership* (pp. 91–106). Litwin Books.

Zurba, M., Land, G., Bullock, R., & Graham, B. (2022). Exploring Indigenization and decolonization in cross-cultural education through collaborative land-based boundary education. *Journal of Cultural Geography*, *39*(1), 8–31. https://doi.org/10.1080/08873631.2021.1999007

Zurba, M., Maclean, K., Woodward, E., & Islam, D. (2019). Amplifying Indigenous community participation in place-based research through boundary work. *Progress in Human Geography*, *43*(6), 1020–1043. https://doi.org/10.1177/0309132518807758

Appendix A

List of the Universities Libraries Examined

- University of California, Berkeley
- University of California, Los Angeles
- Florida State University
- University of Illinois Urbana-Champaign
- Indiana University Bloomington
- University of Iowa
- University of Michigan
- Michigan State University
- University of Minnesota
- University of North Carolina-Chapel Hill
- North Carolina State University
- Ohio State University
- Pennsylvania State University
- University of Pittsburgh
- Rutgers University
- University of Texas at Austin
- Texas A&M University
- University of Virginia
- University of Washington
- University of Wisconsin-Madison

Appendix B

Definitions for theory or framework categories used for data collection:

Land Education — Land-based learning that places emphasis on the social, cultural, spiritual and biological relationship between people, material and the land.

History of Place — Social and historical context of the land the library sits on.

Indigenous knowledges, epistemologies, and ontologies or "ways of knowing" — The ways in which Indigenous peoples define, relate, and explain their lives, society, and the world. We use the plural form of these words to acknowledge the many Indigenous peoples and perspectives.

Indigenous Science — Traditional, environmental, and cultural knowledge that is unique to a group of people, who are a part of a community that has resided within a bioregion over generations.

Land experts — Experts whose discipline of study and/or training focuses on environmental and cultural knowledge of a bioregion.

Western context of knowledge — Fields and/or disciplines that are upheld within the Western canon as universal knowledge production disciplines.

Data Driven — Theories and/or framework grounded in knowledge established from application of Western scientific methods to investigate and contextualize the biological and cultural experience of being.

Bringing the Land into the Library
Land Acknowledgements in an Academic Library

Ashley Edwards, Dr. Julia Lane, Dr. Alix Shield, and Dal Sohal

Land Acknowledgements have become commonplace in many institutional settings, especially at the start of events and the opening of some, often high profile, meetings (Keeptwo [Algonkin/French and Irish], 2021).[1] The Canadian Federation of Library Associations' Indigenous Matters Committee (CFLA IMC/FCAB) recommends including Land Acknowledgements as part of the decolonizing process (n.d.), and Simon Fraser University's Aboriginal Reconciliation Council (SFU ARC) reminds us that Indigenous Peoples' "traditional lands define who they are as a people and are intrinsically linked to their Indigenous cultures, knowledge systems (epistemologies and methodologies), and their ways of knowing, seeing, and doing" (p. 81). As such, Land Acknowledgements can be a way to show respect to Indigenous Nations and their worldviews. Yet, the term "Land Acknowledgement" can easily give the impression that the central purpose of such a

---

[1] In keeping with current practices as outlined by many Indigenous authors (Joseph [Gwawaenuk], 2018; Justice [Cherokee Nation], 2018; Vowel [Métis], 2016b, Younging [Opaskwayak Cree], 2018), the term "Indigenous" will be used when discussing First Nations, Métis, and Inuit Peoples. Additionally, where possible the name of an author's community or Nation has been included the first time we cite them. We are responsible for any omissions or mistakes and apologize in advance for them. In composing this chapter, we referred to author Gregory Younging's 2018 work Elements of Indigenous Style (EIS). When there were discrepancies in publication and style guidelines, we followed EIS.

statement is to simply name the lands[2] on which an event or meeting takes place. Indeed, this approach was taken to its logical extreme by Pride Toronto in 2019. The event's Land Acknowledgement was posted on a sign and prompted readers to:

> Take a moment to connect with the land that you are currently standing on. Now introduce yourself spiritually; build a relationship with Mother Earth that provides for all our relations. No matter what part of Mother Earth our family originates from, we all have a relationship and a responsibility to the land. Let's build a healthy relationship together. ("Pride Toronto apologizes," 2019)

This statement was heavily criticized for failing to mention both Indigenous Peoples and the treaties that currently govern the legal relationship between Indigenous and non-Indigenous Peoples.[3] As Sḵwx̱wú7mesh matriarch Ta7talíya Nahanee has explained, the practice of giving Land Acknowledgements can be about relationships and about building better relations – between non-Indigenous and Indigenous Peoples, *and* between all people and the Land (Auger, 2021).

In *Decolonize First: A Liberating Guide and Workbook for Peeling Back the Layers of Neocolonialism* (n.d.), Nahanee writes:

> A territorial acknowledgment is a personal commitment to and appreciation for the land you are in relations with. It is a way to respect the Ancestors who cared for the land that is now caring for you. It can connect you to the medicine of the land. When you acknowledge the territory in a good way, you build your strength, you give yourself medicine. You also model respectful relations. When you introduce yourself and say where you're from, you can include whose territory you grew up on. A territorial acknowledgment uses the name of the Nation who cares for the land, not the colonial name of the

---

2   Throughout this chapter you will notice that we use both "land" and "territory" when discussing place. In the literature and in practice these terms are sometimes used synonymously. However, some scholars and practitioners have clear preferences for one term or the other. As you will see in our references, some writers use Land Acknowledgement while others use Territory Acknowledgement. We made the choice to use both terms here, as a way of reflecting that our learning about terminology is ongoing. While we employ both terms throughout the paper, we use the phrase "Land Acknowledgement" more than "Territory Acknowledgement" for the sake of clarity and consistency. It is not our intention to suggest that one phrase is preferable over the other.

3   We use the broad terms "Indigenous and non-Indigenous Peoples" intentionally here. We discuss some common identity terms used in Land Acknowledgements later in the chapter.

place. It is a decolonizing practice to be in good relations with land and appreciating Indigenous Peoples['] stewardship is part of that. Territorial acknowledgments have become compulsory email footers but can be so much more. (p. 7)

We quote Nahanee at length because we want to amplify her work and expertise. We are grateful for the knowledge she has shared both with us directly in workshops at the library and indirectly through her published texts and interviews. We appreciate her insights about acknowledgements as a way to give yourself medicine. These are teachings that she carries and that she shares through her work, including through workshops she offers on Territorial Acknowledgements. These are not our teachings and we cannot elaborate on them in this chapter. However, we want to join our voices with Nahanee's in encouraging our readers to take the acknowledgement beyond the "compulsory email footer" by taking up this work as a "personal commitment." In order to come to a place where this practice is about relationality and not simply about reading a script or completing a checklist, many of us need to cultivate a different understanding about what Land Acknowledgements are, why we offer them and to whom, and how to do so differently.

This chapter offers our shared insights for cultivating a reflective practice to guide the work of Land Acknowledgements. It is our intention to support others in libraries to (re)think their practices and approach their acknowledgements with a deepened understanding in order to craft more heartfelt statements. When we talk about statements being heartfelt, we want to specifically encourage readers to think about approaching Land Acknowledgements in a way that is intended to build, nurture, respect, and take care of relationships between people and between people and the land. Writing and speaking such acknowledgements is a process of self-reflection that should result in a commitment or compelling action. The reflective process that we offer has three main stages:

1. Reflect first on yourself and your positionality.
2. Reflect next on where you are and how you have come to be here.
3. Finally, reflect on who you are speaking with or to, why you are speaking in this place, and what you have come to say.

Our own engagement with this process of reflection prompted us to collectively decide *not* to offer individual acknowledgements at the beginning of this chapter because both the "where we are" (in this case expanded to include where we will be read) and "who we are speaking with" are unknown to us in the context of this writing. We want to actively resist the scripted, standardized statement. In its place, we offer brief bios about each co-author in the "About the Contributors" section of the collection. We have crafted these bios specifically to accompany this chapter. They offer some insight into our individual positionality; however, it is worth noting that what we choose to share about ourselves is contextual. The positionality statements that we offer here differ from those that we may share orally as we build relationships through our practices of positionality and acknowledgement.

Situating Our Workplace

> We recognize that we work at a colonial institution whose three campuses occupy the lands of the xʷməθkʷəy̓əm (Musqueam), Sḵwx̱wú7mesh (Squamish), səl̓ilw̓ətaʔɬ (Tsleil-Waututh), q̓íc̓əy̓ (Katzie), kʷikʷəƛ̓əm (Kwikwetlem), qiqéyt (Qayqayt), q'ʷa:n̓ƛ'ən̓ (Kwantlen), Səmyámə (Semiahmoo), and sc̓əwaθən məsteyəxʷ (Tsawwassen) Nations. The province colonially known as British Columbia is home to close to 200 Nations, approximately one third of the recognized First Nations in Canada. There's an amazing diversity of language, art, and cultural practices grounded in the Landscape of this place.

The text above, created by the authors, is a familiar example of an institutional Land Acknowledgement. Our intention in this paper is to differentiate between this type of acknowledgement, which simply names the Nations whose Lands you are on, and a Land Acknowledgement *practice* that involves one's own positionality and comes from the heart. It is our goal to encourage the development of such a practice to deepen our approach to offering Land Acknowledgements. The focus of this practice is a continual reflection on our role(s) in the relationship between ourselves, the land, local Indigenous Nation(s), and the forces of ongoing colonization. This is a process of un-learning and re-learning, and it is for this reason that we resist the "once and for all" approach of scripted Land Acknowledgements that merely list the names of relevant Nations.

The practice of engaging deeply with Land Acknowledgements asks us to perpetually consider and reconsider the layers of meaning, history, and relationship embedded in the Land and our institutions. As we engaged in this work, we have therefore needed to ask more questions about the university where we work. This institution was named for an American-Scottish explorer, Simon Fraser (Simon Fraser University Archives, n.d.). In a 2018 blog post, SFU undergraduate student Georgia Twiss shared research from her honours thesis in History. By consulting the SFU Archives, Twiss found that the name came about by accident, with "Simon" added after realizing that the planned name of "Fraser University" (for the local river) would have the acronym "FU." From there, the university's first president endeavoured to create a sense of tradition by embracing aspects of Scottish culture (Twiss, 2018). This naming occurred in 1965 and demonstrates how contemporary colonialism operates: instead of learning what the local Nations call Burnaby Mountain or the surrounding area, the university president and board embraced European conventions. The practice of naming buildings, streets, cities, etc. after "Very Important (white) People" is a colonial impact on the land, as it reaffirms a European cosmology wherein only people (and not plants or animals) are granted sentience (Geraldine King [Anishinaabe], *All My Relations* podcast, 2021).

For many Indigenous Nations, however, the land and all beings on the land carry their own knowledges. Indigenous naming practices are therefore focused not on imposing names meant to memorialize people, but rather on learning to listen to the land as a practice of coming to know an appropriate place name. With that in mind, our own practice of Land Acknowledgement has been deepened through learning and practicing saying a Skwx̱wú7mesh place name, Lhukw'lhukw'ayten, to refer to the Land the university occupies. This name was suggested by Skwx̱wú7mesh community leader and spokesperson Khelsilem Tl'akwasik̲a̱n as an appropriate place name. It derives from the Skwxwu7mesh word for arbutus, lhulhuk̲w'ay, which comes from lhuk̲w' (peel), and means "always peeling tree" (Bill Reid Centre, ímesh Mobile App).

Who Are We To Do This Work?

While writing this chapter, we experienced a shared discomfort about the authorial role and the way it might set us up as experts. We are not experts in Land Acknowledgements. We approach this work with humility and in the spirit of ongoing accountability to ourselves and others.

We also recognize that as institutions become more active in decolonization, Indigenization, and reconciliation, there is work for both Indigenous and non-Indigenous Peoples to do, and our responsibilities differ. As Carol Arnold (Métis-Cree) writes "the act of acknowledging colonization, theft of land, and the displacement of Indigenous Peoples is for white people, settlers, Europeans, and non-Indigenous members of any assembly" (2021, p. 20). The Decolonizing the Library Interest Group at SFU Library is made up of both Indigenous and non-Indigenous members. We have taken up a shared responsibility to humbly learn, connect, and build relationships to support more meaningful practices of Land Acknowledgement and decolonization, Indigenization, and reconciliation across the library.

Returning to the Pride Toronto example that we discussed in the introduction, it is worth noting that when the society was called out about their acknowledgement, their response was that their statement was "written by an Indigenous person." This response was problematic for a number of reasons, not least because it placed blame solely on the author while the organization refused to be held accountable. A tweet by Nickita Danielle (@auntykita) (Saulteaux) critiquing Pride Toronto's response cites a talk by Dr. Marcia J. Anderson[4] (Cree-Anishinaabe) to explain that, "one of MANY ways organizations get in the way of themselves when 'decolonizing' or 'Indigenizing', is their unwillingness to stand in the fire with us when things get challenging" (2019). In uncritically responding to concerns about their Land Acknowledgement by stating that it had been "written by an Indigenous person," Pride Toronto applies pan-Indigenous logic. This is akin to saying that something was done by a "European." Their response provides us with no information about who wrote it, what community or Nation they are from, or why they were asked to undertake this work on behalf of Pride Toronto. Their response also implies that the work of creating and offering Land Acknowledgements "belongs" (only) to Indigenous Peoples and that there is no work for non-Indigenous people who occupy Indigenous lands to do.

We recognize the leadership, knowledge, and expertise of Indigenous Peoples and are grateful for the opportunities that we have to benefit from each. We also strive to respectfully pick up the pieces of this work that are ours to carry. We believe that challenging ourselves and our colleagues to approach the work of Land Acknowledgements with deeper understanding and more heart is one facet of that work.

---

4 The lecture by Dr. Marcia J. Anderson that Nickita Danielle cites can be accessed here: https://www.facebook.com/IndigenousStudentCentreUofM/videos/367421163855990/

Our Positionality Statement and Land Acknowledgement Workshop

In December 2020, our Decolonizing the Library Interest Group (DIG) offered a Positionality and Land Acknowledgement Writing Workshop. The SFU ARC report recommends that an acknowledgement of the people and land should be done "at the start of meetings, classes, and events" (p. 48). The report states that this recognition is "one of the most important acts of reconciliation" (p. 81). After the inception of the interest group in 2019, we heard regular requests for a Land Acknowledgement workshop, perhaps because our colleagues were eager to enact the ARC's recommendation in a good way. Our planning team agreed that, though we are not experts and none of us are from the Nations whose land SFU occupies, we could create a meaningful opportunity for colleagues to come together to deepen our understanding of the practices of offering Land Acknowledgements. We were also clear that we could not provide insights into any Nation-specific cultural protocols. Learning about those protocols is different work and must be undertaken through consultation with community members and Knowledge Keepers.

Our workshop was designed to engage participants in solo reflection through writing prompts, as well as through discussion with one another. Prior to the workshop, we asked registered participants to engage in some prep work such as finding out whose land they live on (Native Land Digital, 2018), locating the Residential School site closest to where they grew up (CBC News, 2018; see also Indian Residential School History & Dialogue Centre, n.d.), and watching a segment of a talk given by Dr. Kim Anderson (Métis) where she identifies the "glazing over" effect that scripted Land Acknowledgements can have on audiences (Anderson, 2019).

Using a writing activity from Dr. Shield's English 359 course, *Literatures of British Columbia: Place, Space, and Indigeneity,* participants worked to craft their positionality and Land Acknowledgement using the following prompts:

- What is your name?
- Are you a settler/non-Indigenous person?
- Are you Black? Are you a Person of Colour? Are you Indigenous?

- What is your relationship to SFU (Are you student/faculty/staff/etc.)?
- What department are you located in at SFU?
- Whose territory/territories are you located on? Grew up on?
- Why are you engaged in this work/area of study?
- What is your "compelling action" in doing this work? (i.e. how are you engaging in a meaningful relationship with the Land and/or Nations?)

The focus in our workshop was to understand *why* this statement was being written and used. In an interview with CBC Unreserved (2019), Hayden King (Anishinaabe) says that he regrets writing Ryerson University's[5] Land Acknowledgement back in 2012. His regret, he says, comes from how often these statements can become superficial. What is needed is voicing an obligation or, as he says in an episode from *The Red Road Podcast* (Skye & King, 2019), a compelling action. In the context of academia, and libraries, we asked workshop participants to think back to Dr. Anderson's talk and how she connected her Land Acknowledgement to her course lecture.[6]

What Land Acknowledgements Are and What They Are Not

Land Acknowledgements have become a common practice across institutions all over Turtle Island (Robinson, 2018), the name used by some Indigenous Nations to refer to what is colonially known as North America.[7] For non-Indigenous people, the act of providing a Land

---

5 At the time of our writing, this university was also often known as X University. After years of work from Indigenous students, staff, and faculty, the university was engaged in a community consultation process to change its name. Before the chapter went to press, the university announced that it would change its name to Toronto Metropolitan University.

6 For a detailed description of the workshop, please visit our webpage: https://www.lib.sfu.ca/help/academic-integrity/indigenous-initiatives/icrc/Land-acknowledgement-workshop

7 Individual Indigenous Nations have their own distinct creation stories. Some Indigenous Peoples prefer not to use the term "Turtle Island," especially because it can perpetuate pan-Indigenous assumptions and stereotypes. Others embrace the term as a way of referring to this place without relying on colonial references (which "Canada," "the United States of America," and "North America" all are). Turning our attention to creation stories for a moment, here on the Northwest Coast, many Indigenous Nations maintain traditions focused on Raven as the creator of landforms, including mountains and islands such as Haida'Gwaii and the volcanoes along southwest Alaska. You can read the story of how Haida'Gwaii came to be, as narrated by GwaaGanad (Diane Brown, Haida) here: https://www.historymuseum.ca/history-hall/origins/_media/Creation-of-Haidagwaii-EN.pdf

Acknowledgement can be a way to centre Indigenous presence on the lands, express gratitude to the original and ongoing stewards of the land, and take a small step towards reconciliation.

As western colonial institutions have been called to decolonize and Indigenize,[8] Land Acknowledgements have sometimes been misunderstood as enactments of Indigenous cultural protocol or practice. In her 2021 book *We All Go Back to the Land*, Suzanne Keeptwo writes that Land Acknowledgements are relatively contemporary and that it was not until after the release of the Truth and Reconciliation Reports and Calls to Action in 2015 that these statements were offered more widely. Through our work we have come to recognize that there is no such thing as a pan-Indigenous Land Acknowledgement protocol outside of the contemporary, institutionalized practice that is often led and enacted by non-Indigenous peoples. Instead, there are culturally and contextually-specific oral practices that guide and structure events, ceremonies, and meetings within and amongst Indigenous Nations and communities. For example, in the Haudenosaunee tradition, there is the Thanksgiving Address, or the words that come before all else (Stokes and Kanawahienton, 1993; Kimmerer, 2013). As another example, Sxwpilemaát Siyám (Chief Leanne Joe, Sḵwx̱wú7mesh) shares,

> For the Coast Salish People, we would welcome our guests coming to shore on their canoes, by listening to each canoe ask for permission to come to our shore, state their business or purpose and acknowledge their kinship ties to the welcoming Nation. This would be followed by the Chief [...] either denying or welcoming them to their territory, asking them to come and feast with them and do their business. (2020, n.p.)

The orality of these traditions is noteworthy and raises questions about written statements, such as those included on institutional websites and in email signatures. Often, significant time and energy is invested in crafting these written statements to "get them right." Of course, it is important to do the learning required to offer an acknowledgement

---

8   The terms "decolonize" and "Indigenize" are both complex and, at times, fraught, particularly as the terms and the work associated with them are taken up within white colonial institutions, such as libraries. Each term has been defined in a wide variety of ways, sometimes in direct conflict with one another. We encourage readers to start learning and reflecting on these terms and what they might mean within library work by engaging with the work of Indigenous scholars, as in this example: https://www.ictinc.ca/blog/a-brief-definition-of-decolonization-and-indigenization

that is accurate, respectful, and reflective of the linguistic and rhetorical preferences of the Indigenous Nations whose lands and sovereignty are being acknowledged. However, this investment in the writing can have the unintended consequence of reifying the written statement as *the* way that all acknowledgements must be done, resulting in the institutional Land Acknowledgement "script." What is lost in this process of reification is the responsiveness, flexibility, and contextual possibility of acknowledgement as a practice: the understanding that offering acknowledgement can be an opportunity for relationship building in a specific context.[9]

Scripted statements can also end up being delivered by rote or simply repeated, without recognition of the speaker's positionality or reasons for including the acknowledgement at the event. When delivered in this way, Land Acknowledgements can allow us to feel that we have completed our "due diligence" and are somehow excused from complicity in systems and structures that continue to perpetuate and reproduce colonialism. In a blog post, Métis author Chelsea Vowel (2016a) notes that "territorial acknowledgments can become stripped of their disruptive power through repetition. The purpose cannot merely be to inform an ignorant public that Indigenous peoples exist, and that Canada has a history of colonialism." Jennifer Matsunaga (2016), a settler-Canadian of mixed Japanese-British-Scottish descent, adds that Land Acknowledgements remain as mere presentation etiquette if they are not followed through with actions such as developing one's knowledge about the local territory and history and making efforts for deeper engagement with the people of that territory. With this chapter, we raise the question: If acknowledgement is not just about making ourselves feel better, what can we actually do to (re)build relationships and address the ongoing impacts of colonialism? What does this work involve?

What is Positionality? Why Does It Matter in a Land Acknowledgement?

One aspect of making Land Acknowledgements more meaningful comes from the practice of positioning or situating oneself in relation to the land, work, and context. There are two theories at work: positionality

---

9   This tension speaks to the wider conversation about orality and the written word and the ways that each is understood and valued in Indigenous and settler colonial societies, about which much has been said and written.

and intersectionality. In her 2017 book *Network Sovereignty: Building the Internet Across Indian Country,* Marisa Duarte (Pascua Yaqui/Chicana) writes that "the methodology of positionality requires researchers to identify their own degrees of privilege through factors of race, class, educational attainment, income, ability, gender, and citizenship" (p. 135). This recognition helps researchers "understand how their way of making meaning, of framing research, within their conceptual universe is tied to their positionality within an unjust world" (p. 135). How these factors come together is known as intersectionality, a term coined by Black feminist lawyer and scholar Kimberlé Crenshaw in the late 1980s.[10] Intersectionality is how the overlapping facets of one's identity impact their lived experiences and therefore their worldviews. Acknowledging the intersectionality of our own identities is an important part of positioning ourselves. The work of positioning and situating ourselves in a Land Acknowledgement is also a way of demonstrating our relationship with the land and with other beings. In many Indigenous cultures, situating yourself within your community and kinship networks indicates your relationships and accountability (Keeptwo, 2021; Wilson, 2008). Anishinaabe scholar Kateri Akiwenzie-Damm argues that understanding one's position shows an awareness of "the colonial history that may come to bear upon the process and upon [one's] relationships" with Indigenous topics (2016, p. 32). Consider the creation of a "positionality statement" as an opportunity to acknowledge your position and identity in relation to the work that you're doing.

Approaching Land Acknowledgements With Heart

In this section we will use an example to demonstrate an approach to offering Land Acknowledgements that contrasts with the institutional script provided above. This example is included as a way of making some of the conceptual points above more concrete.

> My name is Jaad Les[11] and I am a white settler living on the ancestral, unceded, rightful, and occupied Lands of the ʷməθkʷəy̓əm (Musqueam), Sḵwx̱wú7mesh (Squamish), səl̓ilw̓ətaʔɬ (Tsleil-Waututh),

---

10   See "Mapping the Margins: Intersectionality, Identity Politics, and Violence against Women of Colour" (1991); and "Demarginalizing the Intersection of Race and Sex: A Black Feminist Critique of Antidiscrimination Doctrine, Feminist Theory and Antiracist Politics" (1994).

11   This person does not exist. The name was created by combining letters from the co-authors' names.

and kʷikʷəƛ̓əm (Kwikwetlem) Nations. I was born and raised in Treaty 1 territory in Southern Manitoba. Treaty 1 was signed between representatives from the Swampy Cree Nation, the Anishinaabe Nation, and the Imperial Crown of Great Britain and Ireland. As a descendant of British settlers in this place, I recognize that horrific violence was and is committed against Indigenous Peoples in order to secure the comfort and privilege that I now experience.

As we begin this workshop, I am also reflecting on the fact that these lands that we gather on today have been shared territories for many countless generations. People from the xʷməθkʷəy̓əm (Musqueam), Sḵwx̱wú7mesh Úxwumixw (Squamish), səl̓ ilw̓ ətaʔɬ (Tsleil-Waututh), and kʷikʷəƛ̓əm (Kwikwetlem) Nations all have a long and ongoing connection to this place. Colonially, this place is known as Burnaby Mountain and as Simon Fraser University. Khelsilem (spokesperson for the Squamish Nation) has taught me that it can also be called Lhuḵw'lhuḵw'áyten in the Squamish language, meaning "where the bark gets peeled" in spring. The name is derived from the Squamish word for arbutus, lhulhuḵw'ay, which comes from lhuḵw' (peel), and means "always peeling tree." This information is also on the Bill Reid Centre's website (2022), which provides useful resources for learning more about Coast Salish place names and about the Indigenous art on SFU's campuses. We are privileged to learn together on these lands and I recognize my own responsibility to continue the work of learning how to live well in shared territories. I also commit myself to engaging with both the histories and contemporary realities of the Indigenous Nations whose lands I occupy to better uplift the sovereignty of those Nations and take up my responsibilities as a settler living in an Indigenous place.

In this example, our fictional speaker positions themself in relation to the Indigenous lands they occupy. We learn that the speaker identifies as a white settler and they provide information both about the lands where they were raised and where they are currently offering the workshop.

There are several language choices that a speaker must make when offering a Land Acknowledgement. In the example above, Jaad has chosen to position themself as a "white settler." The term "settler" has become increasingly widespread but it can cause confusion and a sense of disconnection or alienation. In *Indigenous Writes* (2016b), Vowel unpacks the term. She writes that when we consider the identities and trajectories of the peoples who live in what is colonially known as Canada, "we are left with three broad, unsatisfactory, but possibly usable categories: settlers (the non-Indigenous peoples living in Canada who form the European-descended socio-political majority), non-Black persons of colour (hereafter, non-Black POC), and Black people" (p. 17). She further articulates that these distinctions are necessary because "the term *settler* does not, and can never, refer to the descendants of Africans who were kidnapped and sold into chattel slavery. Black people, removed and cut off from their own indigenous lands — literally stripped of their humanity and redefined legally as property — could not be agents of settlement" (2016b, p. 17). Tuck (Unangax̂) and Yang (2012) also draw a distinction between settlers and immigrants, suggesting that settlers are those who applied colonial logics to exert control and enforce their own systems of governance over those that already existed in this place. Immigrants are those who arrive in this place with the expectation that they will live according to the existing laws and customs.

In addition to identifying themself as a settler, Jaad has also added the racial qualifier, "white." Vowel suggests that "a strong argument can be made that non-European-descended peoples who come to live in Canada are also settlers" (2016b, p. 17), demonstrating a different understanding than the one advanced by Tuck and Yang and articulating that "settler" can be used as a relational term, rather than a racial category. Understood in this way, it is possible for individuals to identify as both a Person of Colour[12] and a settler in Indigenous territories. Furthermore, within white supremacist societies, white is often the unnamed and unacknowledged racial category. Choosing to name one's self as white and/or as a settler can signal a person's critical awareness of the impact that their presence and their speaking a Land Acknowledgement, especially in a colonial institution, may have on others. The naming of whiteness is an important practice, especially in contexts where white has been assumed to be neutral or the default. The practice of naming whiteness can be deepened in an acknowledgement that specifically addresses the harms perpetuated in the name of white supremacy, through European settlement of these lands and beyond (Lowman and Barker, 2015). The complexity of these identity categories and language choices clearly demonstrates

---

12 Person of Colour: Used to refer to a person who is not white. This term is often used to signal shared experiences of systemic oppression and racism in a culture of white supremacy.

the personal work that must go into crafting a meaningful, heartfelt Land Acknowledgement–work that includes learning more about how you and your family came to these lands and coming to understand how you have benefitted from (and also potentially been harmed by) the ongoing colonization of the place where you live (Singh, 2019).

Some other terms worth noting in Jaad's Land Acknowledgement are "unceded" and "occupy." In most parts of British Columbia, you will hear the word "unceded" in Land Acknowledgements. Unceded means that the Nation(s) being acknowledged never surrendered their rights or ties to the Land. It effectively means the land is occupied by the colonizer government (British, and then Canadian), and by those non-Indigenous peoples living on it. In other parts of this country, there is a long history of treaties being signed between governments and Indigenous Nations, as Jaad also references by acknowledging Treaty 1 territory.[13] While it is important for non-Indigenous peoples to recognize whether land is treatied or unceded, both terms are insufficient for a full understanding of historical and contemporary land politics. The words that a speaker chooses to use in their Land Acknowledgement can signal their own understanding of and relationship to these land politics. Consider, for instance, the difference between simply stating that land is unceded as compared to saying that it is "unceded and occupied" or even dispensing with the esoteric legal term "unceded" and stating that the land has been stolen.

What becomes clear in working through this example is that the words we use in Land Acknowledgements are powerful and must be chosen with thought and care. When making these decisions, we should keep in mind some key questions:

1. What is the work that we want our Land Acknowledgements to do?
2. What language choices can we make to reflect this work and positioning?

When our language choices are made in line with those questions, the words we use can extend what we share directly about ourselves to

---

13   There has been sustained criticism of the treaties related to broken promises, forced signatures, and misinterpretations of intent (both deliberate and unintentional) stemming from language and cultural differences. The modern treaties that are being negotiated for unceded Lands are often significantly different from the historical treaties. The Canadian Encyclopedia provides a starting point for learning about the history of treaties here: https://www.thecanadianencyclopedia.ca/en/article/aboriginal-treaties

position us in relation to the land, the Indigenous Nations of that land, and those in attendance.

It is also worth noting that Jaad's acknowledgement provides significantly more information than is generally furnished in an institutional script, including a local Indigenous language and a resource those in attendance can access to learn more. Finally, Jaad makes a public commitment to continue their work. What is clear in this example is that the work is not completed at the end of the speech act. Instead, the acknowledgement is an opening to further learning, relationship building, and commitment.[14] In short, the spoken Land Acknowledgement is only one piece of a larger *practice* of acknowledgement and action.

What Does it Mean for Libraries to be on This Land and to Give Land Acknowledgements?

Libraries are places of learning. As perceived gatekeepers of information, libraries are also complicit in the attempted assimilation of Indigenous Peoples. Recognizing and understanding the colonial roots of educational institutions is an important step in decolonizing. Libraries are not, and have never been, neutral spaces. Through our collections, the English language and written works have been prioritized, leaving little room for other languages and other ways of engaging with information. As Daniel Heath Justice writes, "literature as a category is about what's important to a culture" (2018, p. 20), and Indigenous literatures can be found in "texts, such as cane baskets, wampum belts, birchbark scrolls, gourd masks, sand paintings, rock art, carved and painted cedar poles, stones and whale bones, culturally modified trees, and so on" (p. 22). Where are these forms of knowledge and literature in libraries?

A meaningful Land Acknowledgement practice requires us to ask critical questions about ourselves, our work, and our institutions. Working as we do for an academic library, our own practice of Land Acknowledgement has led us into deeper engagement with understanding education as a colonial and assimilative system. The history of education provided to and forced upon Indigenous Peoples is full of trauma. Dating back

---

14 We also want to be clear that we are not suggesting that this is a perfect Land Acknowledgement. The central focus of this chapter is on resisting the notion of a singularly defined, "once and for all" approach to Land Acknowledgements. We offer this example only to demonstrate an approach to offering acknowledgement and the kinds of personal reflection, research, and commitment-making that can accompany heartfelt, meaningful Land acknowledgement practices.

to the mid-1800s, education was used to attempt to assimilate Indigenous children through Residential Schools and boarding schools run by religious institutions with support from the government (Battiste, 2013; Cote-Meek, 2014; Joseph, 2018; Maracle, 2017; Vowel, 2016b). Stó:lō storyteller Lee Maracle (2017) uses the United Nations definition to label these assimilationist tactics "acts of genocide." While people often celebrate the ways that the education system has improved, the authors of *The Equity Myth: Racialization and Indigeneity at Canadian Universities* (2017) demonstrate how education-as-assimilation continues to this day. Mi'kmaw scholar Marie Battiste has described this ongoing process as "cognitive imperialism" (2013) – a eurocentric, westernized curriculum that leaves little room for Indigenous Knowledges and voices.

Recognizing and acknowledging this ongoing assimilation is the first step in taking up the broader engagement with reconciliation and decolonizing work that should be implied by practicing Land Acknowledgements within libraries. Q'um Q'um Xiiem (Dr. Jo-ann Archibald, Stó:lō) talks about the tradition of sharing information and knowledge (2008), which is also at the heart of what libraries strive to do. When giving a Land Acknowledgement at a library, it is therefore important to think about who or what the library is in relation to the land on which it is located. For example, you could consider whether materials created by members of the local Nations are included in the collection, or if library programming includes (paid) speakers from the Nations where the library is located. If not, what initiatives could be undertaken to change things? As mentioned previously, a strong and heartfelt Land Acknowledgement includes a compelling action reflective of the institution, the person offering the acknowledgement, and the specific event.

Our Compelling Action

One critique of Land Acknowledgements is that they have become statements devoid of both action and heart, rendering them essentially meaningless. Courtney Skye and Hayden King (2019) encourage us to counteract this trend by including a "compelling action" in our acknowledgements – an action or call to action that deepens the relationship between the speaker and the land and Nation(s). This chapter acts as part of our own compelling action, and was written in the spirit of knowledge sharing (Archibald, 2008). It is our hope that this work inspires other libraries and library staff to examine and ultimately deepen their engagement with Land Acknowledgement practices.

Land Acknowledgements can become a practice through which libraries and library staff come to recognize not just our place and our relationship to this place, but also the value of knowledge traditions beyond what libraries have conventionally collected (the written word). This would be another step towards decolonizing, recognizing that the land itself plays the role of library for many Indigenous cultures. As we step into this work, we must engage in an ongoing reflective practice that challenges us to examine our relationship and the relationship of our institutions with Indigenous lands, Indigenous Nations, and Indigenous Peoples. Significantly, we must start to recognize that the work of delivering meaningful, heartfelt Land Acknowledgements begins well before words are spoken at an event. Furthermore, the work that the Land Acknowledgement represents must extend well beyond the few moments required to complete the speech act. Instead of thinking about Land Acknowledgements and the larger work of decolonization and reconciliation as projects to complete, we encourage readers to understand each as a practice that we perpetually take up, re-committing ourselves to building healthier and stronger relationships with one another and with the Land.

In this way, the work of Land Acknowledgements embodies the work of decolonization and reconciliation. None is a destination at which we can arrive. Instead, each is a practice that we perpetually take up, as we commit ourselves to the ongoing work that needs to be done.

Acknowledgement

Our colleague Jenna Walsh contributed knowledge and labour to both the workshop and our discussions during the planning stages of this chapter. Her insights and guidance have grounded our thinking throughout this process. We are grateful to have her support and encouragement in this work. *Kitchi-marsii* Jenna.

References

Akiwenzi-Damm, K. (2016). "We think differently. We have a different understanding.": Editing Indigenous texts as an Indigenous editor. In C. Verduyn, D.J. Irvine, & S. Kamboureli (Eds.), *Editing as cultural practice in Canada* (pp. 29-39). Wilfrid Laurier University Press.

Anderson, K. (2019, March 14). *Indigenizing curriculum.* https://www.youtube.com/watch?v=EmpyOZm7sQ0

Anderson, M.J. (2019). "Ten ways organizations get in their own way on 'Indigenous achievement' / 'reconciliation' / 'diversity' / 'inclusion' / 'anti-racism'." home [facebook page] Facebook. Retrieved May 1, 2021, from https://www.facebook.com/IndigenousStudentCentreUofM/videos/367421163855990/

Archibald, J. (2008). *Indigenous storywork: Educating the heart, mind, body, and spirit.* UBC Press.

Arnold, C. (2021, May/June). The art and heart of land acknowledgments. *BCTF Teacher*, 20-21.

Auger, O. (2021, May 14). Land acknowledgements are about better relations, not just checking a box. *APTN National News*. https://www.aptnnews.ca/national-news/Land-acknowledgements-british-columbia/?fbclid=IwAR0nkh-WfHNmdLrNcfk4VuQGcVabrVvks8f2Pw_t0yVvnKs8ZJXUTErzAZs&utm_source=ActiveCampaign&utm_medium=email&utm_content=March+2021+news+++events&utm_campaign=March+News

Battiste, M. (2013). *Decolonizing education: Nourishing the learning spirit.* Purich Publishing Limited.

Bill Reid Centre. (n.d.) ímesh mobile app. *Simon Fraser University.* http://www.sfu.ca/brc/imeshMobileApp.html

Bill Reid Centre. (n.d.). Lhukw›lhukw›ayten–Burnaby Mountain, Burnaby, British Columbia. *Simon Fraser University.* https://www.sfu.ca/brc/imeshMobileApp/place-names/lhukwlhukwayten.html

CBC News. *Did you live near a residential school?* https://www.cbc.ca/news2/interactives/beyond-94-residential-school-map/

CBC Radio, Unreserved. (2019, January 18). 'I regret it': Hayden King on writing Ryerson University›s territorial acknowledgement. https://tinyurl.com/y9wz2zf3

Canadian Federation of Library Associations Indigenous Matters Committee. (n.d.). Truth and reconciliation report and recommendations. https://cfla-fcab.ca/en/indigenous/trc_report/

College of Social and Applied Human Sciences. (2019, March 14). *Indigenizing curriculum* [Video]. YouTube. https://www.youtube.com/watch?v=EmpyOZm7sQ0

Cote-Meek, S. (2014). *Colonized classrooms: Racism, trauma and resistance in post-secondary education.* Fernwood Publishing.

Crenshaw, K. (1991). Mapping the margins: Intersectionality, identity politics, and violence against women of color. *Stanford Law Review, 43*(6), 1241-1299. doi:10.2307/1229039

Crenshaw, K. (1994). Demarginalizing the intersection of race and sex: A Black feminist critique of antidiscrimination doctrine, feminist theory, and anti-racist politics. In *Living with Contradictions* (1st ed., pp. 39–52). Routledge. https://doi.org/10.4324/9780429499142-5

Duarte, M. E. (2017). *Network sovereignty: Building the Internet across Indian Country.* University of Washington Press.

Frances, H., Enakshi, D., James, C.E., Kobayashi, A., Li, P., Ramos, H., Smith, M.S. (2017). *The equity myth: Racialization and Indigeneity at Canadian universities*. UBC Press.

GwaaGanad (Brown, D.) (n.d.). The creation of Haida'Gwaii (Haida). https://www.historymuseum.ca/history-hall/origins/_media/Creation-of-Haidagwaii-EN.pdf

Hall, A.J. (2011, June 6). Treaties with Indigenous Peoples in Canada. *The Canadian Encyclopedia*. https://www.thecanadianencyclopedia.ca/en/article/aboriginal-treaties.

Indian Residential School History & Dialogue Centre. *Find schools*. https://collections.irshdc.ubc.ca/index.php/Browse/schools

Indigenous Corporate Training. (2017, March 29). A brief definition of decolonization and indigenization. *Working Effectively with Indigenous Peoples*. https://www.ictinc.ca/blog/a-brief-definition-of-decolonization-and-indigenization

Joseph, R. P. C. (2018). *21 things you may not know about the Indian Act : helping Canadians make reconciliation with Indigenous Peoples a reality*. Indigenous Relations Press.

Justice, D.H. (2018). *Why Indigenous literatures matter*. Wilfrid Laurier University Press.

Keeptwo, S. (2021). *We all go back to the Land: The who, why and how of Land acknowledgements*. Brush Education.

King, G. (Guest). (2021, May 17). All my loving relations [Audio podcast episode]. In *All My Relations*. https://www.allmyrelationspodcast.com/podcast/episode/48f75f91/all-my-loving-relation

Kimmerer, R.W. (2013). *Braiding sweetgrass: Indigenous wisdom, scientific knowledge, and the teachings of plants*. Milkweed Editions.

Lowman, E.B. and Barker, A.J. (2015). *Settler: Identity and colonialism in 21st century Canada*. Fernwood Press.

Matsunaga, J. (2016, May 27). Thinking outloud about the "Guide to Acknowledging Traditional Territory". *Reconciling truths and accounting for the past: Community interactions with the government*. https://jennifermatsunaga.com/2016/05/27/thinking-outloud-about-the-guide-to-acknowledging-traditional-territory/

Maracle, L. (2017). *My conversations with Canadians*. BookThug.

Nahanee, T. (n.d.). *Decolonize first: A liberating guide and workbook for peeling back the layers of neocolonialism*. Nahanee Creative.

Native Land Digital. (2021). *Native Land*. https://native-Land.ca/

Pride Toronto apologizes for Land acknowledgement that 'failed to recognize' Indigenous people. (2019, June 24). *CBC News*. https://www.cbc.ca/news/canada/toronto/pride-toronto-indigenous-Land-acknowledgement-1.5188127

Robinson, A. (2018, November 6). Turtle Island. The Canadian Encyclopedia. https://www.thecanadianencyclopedia.ca/en/article/turtle-isLand

Ryerson Today. (November 16, 2021). Update on finding a new name for the university. https://www.ryerson.ca/news-events/news/2021/11/update-on-finding-a-new-name-for-the-university/

Simon Fraser University, Aboriginal Reconciliation Council. (2017). Walk this path with us. https://www.sfu.ca/aboriginalpeoples/sfu-reconciliation.html

Simon Fraser University Archives. (n.d.). Simon Fraser, the explorer. https://www.sfu.ca/archives/archives-program/outreach-education/simon-fraser-the-explorer.html

Simon Fraser University Library, Indigenous Curriculum Resource Centre. (2021, April 19). Positionality statement and Land acknowledgement workshop. https://www.lib.sfu.ca/help/academic-integrity/indigenous-initiatives/icrc/Land-acknowledgement-workshop

Singh, A. (2019). The racial healing workbook. New Harbinger Publications.

Siyám, S. (2020, June 17). Beyond Land acknowledgments. SFU Community Economic Development. https://www.sfu.ca/ced/economic-reconciliation/transformative-storytelling/beyond-Land-acknowledgments.html

Skye, C. and King, H. (Hosts). (2019, June 28). Beyond Land acknowledgements (season 2, episode 6) [Audio podcast episode]. In The Red Road. https://podcasts.apple.com/ca/podcast/the-red-road-podcast/id1440299794

Stokes, J. and Kanawahienton. (1993). *Thanksgiving address: Greetings to the natural world*. Six Nations Indian Museum and the Tracking Project.

Twiss, G. (2018, November 14). A tale of two Simon Frasers: The invented and contested Scottish tradition of SFU. *Scots in British Columbia*. https://scotsinbritishcolumbia.com/2018/11/14/a-tale-of-two-simon-frasers-the-invented-and-contested-scottish-tradition-of-sfu/

Tuck, E., & Yang, K. W. (2012). Decolonization is not a metaphor. *Decolonization: Indigeneity, education & society, 1*(1).

Vowel, C. (2016a, September 23). Beyond territory acknowledgements. *âpihtawikosisân*. https://apihtawikosisan.com/2016/09/beyond-territorial-acknowledgments/

Vowel, C. (2016b). *Indigenous writes : A guide to First Nations, Métis & Inuit issues in Canada*. HighWater Press.

Wilson, S. (2008). *Research is ceremony: Indigenous research methods*. Fernwood Publishing.

Younging, G. (2018). *Elements of Indigenous style: A guide for writing by and about Indigenous Peoples*. Brush Education.

Downstream

Danielle Marie Bitz

We had intended to spend our first night on the river in the area of the Hague Ferry crossing, roughly 25 kilometers downstream of the Clarkboro Ferry, where we had launched the canoe and two kayaks in which our party was traveling. However, when we reached the Hague Ferry crossing before noon it took very little discussion to decide that we would push on. Not only was there at least eight hours of daylight left, but also the next day's forecast called for high winds and possibly rain, a combination that can drastically slow the progress of a boat on the river, even if that boat is moving with the current, travelling downstream. We agreed on another hour or two of paddling, maybe 10 or 15 kilometers, but the shifting shorelines, sandbars, and islands that line and dot the South Saskatchewan River left us very little in the way of options for campsites. When we finally pulled the boats from the water onto the sandbar at the place we had originally planned to camp on our second night—roughly 45 kilometers from where we launched that morning—we were tired and hungry and victorious.

In preparation for this trip, knowing that the section of the river we would be paddling is central to Métis history, and a large part of my own history, I had read the descriptions of the "historical sites" in various canoeing brochures and maps, on the blogs of other paddlers, and in the content posted on the Saskatchewan Government's website. I had sought out and read different accounts of the North-West Resistance. In my mind, I had gone back over the stories I had been told about the Big Battle at Batoche and about how, in the aftermath, much of our family had fled south to Montana to escape persecution by the Canadian state and its military. It seemed surreal to be pitching camp a stone's throw from Petite Ville, one of the first Métis wintering (hivernant) villages in the area.

We spent two nights at this camp, owing primarily to our proximity to Gabriel's Crossing (we were about 7 kilometers upstream), where we were scheduled to meet our cache drop at noon on the third day of our trip. The site we chose for our tent and cook fire was on a sandbar on the lee side of a small island in a bend of the river, a short distance from the site that was Petite Ville. If we stood facing the main trunk of the river, behind us was a narrow and shallow channel that was just wide enough to discourage visits from the RV camping crowd that had set up atop some nearby cliffs. In front of us the main body of the river curved around a reedy bank that rose up to a wide, partially-treed floodplain at the base of the surrounding slopes. A flat sheltered expanse, just to the north of us is the site that an hivernant community of Métis hunters and traders called home for the winter.

On paper, Petite Ville is a "Métis archeological site near Batoche, Saskatchewan" that was designated as a "Provincial Heritage property" in 2005 (Government of Saskatchewan, Ministry of Tourism, Parks, Culture and Sport, 2008). In a press release on the Government of Saskatchewan's website, Petite Ville is described as an archaeological site containing "information on a pivotal period in the history of the Métis–their transition from nomadic buffalo hunting to a sedentary agricultural existence" (Government of Saskatchewan, Ministry of Tourism, Parks, Culture and Sport, 2008). The canoeing guides produced by the Meewasin Valley Authority (1998) describe the site as follows:

> Petite-Ville, established in the 1860s, was the first semi-sedentary wintering village (hivernement) of those families who later founded the St-Laurent settlement. These hivernant villages were unorganized clusters of mud-plastered cabins, abandoned during the summer months and re-occupied after the fall hunt. The natural shelter along the river was likely the key attraction. (p. 16)

On one level, there is a great deal to unpack solely in the language of these descriptions. For example, just because an archaeologist doesn't understand the way that a village has been organized, does not mean that it is "unorganized." When a family closes up a lake house or a cabin for the winter, would it ever be described as "abandoned?" In one's imagination, does describing the filled cracks between logs in a cabin wall as "mud-plastered" carry the same connotations as *clay-chinked*?

Viewed individually, each of these examples is simply an incident of poor word choice; collectively, however, these incidents demonstrate a pattern of bias. In highlighting the need for their thesis, *Petite Ville: A Spatial Assessment of a Métis Hivernant Site,* Kim Weinbender (2003) asserts that "Historically, not much is known about the spatial nature of hivernant settlements and structures. The few existing descriptions are usually quite biased by the observer's European background and are typically derogatory in nature" (p. 3). While this bias is problematic, it is nowhere nearly as damaging as the omissions it both allows and depends on.

None of these tourism documents mention that many of the families that formed the communities along the South Saskatchewan River during the late 1860s and early 1870s were refugees from the Red River area. Also omitted from this narrative of migration and settlement are the actions of the Canadian state during and following the Red River Resistance of 1869-70, and the subsequent military campaign commanded by Col. Garnet Wolseley against the Red River Métis, a time that is still referred to as the reign of terror in Métis history (Barkwell, 2017; Royal Canadian Geographic Society, 2018c).

Instead, the Meewasin Valley Authority's River Guide mentions the declining population of bison as a factor influencing the decision of the Métis to move into farming settlements. However, this narrative too is incomplete. It omits the over hunting of the bison by non-Indigenous hunters who took the furs and left the meat to spoil or poisoned it to kill the wolves that would feed on the discarded carcasses so that their pelts might also be collected. It additionally fails to mention the United States Government policy of removing the bison, migratory herd animals that did not respect colonial state-lines, as a food source for the Plains Peoples so that they might be subdued through starvation (Royal Canadian Geographical Society, 2018b). These pamphlets, maps, and government reports and pages, incomplete and biased as they are, remain the sources most readily available to the public, easily accessible through a basic internet search. The narrative that is created and supported in these texts is of a primitive, irreverent people that evolved from a nomadic hunter-gatherer existence to a more advanced one, rooted in agriculture and Christian observance.

This narrative, in turn, sustains several of the foundational elements in the mainstream portrayal of western settlement in what is now Canada. It holds that there is not only a dichotomy between the wilderness and that which is settled, between that which is savage and civilized, but also that societies evolve from savage to civilized through a process of detaching themselves from, and then taming and settling, the wilderness. There are tenets built into this narrative that define what it is to be an evolved and contemporary human, including the assumption that a sedentary existence is more evolved than a nomadic one and that monotheism and atheism are more evolved than animism and polytheism.

I don't think that it is unfair to suggest that libraries, especially academic libraries, have in the past and continue today to contribute to this narrative. We, as librarians, tend to think of ourselves as a civilizing influence, as part of a democratizing institution and we promote that image to the larger public. The American Library Association's (ALA) *I Love Libraries* website asserts that "Libraries level the playing field. As great democratic institutions, they serve people of every age, income level, location, ethnicity, and physical ability, and provide the full range of information resources needed to live, learn, govern, and work" (ALA, 2022). We believe that we improve the lives of people who come into and make use of our spaces—and we do, in the ways that we know. We provide access to information, we teach people how to find the information they want or need, and how to evaluate the sources of that information. However, in doing so we also produce a narrative that dictates what counts as knowledge. If we assert that we "provide the full range of information resources needed to live, learn, govern, and work" (ALA, 2022) then knowledge that we can't provide access to is, by default, either unnecessary or not knowledge.

Much of our work in academic libraries is based on preserving the primacy of text-based culture and an understanding of knowledge that is solely intellectual. As members of the academic institution, we teach and enforce a structure of knowledge creation that is both anthropocentric and excludes those forms of knowledge that live in the body, in the land, and in the spaces of relationality (Duarte & Belarde-Lewis, 2015; Loyer, 2021; Wilson, 2008). In the maintenance of these ways of knowing we deterritorialize (Simpson, 2017) the process of learning, the act of sharing knowledge. If we continue to insist that "all knowledge in the world can be represented in document form" (Duarte & Belarde-Lewis, 2015) we uphold the narrative of settlement; of what is now Canada as a once-wild space that has been civilized through the introduction of knowledge.

* * *

My name is Danielle Marie Bitz; I am a citizen of the Métis Nation and a Canadian of mixed Métis and German-Ukrainian descent. I have familial ties to both settler and Michif/Métis communities across the Métis homeland including those in the Red River Valley, St.François Xavier, Skull Creek in the Cypress Hills, Montana, and what is now Balgonie, Saskatchewan. For my Métis relatives: my Métis family tree includes the names Swain (Swan), Breland, Dauphinais, Desmarais, and Grant.

I currently hold the position of Indigenous Engagement Librarian at the University of Winnipeg; I have worked in libraries for a decade now. I completed the coursework for my Master of Library and Information Studies (MLIS) in April of 2020, a month into the first COVID-19 pandemic lockdown, two weeks prior to my 42nd birthday, and about three and a half months before the canoe trip that I discuss here. The events and circumstances of this journey have (re)shaped my knowledge of the relationship between librarians, libraries, the land, and the knowledge that exists in their connection.

For almost ten years now I have lived on the banks of rivers that are central to Métis identities, narratives, economies, and resistance in both Winnipeg and Saskatoon. I currently rent an apartment that overlooks the last big curve in the Assiniboine River, on the east side of Armstrong point, just before it joins the Red. I am a (long) day's paddle downstream of what is now St.François Xavier, the place that was Grantown when founded by my ancestors. These are the traditional territories of the Anishinaabe, Cree, Oji-Cree, Dakota, and Dene Peoples, it is also the birthplace and homeland of the Métis Nation. I have a complicated relationship with this space, the City of Winnipeg. I both see and feel the social strata here more than anywhere else I have ever lived. I feel at once like I belong here and yet insecure in my right to feel that way. I am reasonably comfortable; I am perpetually homesick for the foothills and the eastern face of the Rockies. Regardless (or perhaps because) of this difficult relationship, the fact that I am able to live in this space fills my heart with a sense of gratitude and kinship that I have not found elsewhere. Despite the gravity that Winnipeg holds for me, I still consider myself a guest here, and as a guest I am trying to learn the ways of being here in a good way, and to support others in their learning.

I was born and raised in Calgary, the place where both sets of my grandparents had moved their families from Southern Saskatchewan in the 1960s, about three quarters of a century following the North-West Resistance. Mohkinstsis, the Siksiká name for the area, refers to where the Bow and the Elbow rivers become one before turning south to meet the Oldman River (a confluence that ends both tributaries and creates the South Saskatchewan River). As a child in the 1980s and a teen in the 1990s I had a relatively free-range upbringing—if I could get there and back on my bike or on the bus, I was allowed to go. As a result, I spent an exorbitant amount of time in the parks and on the pathways that surrounded the rivers in Calgary and later in the foothills and mountains to the west; those spaces are fundamental to my understanding of the city, the land that hosts it, relationality, and what it is to be downstream of something.

I was four years old in 1982 when the Canadian Constitution was patriated, and the Métis were officially recognised by the Canadian Government as one of the *Aboriginal* Peoples in what is now called Canada. I grew up on stories shared by my grandmother and my mother of the family legacy of Métis resistance that began in 1816 with the Battle of Seven Oaks. It included our family's return from the United States in the late 1800s—once the Canadian Government and settler communities had stopped actively persecuting the Métis for their resistance at Batoche (Reed, 1986; Royal Canadian Geographic Society, 2018a). The very first book I borrowed and neglected to return was D. Bruce Sealey's *Cuthbert Grant and the Métis* (1976). I may have been eight, maybe ten years old, and I still wonder if my grandmother ever figured out what happened to it (I still have it—sorry, cousins!). But I also learned at a very young age not to share these stories, that teachers, mainstream community members, and non-Métis family members considered them irrelevant or even fabricated.

This year we are 40 years downstream of the Canadian state's recognition of the Métis Nation as an *Aboriginal* [Indigenous] Nation from these lands. That recognition has allowed for huge gains in the visibility, rights, and sovereignty of my people in what is now Canada. It has also made discernible and legally tenable the rights that were denied to the Métis/Michif people by a colonial government intent on seeing Indigenous title to the land extinguished (Royal Canadian Geographic Society, 2018d). Yet in spite of the gains that the nation has made in the realms of visibility and sovereignty, the way that a flood (re)shapes a river cannot be undone. Many of us, born and raised in urban environments, will spend our lives in a liminal space either denying our heritage or wondering if we are Métis enough. Others, with no kinship, cultural, or community connections, will attempt to claim citizenship in our nation in order to have access to our recognition as

Indigenous people and our right to treat with the Canadian government on a nation-to-nation basis for the benefit of Métis citizens.

* * *

Land is irrevocably tied to all Indigenous ways of knowing and being; we only learn, we only exist through our relationship to the land (Adese, 2014; Bowra, Mashford-Pringle & Poland, 2021; Fellner, 2018; Loyer, 2018; Simpson, 2017; Wilson, 2008). This is self-evident. That I, a Métisse living in the Métis Homeland, must cite texts published in an academic context, in order to make that assertion in this piece of writing and have it respected is evidence of how marginalized Indigenous way of knowing and being are. It is evidence of the deficit-based thinking that is at the center of Western pedagogical frameworks. It speaks to an underlying assumption that Indigenous ways of learning, knowing, and being must be *lifted up to the level* of Western epistemologies and ontologies.

Leanne Simpson (2017) tells us that:

> We cannot just think, write, or imagine our way to a decolonized future. Answers to how to rebuild and how to resurge are therefore derived from a web of consensual relationships that is infused with movement (kinetic) through lived experience and embodiment. (p. 162)

In short, to decolonize, we must learn to Indigenize our ways of learning, of knowing.

I have heard multiple authors, thinkers, and elders speak to a similar idea: a reality in which we learn as we move across the land. There is a particular knowledge that is gained when we take the time to experience the spaces we move through as a component of the teachings that belong to them. There are very particular relationships that are formed when children begin receiving knowledge across generational lines, from relatives as they ride in or walk beside a cart, moving with the season to the next camp. In this way of being, knowledge is living, and it is layered into our minds and bodies through stories that are retold each year in the same space and season, both drawing on and contributing to what has been and what will be learned from each iteration.

For years, the idea of building layers of embodied knowledge that is tied to places we visit cyclically has been part of *the "stuff" teachers have put into my memory* where it sat waiting for me to *have the experience to understand it* (Campbell, 2010, p.4). In the winter of 2020/2021, I heard Maria Campbell speak, and as a preface to what she was saying she described our ways of land-based learning; I didn't understand it then, but that moment brought the *stuff* in my memory and my experience together. Over the next few months, I would think frequently of my mother and of the dream visits she received from her grandfather, Peter Swain, at a time in her life when she felt particularly alone. I spoke to my mother about this and, in particular, about grandpa's teachings about pine trees—the medicine in pine needles, in pine sap, the structure of trees, and how they grow in rings adding a unique layer each year.

In the summer of 2021 I moved back to Winnipeg to begin the work of my first job as an academic librarian. On one particularly glorious morning, about a month into my return, I was standing in my kitchen sipping coffee, gazing out of my kitchen window at the shadows dancing with currents on the Assiniboine river, and envisioning my ancestors paddling past that exact spot, the last big bend in the water on their way into The Forks (a meeting and gathering place for Indigenous peoples in the area since time immemorial). And while standing there contemplating the distance between St.François Xavier and the heavily treed shoreline just steps away, that spot in the circle came around again.

Almost exactly a year following my canoe trip on the South Saskatchewan, I stood overlooking a different river, another Métis travel corridor, another site of resistance. I could feel the paddle in my hand and see the safe channels through the river. I could feel the connection I had built with this place before having moved to Saskatoon for five years; I could feel the complicated history my ancestors had been a part of, one that I am still living today. Standing there in my kitchen, I could hear Maria's words and smell pine needles. I could see my mother folding towels and talking about Grandpa Swain. I could feel the canoe sliding through the current, and I understood that we are still resisting.

* * *

Have you ever tried to walk while thinking about how to walk? When I try to do it, it is not pretty; it's like I have forgotten how legs work. How hard is it to see someone you love smile and not smile back? There is a type of knowledge, an understanding of the physical spaces we occupy, the way we relate to those spaces and to those who share them, that lives not in the abstract intellect that we think of as our minds, but rather in our physical bodies. This knowledge grows into our bodies through "a web of consensual relationships that is infused with movement (kinetic) through lived experience" (Simpson, 2017, p. 162). When we intentionally engage with Indigenous ways of knowing and being, with the medicines, with the spaces in which we exist—conscious of the reality that we are both a part of and in relation with those spaces—we embody what we learn and what we learn becomes embodied (Fellner 2018; Simpson, 2017).

Similarly, there is a meditative state that I can enter when engaged in any repetitive movement where the knowledge of how to do that movement lives in my body. It is not that the movement is so boring that my mind wanders off, it is more that there is a clarity that is arrived at only through physical movement in space. If I am struggling with something I will go for a walk, a bike ride, or in the winter for a ski. Seated in the bow of a canoe, paddle in hand, suspended both in and above the water I am travelling, this state comes once I have worked through intellectualizing each movement. Once I have stopped thinking through how the grip of the paddle should feel against the palm of my hand and how far into the water the blade should disappear, how and when to pull or to push instead. There comes a point where the calculations for each stroke of the paddle are made by muscle and sinew. On the first day of this expedition, we had paddled over 30 kms before I found that point.

At the beginning of this trip, I was not a strong river paddler. The majority of my experience had been on lakes, and the few rivers on which I had spent any time in any watercraft had been faster and rock bottomed. The surface of the Bow, which rolls over a gravel and rock bed, reads more definitively than that of the South Saskatchewan where the water runs over a clay and sand bottom that is dotted with shifting sandbars, boulders, and various hazards. Whereas the Bow changes noticeably in a flood year, the South Saskatchewan can change from week to week.

I was keenly aware of my lack of experience compared to that of the other members of our party and really wanted to prove that I was competent; I honestly believed that the experience I did have would translate directly to this trip. I was wrong. I made several errors on that first day, but only needed to get out of the canoe twice to manoeuvre it off a sandbar. I also bounced the hull off a boulder (just once, with no measurable damage to the canoe or myself). I just could not find the place in me that knew how to do this.

My navigational errors were, almost exclusively, the result of not attending to the little twinges in my gut that pulled me towards one channel rather than another, and instead trusting that the canoe could follow the kayaks in our party. It took some time for me to internalize that the kayaks were significantly lighter, travelled higher in the water, and were captained by paddlers with substantial experience on this river. After realizing my mistake a little more than halfway through the day, I was able to improve my practice of navigating the river considerably. In the end, I had to build my own relationship with the river, not rely on the relationship that the other paddlers had with it. I had to learn to trust myself, to hear and to trust what the river was telling me.

Through all of this, the person paddling in the stern of the canoe with me, remained gentle and jovial. They were happy to provide instruction when asked; they were equally happy to let me figure out what I was doing through trial and error. If I was missing something important in my read of the river, they would say something to the effect of, "I think I see a boulder at your 11, what's your read?" Even when my misreading of the river saw us so far grounded on a sandbar that we both had to get out and push, there was only light-hearted grumbling about needing to stand up anyway given how far asleep their bottom was. This cheerful approach made a huge difference in my learning; it was a level of respect for my need to learn how to be in relation with this space that I didn't recognise at the time. Had the person paddling in the stern been inclined to chastise my errors or insist on telling me how to read the river, they would have interfered with my ability to learn how to relate to the space and my movement through it.

* * *

In her text *As we Have Always Done: Indigenous Freedom Through Radical Resistance* (2017), Leanne Betasamosake Simpson speaks extensively about the ways in which teaching and learning happen within Nishnaabeg ways of being and knowing. Through storytelling and discussion, Simpson articulates the spaces and conditions that foster Nishnaabeg intelligence and brilliance. I revisited the chapter "Land as Pedagogy" following my trip on the South Saskatchewan and returned to it again when I started to write this piece. I believe that everyone living on Turtle Island should read this book, but "Land as Pedagogy" is a particularly necessary chapter for educators, caregivers, and all professionals who work with knowledge.

"Land as Pedagogy" offers a critical reading of Western structures of knowledge and meaning from a Nishnaabeg perspective. Simpson highlights the extractive nature of Western ways of learning and knowing, and instead centers holistic experience as the key that creates meaning:

> Meaning, then, is derived not through content or data or even theory in a Western context, which by nature is decontextualized knowledge, but through a compassionate web of interdependent relationships that are different and valuable because of difference. Individuals carry the responsibility for generating meaning within their own lives; they carry the responsibility for engaging their minds, bodies and spirits in a practice of generating meaning (Simpson, p. 156).

Simpson situates the responsibility for engaging in a process of generating meaning in the individual; however, the process itself is found in that individual's kinship relationships—human or otherwise—with the source of that meaning being the land. For Métis people this web of human and non-human kinship and the laws that govern it can be described in the phrase *All my relations* or the word wahkootowin (adopted from the Cree: wahkotowin). Brenda Macdougall describes this web as "extensive kinship networks and shared experiences," she notes that:

> The emphasis on the extended family was fostered through the creation of physical and spiritual relationships between people (living, ancestral, those still to come), land, the spirit world, and creatures with whom they shared physical space. Everyone, therefore, was taught that who they were as individuals could only be understood in relation to their family relationships and which, in turn, reflected relationships to the community, environment, sacred world, and outsiders. (2017, p. 9)

In libraries, particularly academic libraries, we tend to think of knowledge as residing in texts and text-based resources, and we continue to believe that "all knowledge in the world can be represented in document form" (Duarte & Belarde-Lewis, 2015). We situate the source of knowledge in the output of scholars, and the conversations that scholars have with and about knowledge take place by extracting citations and ideas from texts written by others and performing comparative analysis in the hopes that new ideas are realized in that conversation. Contributions to this text-based framework are evaluated in terms of what is produced—papers, grants, and funding—and have consequently become competitive and results-driven.

This "publish or perish" model which demands "new contributions to a field," especially from emerging scholars, disrupts the possibility for cyclical learning, or for any real diversity of ideas. Not only does this model of scholarship deterritorialize (Simpson, 2017) knowledge and the act of sharing it, but it also both draws on and reinforces capitalist paradigms of knowledge production which in turn treat scholars and their outputs as a commodity. Loyer (2018) asserts that this model also results in significant trauma for Indigenous researchers:

> As librarians teaching information literacy, we seldom reflect on how the work of a university sees Indigenous people primarily as Othered objects of research and rarely as researchers. To be Indigenous in Canada is to be inherently political: my body and my legal identity is regulated by the state through biopolitical processes such as the inheritance of Indian Status. If I want to research even my own family history, trauma is inevitable; to research as an Indigenous scholar is to confront horrific stories, many of them directly tied to my own experiences or the experiences of people I love. (p. 147)

Viewed as "Othered objects of research" in many of the library and archival materials that we have access to, Indigenous students and scholars see themselves dehumanized on a regular basis. Like the land the library sits on, we become a resource to be harvested in the production of a commodity. How do we, Indigenous scholars, live in relation with our peers and colleagues, the spaces we occupy within the academy, and our relations outside of the library/the academy when all of these are situated within a system that continues to view us as located on a spectrum somewhere between scholar and Indigenous person?

* * *

The second distraction that I had to overcome in order to settle into that state of bodily knowing was my drive to document everything. I had been taught, at least implicitly, that without documentation experience could not be counted as knowledge gained. Not only do we believe that "all knowledge in the world can be represented in document form" (Duarte & Belarde-Lewis, 2015), but we also tend towards the assumption that if it is not documented, then it is not knowledge.

I knew that people who work in the academy generally have to move for their first few positions, and so I expected to be leaving Saskatoon at some point in the near future. I didn't know if I would ever get a chance to repeat this trip, and I was absolutely determined to make it meaningful, which to me—when I started out—meant documenting all of it. That ended at Fish Creek/Tourond's Coulee (about 35 km in). We stopped at Fish Creek hoping to camp there; however, once I was standing there on the land, I couldn't get away fast enough.

Fish Creek is the site of one of the multiple skirmishes that occurred in the spring of 1885 leading up to the Big Battle at Batoche. It is the place where roughly 150 Métis, Cree, and Dakota fighters, under the command of Gabriel Dumont, dug rifle pits into the sides of Tourond's Coulee and ambushed the Canadian Forces commanded by General Middleton. Middleton's company was forced into retreat and their advance on Batoche was briefly stalled (Middleton, 1885).

I was completely unprepared for the weight of standing at that site.

Prior to this trip, I had visited Batoche during Back to Batoche days, had participated in the cultural events at the campground just down the road from the Batoche National Historic Site, and had made the trek to the townsite and the graveyard on the last day to recognise the Métis that died resisting the annexation of their lands by the Canadian state. Batoche was in 1885–and remains today–a site of loss, resistance, and continued tension. Fish Creek is something else. It is a space where military men were stopped with guerilla tactics. It was a win for the Métis, but it only delayed their defeat at Batoche (Parks Canada, n.d.).

I suspect that, like many Canadians, I tend to think of history as something that happened to someone else in another time and place; history as a cautionary tale. Standing there on the bank of the South Saskatchewan River, 135 years later, I was overwhelmed with how present these events seemed. The narrative surrounding the North-West

Resistance has seen dramatic revisions in recent years, largely as a result of the ongoing work of Métis Elders and scholars digging through the archives of institutions and the archives of oral histories (by which I mean the old people) to recover, reclaim, and (re)tell our stories. Elders like Marjorie Beaucage, Norman Fleury, and Maria Campbell continue to teach and share the knowledge, the history, and the stories they carry with them. Métis institutions like the Louis Riel Institute and the Gabriel Dumont Institute are preserving—and through digitization increasing access to—the documents and recordings that represent us as a nation in the larger cultural archive. Current scholars like Jean Teillet, Brenda Macdougall, and Chris Andersen are compiling and engaging with these histories so that we might both better understand ourselves and be better understood in what is now Canada.

As a child at school, I was taught that "the halfbreed rebels," who embodied the worst traits of both the Indians and the white men, refused to give up their nomadic ways and rebelled against "the civilizing influence" of the Canadian state. According to this telling, in a glorious victory the Rebellion was crushed at Batoche, the leaders were executed, and the halfbreeds were forced to assimilate. Middleton's retreat at Tourond's Coulee was absent from that narrative, as was the appropriation of Métis land, along with the intentional disruption of the river Lot system of land use employed by Métis communities.

Following our stop at Fish Creek, it did not seem to matter how many eagles flew overhead, or even whether or not I managed to take pictures of the landscape or our party—I knew that there was no way for me to document this experience adequately, and that attempting to do so was disrupting, deterritorializing the knowledge I was gaining in the experience. I think that it was this realization which allowed me to move the knowledge of paddling this river from something I had to concentrate on to a knowledge that inhabited my physical body. However, it also bound my understanding of the North-West Resistance to that knowledge—I don't know if I will ever hold a paddle again and not feel The Resistance in each stroke. The weight of the place settled into my consciousness, and I spent the last leg of that day's river time thinking about my mother, her family, and the stories that came from them.

Both my mother and my Elder Sharron have spoken of the ways that our understanding of time as a linear series of events that becomes static or immutable as it passes from present into past tense is incomplete. They say that past, present and future are all happening simultaneously feeding into each other, being made and remade in each (re)telling, building the realities that we individually experience. Before Fish Creek, I believed whole-heatedly that I understood this; in the two years since that understanding has seemed increasingly elementary.

* * *

Since very early in life, I have been very conscious of the liminal space I inhabit. I am Métis; I have a German surname. I am white-coded and have elected to pass in some (maybe too many) situations and am now (perhaps, as a result) very vocal about the Indigenous ways of thinking and being that I inhabit, that I have intentionally learned and embraced. I am very conscious of the privilege afforded me by an urban, working-class upbringing and education; I have seen that privilege negated when a person in a place of power understands that I am an Indigenous person. In many ways, this liminality is at the core of my existential dilemma. How do I exist both as a contemporary person, raised urban, now in possession of a level of Western education that we in the academy forget is inaccessible or otherwise unattainable to a large majority of people, and with a worldview that is predominantly perceived as being less evolved, or, at best, as naïve?

In many ways, my choice to attend library school was both a result of and a galvanizing influence on this acceptance of my own liminality—although I did not understand that at the time (and I am certain that by the time I am 50 my understanding of my positionality will have changed again). When I applied to library school, I had already spent almost six years working as a Library Page and Library Assistant in public and academic libraries. This trajectory started with a three-year stint at the University of Calgary as a student-assistant in the Interlibrary Loans/Document Delivery Services department. A lot of what I did in this position was to collect texts from the stacks that would either be sent to other libraries on loan, or have a chapter scanned from them and sent electronically to another library for use by one of their patrons.

It was in this job that I began to notice that almost all of the books relating to Indigenous Peoples in what is now Canada (and the United States) were shelved in the history section. Later I would see all the Indigenous-related resources pulled from the regular stacks and shelved in a separate "Indigenous resources section" in public and in some academic libraries. While an Indigenous resource section did have the effect of pulling resources out of History, it also had a second, unintended, effect: the Indigenous resources sections effectively became Indigenous Sections that were easily and frequently avoided by non-Indigenous peoples.

While I was working at the University of Calgary, I was also completing an English Honours Degree as a mature student in my thirties. While I had spent years working in Indigenous social and cultural services organizations, as well as participating in a growing Métis cultural reclamation and resurgence movement, I had not integrated my identity as a Métisse into my academic studies and life. I existed somewhere between these two spaces, and their interplay shaped much of my relationship to the academy and to libraries generally.

Ten years ago, when I was finishing my undergraduate degree, universities were working alongside Indigenous Nations to make post-secondary education more available to Indigenous students. There were scholarships, mentorship programs, and targeted recruitment partnerships with the private sector. These efforts improved enrollment rates but continued to rely on a deficit-based framework of education—at their core these frameworks failed to acknowledge the strength, knowledge, and brilliance of Indigenous individuals and communities. Many institutions (and Indigenous communities) perceived (and continue to perceive) accessible post-secondary education as a way to pull Indigenous Peoples into the 21st Century, a position that Chelsea Vowel (2022) addresses directly in the introduction to her collection of short stories, *Buffalo is the New Buffalo*:

> "Education is the new buffalo" is a metaphor widely used among Indigenous peoples in Canada to signify the importance of education to our survival and ability to support ourselves, as once Plains nations supported ourselves as buffalo peoples. Variations of the phrase have sprung up with increasing frequency, including a particularly vomitus version, "pipelines are the new buffalo." The assumption is that many of our pre-Contact ways of living are forever gone, and we must accept this and adapt. The phrase "buffalo is the new buffalo," however, asserts that we can and must do the work to repair our kinscapes, basing our work in wâhkôhtowin (expanded kinship) to expand our reciprocal obligations to our human and non-human kin. Instead of accepting that the buffalo and our ancestral ways will never come back, what if we simply ensure that they do? (p. 21)

Vowel challenges the idea that the solution to marginalization is for Indigenous Peoples to fully accept and adapt to functioning within the neoliberal capitalist framework. *Buffalo is the New Buffalo* puts forward an alternative—a way to imagine otherwise—in which Indigenous ways of knowing and being offer us a site of rupture and an opportunity for change.

While I was completing my undergraduate studies (2012), the work on building education systems that are culturally-inclusive to Indigenous students was already underway; however, the primary narrative was still one of assimilation. Since the release of the Truth and Reconciliation Commission of Canada's Final Report in 2015, all educational institutions have been taking a long look at the way we engage and support Indigenous students, staff, and faculty to be who they are. We have had to reconsider and reconstruct the narratives about Indigenous Peoples, cultures and communities that we perpetuate. We have started to seek out opportunities to build inclusive, non-assimilative spaces, collections, and programs.

In the space between my identity as a Métis person and my identity as a librarian exists one of the connections in the "compassionate web of interdependent relationships" to which Simpson (p. 156) refers. The relationship that I have built between my identities is, in part, the knowledge I have gained by consciously engaging in a process of making meaning. In many ways, the sum of that knowledge is the realization and the *embodiment* of walking in two worlds; it is a practiced and internalized understanding that neither cognitive dissonance nor liminality is a problem to be solved.

* * *

The first time I visited Batoche, I approached across the land, one foot in front of the other, the prairie grasses crisp beneath my steps. I had been in Saskatoon for about two weeks. I had started my job at the University of Saskatchewan, but not the course work for my MLIS. There were still saskatoon berries on the bushes beside the path; the grasshoppers were just learning their summer songs. I walked through the graveyard gate and stood in front of the mass grave. At one point an old woman came and stood beside me. Without introduction she told me of how the site was owned by the Canadian government and that was why we held the Back to Batoche gatherings down the road: we aren't allowed to have them here. She said that they preserved the town as a historic site to prove that we weren't here anymore, that they wanted to keep the moment of their perceived victory present in everyone's mind and erase all that had come before and all that had come after. And then she wandered away. I stood there blinking in the sunlight.

After the ceremonies were finished and the graveyard had mostly emptied, I wandered to the back and stood beside Gabriel Dumont, overlooking the river. I offered him a cigarette and lit one of my own, saying "Nice spot you got here, Gabe." And for a moment I stood there looking out over the river valley, trying to imagine the changes the old man must have seen from this vantage point.

Later that day, back at the campgrounds, I would have a similar conversation with a Métis writer that very kindly showed me around and introduced me to the events and the people there. I had mentioned that I was really enjoying the day and the feel of the event—that it felt more *resistance-y* than other Métis events that I have attended. In response to my observation, she spoke about the way that the resistance never really ended, that following the 1885 battle on this site the Métis were branded rebels and ostracized by both the government and the settler community. She also spoke to the way that the people here came back every year as an act of protest against their removal from this space, and about how the Canadian government's refusal to return the site to the Métis nation demonstrated a desire to control the narrative and an ongoing attempt to erase our stories from this land.

Four years later, when I approached Batoche from the water, it was hard for me to even recognize the place. Had someone not pointed out the gravestones at the top of the hill to me, I may have missed it all together. The approach from the water made it seem further away, but it also hid features and buildings that were visible from the land route. My inability to recognize Batoche was something that earned me some good-natured, well-deserved teasing. During our stay at Petite Ville I had been asked what I knew about Batoche, and I had recounted everything I could remember. When I finished, one of our party members said, "Huh, so this trip is kind of a pilgrimage for you?" and I shrugged, saying, "I guess so. Yeah."

"Think you'll recognize it?" I didn't know what to say. I mean, I was pretty sure that I would have, before they asked, but there was something in their grin that chewed away at my confidence. The next day when we passed Batoche and I failed to recognize it, the other paddler smirked at me, "It's almost like things look different from this angle, isn't it?"

In the couple of years since, that quip has become something of a refrain for me. On a personal level it's a humbling reminder that I can believe that I have a pretty good grasp on a situation, but all it takes is a perspective shift and I may have to start over. On a more professional level I think about how narratives can be hidden in plain sight when our relationship with the land breaks down or is intentionally removed. If Batoche had been occupied by Métis people, there would be trails up and down the riverbanks. It would probably also have a boat house at the river's edge, so it would be recognisable the way that other towns on the route were. The absence of people living in community with each other and the space around them made Batoche invisible to me. However, that absence should have been glaringly obvious, especially because the rest of the shoreline was so obviously occupied, but this is how erasure works.

A few short blocks west of where I currently live in Winnipeg, there is a neighbourhood that is affectionately referred to by locals as the granola belt. The residences are primarily well-kept two and three-story detached houses with yards; some have been divided into suites, but many remain single-family homes. The apartment buildings there are primarily historic brick and/or Tyndall Stone structures. Among other shops and businesses there is a yoga studio, a new age bookstore, an organic food co-op, a yarn store, a coffee shop, and a bakery. In the summer, there is a farmers market that operates at the community centre two nights a week. Some houses fly pride flags next to prayer flags, some hang orange shirts in their windows year-round. This lovely community of progressive liberalism and the main road that winds through it are both officially called Wolseley.

When I first moved to Winnipeg in 2012, I was aware that there had been a time following the Red River Resistance in which Métis people were ostracised and subjected to discrimination. It wasn't until I moved to Saskatoon in 2016 and visited Batoche for the first time that I learned that particular period of Resistance was dubbed 'the reign of terror' by the Métis and was an intentionally orchestrated campaign of violence and intimidation. Colonel Wolseley and his men were sent to remove the Métis from the land that they had been granted by the Canadian state with the signing of the Manitoba Act, and it had worked–many families moved to communities in what is now Alberta and Saskatchewan.

I have been back in Winnipeg for a year now, and every time I hear someone say Wolseley, I have a physical reaction. In part that reaction is to who Colonel Wolseley was, but beyond that I am reacting to the erasure, the white-washing of the history of this place that allows some residents of the city to have a positive relationship with it, naïve of what its name denies others. For most Winnipeggers, Wolseley has become synonymous with liberalism and with community. The city has forgotten that the name celebrates the annexation of land for settlers through violence and intimidation, and it stands as a veiled threat against contemporary resistance. How do I build a reciprocal relationship with a space when I cringe each time it's mentioned? How do I engage in a place-based practice of librarianship when the library I work at borders a neighbourhood named for the man who led the charge to remove my nation from this place? How am I, as a librarian in this place, contributing to the maintenance of the narrative which erases that history simply by not actively working against it?

* * *

The last stretch of the river we paddled was between the St. Laurent Ferry and the town of St. Louis. Like the other shorelines we had passed in the previous days, this stretch was divided into a variety of riverfront spaces: farms, ranch lands, First Nations reserve lands. There were a number of historic trading posts and even a winery. The coulees and the brush lands were divided up into lots by barbed wire fences and lined with service roads, ATV tracks, and/or foot trails. After five days and 105 km of shoreline, I was amazed how little space there had actually been on our trip that did not show visible signs of being inhabited, or at least used by people. As an urban-raised hiker, backpacker, and camper, I have to work to maintain an awareness of my tendency to think of "the land" as wild spaces that are uninhabited by humans. Moreover, I have had to unlearn the false person–land dichotomy.

We tend to think of "the land" as synonymous with wilderness, to which we apply words like pristine and untouched. This false equivalency prevents us from understanding the place in which we stand at any given moment as being part of the land. Even if we are standing 30 stories above a concrete covered expanse, the land is still there. We are still a part of it.

During the initial colonization of Turtle Island, the British and the French used connections and kinships that the First Peoples had (and continue to maintain) with the land as a reason to see them as less than human. And as less than human, First Nations Peoples were denied many of the rights of personhood by the Europeans and were instead perceived as commodities. The bodies of the First Nations, and later the Inuit and Métis Peoples, became commodities in an extractive economy. Following the river through the spaces where the Métis live(d), the spaces we defended against the encroachment of the Canadian state makes this reality undeniable.

Much of what we do in contemporary libraries, especially those attached to universities, continues to enforce a human/non-human binary. We continue to situate knowledge as a product created through human intelligence disconnected from land, from our bodies, and from the web of kinship that is fostered and maintained as we move through the spaces that create and nourish our connections and reciprocal relations. One of the places we can observe this disconnect is in how we teach research and information literacy skills, including how we define scholarly sources. As Marsh (2019) notes, "Information from Indigenous voices and sources or the use of Indigenous research methodologies is often devalued because it does not conform to universalist, 'standard', Western forms of scholarship." We have only recently developed citation formats for Elders and Knowledge Keepers (maarsii, Lorisia MacLeod), and using our personal experience can see us accused of a lack of objectivity. In the same vein, the practice of including a statement of identity and positionality can be seen as excessive or self-indulgent.

What would libraries look like and what would be the role of the librarian if we were to make space for the diversity of knowledges created through relationships and reciprocity? How would research change? How would we use the tools we have to foster new ways of learning, knowing, and being? The answer is—by necessity—*different in every city, in every library*. It always begins with using the skills of critical librarianship to interrogate academic power structures, the systemic exclusion of marginalized peoples, and colonial methods of scholarly production (Marsh, 2019). It requires us to investigate the histories of the spaces we occupy and our involvement in shaping or erasing contemporary narratives stemming from those histories. It obligates us to work with land and place/space-based learning scholars and practitioners to create frameworks that allow us to perceive these ways of learning and knowing as valid and a necessary part of education and research paradigms.

* * *

Lying on a sand bar surrounded by the currents of the South Saskatchewan River, Petite Ville is an eerie and surreal place, and the fact that our first two nights on the river were spent there affected the entire fabric of the trip for me. On the first night, following a dip in the river, dinner, and a fireside visit we retired to the tent and my three friends were quickly asleep. I lay listening to the river lapping against the edges of the sandbar. I may have dozed, but I don't think I had slept much before the owl started calling. After the owl quieted down, which was well after midnight but before the first light, the coyotes started. On the second night, after the owl once again stopped calling, I kept waking up, hearing footsteps in the sand around us and men talking. On three different occasions I left the tent to check, but found no unusual tracks, no animals, and no people on the tiny island on which we were camped.

Finally, it occurred to me that I had neglected a fundamental part of reciprocal relationality: a gift or an offering that acknowledged the presence and agency of my non-human kin in this place and allowed me to introduce myself, a measure which demonstrated my gratitude for their hospitality and my commitment to behaving in a good way while in their space. I left the tent, broke open one of my cigarettes, and put down a little tobacco in the way I had been taught, as well as some of the candy I had squirreled away in the food box. I spoke my salutations, my introduction, my gratitude, and my commitment to being a good relative in this space. I apologised for my failure to do so earlier. I returned to the tent and immediately fell asleep.

Up to that point I had been behaving poorly; essentially, I had walked into my neighbour's unlocked apartment, sat down on their couch without even acknowledging their presence, and spent an entire day watching TV there. My relatives were not happy about it and they let me know. After that second night I would volunteer to dig the latrine pit at each site and would do the same while I was by myself a short distance from camp. I still don't know if I believe in little people or tricksters in any concrete physical form. I do believe that they exist—at least as metaphors, as cultural icons—to remind us that the land is more than we can imagine, that it is alive, that it has knowledge that we need and to which we only have access when we form reciprocal relationships.

References

Adese, J. (2014). Spirit gifting: Ecological knowing in Métis life narratives. Decolonization: Indigeneity, Education & Society, 3(3), Article 3. https://jps.library.utoronto.ca/index.php/des/article/view/22191

American Library Association. (2022). What libraries do. I Love Libraries. https://ilovelibraries.org/what-libraries-do/

Barkwell, L. J. (2017). The reign of terror against the Métis of Red River. https://www.metismuseum.ca/resource.php/149078

Bowra, A., Mashford-Pringle, A., & Poland, B. (2021). Indigenous learning on Turtle Island: A review of the literature on land-based learning. The Canadian Geographer / Le Géographe Canadien, 65(2), 132–140. https://doi.org/10.1111/cag.12659

Campbell, M. (2010). Stories of the road allowance people (Rev. ed). Gabriel Dumont Institute.

Campbell, M. (2021). [Untitled talk]. [Live Online Talk]. University of Saskatchewan, Indigenous Advisors Circle.

Duarte, M. E., & Belarde-Lewis, M. (2015). Imagining: Creating spaces for Indigenous ontologies. Cataloging & Classification Quarterly, 53(5–6), 677–702. https://doi.org/10.1080/01639374.2015.1018396

Fellner, K. D. (2018). Embodying decoloniality: Indigenizing curriculum and pedagogy. American Journal of Community Psychology, 62(3-4), 283–293. https://doi.org/10.1002/ajcp.12286

Government of Saskatchewan, Ministry of Tourism, Parks, Culture and Sport. (2008, July 26). Petite Ville Heritage Plaque Unveiled. Government of Saskatchewan. https://www.saskatchewan.ca/government/news-and-media/2008/july/26/petite-ville-heritage-plaque-unveiled

Loyer, J. (2018). Indigenous information literacy: nêhiyaw kinship enabling self-care in research. In K.P. Nicholson and M. Seale (Eds.), The Politics of Theory and the Practice of Critical Librarianship. (pp. 145-156). Library Juice Press. https://mru.arcabc.ca/islandora/object/mru:237

Loyer, J. (2021). Collections are our relatives: Disrupting the singular, white man's joy that shaped collections. In M. Browndorf, E. Pappas, and A. Arrays (Eds.), The collector and the collected: Decolonizing area studies librarianship. Library Juice Press. https://mru.arcabc.ca/islandora/object/mru:793

Macdougall, B. (2017). Land, family and identity: Contextualizing Metis health and well- being. National Collaborating Centre for Aboriginal Health (NCCAH). https://www.ccnsa-nccah.ca/docs/context/RPT-ContextualizingMetisHealth- Macdougall-EN.pdf

Meewasin Valley Authority. (1998). South Saskatchewan River Ecocanoe Tour Map Guide. Meewasin Valley Authority. https://meewasin.com/wp-content/uploads/2019/11/RiverEcocanoeGuide-Mapshigh-complete.pdf

Marsh, F. (2019, November 27). Indigenous knowledge & decolonising through critical information literacy. Decolonising through Critical Librarianship. https://decolonisingthroughcriticallibrarianship.wordpress.com/2019/11/27/indigenous-knowledge-decolonising-through-critical-information-literacy/

Middleton, F. (1885, April 24). CPR Telegraph Ledger—Battle of Fish Creek (April 24). http://www.saskarchives.com/node/558#overlay-context=node/559

Parks Canada. (n.d.). Battle of Tourond's Coulee / Fish Creek National Historic Site of Canada. Parks Canada Directory of Federal Heritage Designations. https://www.pc.gc.ca/apps/dfhd/page_nhs_eng.aspx?id=739

Reed, H. (1986). Document One: Memorandum for the Hon[uorable] the Indian Commissioner Relative to the Future Management of Indians. Native Studies Review, 2(2), 127–130. http://iportal.usask.ca/docs/Native_studies_review/v2/issue2/pp127-130.pdf

Royal Canadian Geographical Society. (2018a). Aftermath of 1885. In Indigenous Peoples atlas of Canada. https://indigenouspeoplesatlasofcanada.ca/article/aftermath-of-1885/

Royal Canadian Geographical Society. (2018b). Bison hunting. In Indigenous Peoples atlas of Canada. https://indigenouspeoplesatlasofcanada.ca/article/bison-hunting/

Royal Canadian Geographical Society. (2018c). Red River Resistance. In Indigenous Peoples atlas of Canada. https://indigenouspeoplesatlasofcanada.ca/article/red-river-resistance/

Royal Canadian Geographical Society. (2018d). Scrip. In Indigenous Peoples atlas of Canada. https://indigenouspeoplesatlasofcanada.ca/article/scrip/

Simpson, L. B. (2017). As we have always done: Indigenous freedom through radical resistance. University of Minnesota Press.

Vowel, C. (2022). Buffalo is the New Buffalo. Arsenal Pulp Press.

Weinbender, K. D. (2003). Petite Ville: A spatial assessment of a Métis Hivernant site. https://harvest.usask.ca/handle/10388/etd-03042009-133642

Wilson, S. (2008). Research is ceremony: Indigenous research methods. Fernwood Publishing.

Refusing Growth
Cloud Technology, Climate Change, and the Future of Libraries and Archives

Ariel Hahn

Introduction

In contemporary library and archival work, our technological dependencies are immense and include everything from cataloging software, cloud storage, and task management platforms to credit card machines, scanners, and electronic communication systems. A core link between these tools and their connection to libraries, archives, and information work is "the Cloud." Though invoked – almost poetically – as a singular, seamless piece of infrastructure, the Cloud is far from floating vapor. Marketing firms and technology corporations often employ the Cloud or cloud-based services as an environmentally conscious solution for the modern workplace; however, popular imaginings like this one mystify its true nature as well as its role in furthering climate change. The Cloud, instead, possesses deep ties to oil and gas extraction in addition to a profound physical and resource-heavy footprint. Moreover, as an armature of Big Tech – including as the largest source of Amazon's increasing value (Markman, 2021), for instance – the Cloud is firmly embedded within the inner workings and assumed growth of the United States Military. These carbon-intensive entanglements are an ironic reality since cloud infrastructure also enables the advanced scientific modeling necessary to understand our increasingly unpredictable climate future (Edwards, 2017, pp. 36–37; Emanuel, 2019; Mattern, 2017).

Evidence of our shifting climate can be found through crushing heat waves and wildfires, alongside dying ocean life, in clear cut forests and empty water reserves, as well as anywhere that has been touched by intense hurricanes, flooding, mudslides, drought, low crop-yields, snowstorms, or freezing temperatures (Fountain, 2022; Irfan, 2021a; Leahy, 2021; Lewis et al., 2019). Carbon-driven climate change is not imminent; rather, climate change is both already present and accelerating rapidly (*United Nations*, 2021; Irfan & Leber, 2021b). Because of this uncertain environmental future, many industries – including libraries and archives – have now arrived at or are making their way towards a critical inflection point wherein massive adaptation and adjustment is required. So, for those of us using cloud technology in our day-to-day work – as is required by much of librarianship and archivy – where does our responsibility amidst these powerful entities, systemic issues, and stark futures lie?

In the following chapter, I engage with some of the ways that information and memory work actively contribute to climate change through our technological dependencies. To reveal these connections, I first diagram the materiality of the Cloud, reasserting its carbon and land-based footprint. I also directly address the connection between the Cloud and fossil fuels. I then examine recent literature and climate-related actions taken across libraries and archives, exploring the collective necessity for an ethos of both critical refusal and degrowth as tangible field-based responses to climate change. Lastly, I close this chapter by discussing potential paths forward, including scaling back our technological investments, restructuring how we work, as well as taking the maintenance and repair of our systems, spaces, and materials more seriously.

The Cloud

Despite possessing a name that evokes ephemerality, cloud technology, or "the Cloud," is a highly material form of networked computing comprised of an immense chain of geographically-dispersed data centers – a "global archipelago of warehouses that collectively coordinate the world's computing power" (*Very Like a Whale*, 2022, para. 6). Connected through seas of vinyl cables, these data centers each house server after server and are often kept cool through energy-intensive means like constant fan usage, air conditioning, and/or chilled water (Burrington, 2015; Carruth, 2014; Gonzalez Monserrate, 2022;

Johnson, 2019; Starosielski, 2015). Since the Cloud most often takes up space in unassuming or unmarked office complexes around the world (Burrington, 2016; Hogan, 2015a), our capacity to recognize it, and thus question it, is frequently mired. In *Prehistory of the Cloud*, media scholar Tung-Hui Hu (2015), asserts that, "the cloud has become so naturalized in everyday life that we tend to look right through, seeing it uncritically, if we see it at all" (p. 10). Though this status of quasi-invisibility is key to all facets of infrastructure – invisible until broken (Bowker et al., 2016) – the Cloud's suggested ethereality is particularly key in how powerful American technology corporations[1] are able to hide away its overwhelming ecological impact (Taylor, 2019; Vonderau, 2019).

When examined on a deeper level, the physical footprint, environmental consequences, and geopolitical realities associated with the Cloud become difficult to ignore.[2] Political geographer Louise Amoore (2018) states that, "the whereabouts of 'unseen computers' is not unknown at all, but rather the Cloud is actualized in data centres, located in places with plentiful land, favourable tax rates, affordable energy, water for cooling, and proximity to the main trunks of the network" (p. 8). Every individual data center is a place-specific piece of infrastructure that can either gradually or rapidly influence its surroundings. Data centers exist in the middle of the desert, under the cover of ocean water, and buried in isolated snow and ice – though the information stored within their walls may originate thousands of miles away.[3] The more granular material components of the Cloud are no different. Planned obsolescence plagues the computers, magnetic tape, and drives that make the Cloud function, resulting in both unnecessary and somehow unavoidable excess. The rare earth minerals required for much of this technology are mined under harsh and hazardous conditions.[4]

---

1 The specific "American technology corporations" I am referencing are Amazon, Google, and Microsoft – which I will refer to as "cloud corporations" for the remainder of this chapter.

2 For additional writing on the ecological, sociological, and material impact of the Cloud, see Gonzalez Monserrate, 2022; Pasek, 2019; Taffel, 2021.

3 Though beyond the scope of this chapter, data centers are built just about everywhere, including in wildfire and drought heavy regions in the United States like California, Utah, Oregon, and the deserts of Arizona. To keep these energy intensive machines cool, many data centers rely on access groundwater for evaporative cooling – the amounts of which companies like Google and Meta/Facebook fight to keep private. Both companies have identified this kind of information as a proprietary trade secret. See Hogan, 2015b; Parks, 2021; Solon, 2021.

4 For more on computing, cloud technology, waste, and mining for renewables, see Ensmenger, 2018; Liboiron, 2018; Riofrancos, 2019.

And, even if declared carbon-neutral, any data center will continue to consume non-renewable resources.[5] Quite literally, all aspects of the Cloud's material footprint are marked by waste and toxicity.

Concerned with their public image, more and more cloud corporations appear to be moving away from "dirty" energy in favor of "clean" methods of power. Currently, Amazon, Google, and Microsoft – the three field leaders – are seeking renewable ways to power and maintain their data centers, some even constructing or investing in wind and solar farms (Ambrose, 2019; Gonzalez Monserrate, 2022). Writer Ingrid Burrington (2015) critiques this kind of greenwashing by arguing that, "while underwriting the cost of a wind farm is laudable, it only addresses one kind of environmental impact, focused on one particular set of metrics" (para. 15). Unsurprisingly, these three cloud corporations actively compete to be the "greenest" among them. Through their renewable energy investments as well as initiatives like internal recycling campaigns, cloud corporations appear to center climate action and distance themselves from the waning popularity of the fossil fuel industry (Amazon, n.d.; Google, n.d.; Microsoft, n.d.; Taylor, 2019; Zero Cool, 2019). However, these "environmentally-conscious" endeavors simply distract from the numerous cloud-based tech solutions that have evolved to make Big Oil more profitable.

In their 2020 report, *Oil in the Cloud*, Greenpeace examines how Amazon, Google, and Microsoft all have high-valued contracts with oil and gas conglomerates, thus cementing the Cloud's role in furthering climate change. Citing industrial case studies, recent news articles, and corporate press releases, Greenpeace claims that many of these contracts "specifically aid in the exploration or production of oil" (Donaghy et al., 2020). For Big Oil, the Cloud is not just utilized to store data. Rather, this networked technology enables oil and gas conglomerates to obtain strategic information about new, exceedingly difficult to extract, and/or under-utilized oil wells through data-intensive machine learning processes, artificial intelligence, and predictive analytics (Munn, 2021, pp. 216–218). These tactics, which media studies scholar Luke Munn (2021) identifies as "petrotechnical violence" (pp. 218–221), ensure fossil fuel extraction for many decades to come. In their essay, "Oil is the New Data," Microsoft engineer Zero Cool

---

5 For a brief overview of carbon credits – the method through which most carbon neutrality is "earned" – see Buck, 2022; Elgin & Mider, 2020; Greenfield, 2021; Miller, 2021; Song, 2019.

(2019) captures the futility of these eco-initiatives by asking, "Why go through the effort of using clean energy to power your data centers when those same data centers are being used by companies like Chevron to produce more oil?" (para. 40). Acknowledging these conflicts of interest requires us to actually see the complex material, ecological, and political mechanizations that create and are reproduced through cloud technology.

For a further example, in late 2018, the United States Department of Defense released an unclassified Cloud Strategy report arguing the necessity and potential efficacy of committing to data-intensive, cloud-based warfare across the entire military. Some of the key arguments highlighted for militaristic cloud adoption were the potential to "enable exponential growth" (Department of Defense, 2018, p. 3) as well as utilize artificial intelligence and machine learning in support of warfighting. [6] The document claimed that "in the last two years, the world produced 90% of all existing data. This is a trend that has been going on for a decade, with no end in sight" (Department of Defense, 2018, p. 3). If we are to believe that cloud-based global data growth is both exponential and unending, then the latter statement promises the catastrophic end of life in two distinct ways: an increasingly "lethal, resilient, and innovative" (Department of Defense, 2018, p. 10) technocratic U.S. military and an accelerating climate crisis that endangers the lives and ecosystems of every being on the planet. Digital media and ecology scholar Sy Taffel (2021) succinctly captures and analyzes this dichotomy, stating that "the rhetoric of ongoing exponential increases in digital data is fundamentally incompatible with addressing Anthropogenic ecological crises; it forms a capitalist-colonialist fantasy that sustains the myth of perpetual economic growth without material limitations" (p. 2).

---

6   Countless technology experts have written about how flawed our societal assumptions around AI and machine learning truly are. From predictive policing to automated warfare, contending with the flaws within these systems and the false premises under which they have been created is tantamount to building a more just world. Specifically related to warfare, Lucy Suchman offers that, "the promotion of automated data analysis under the rubric of artificial intelligence, and in the name of accuracy, can only serve to exacerbate military operations that are demonstrably discriminatory in their reliance on profiling, and indiscriminate in their failures to adhere to international laws of war" (Suchman, 2020). For more on the general topic of ethics and AI, look to the work of Ruha Benjamin and the Ida B. Wells Just Data Lab (Ida B. Wells Just Data Lab, 2021), Meredith Whitaker and the AI Now Institute (AI Now Institute, n.d.), as well as Timnit Gebru and the newly formed DAIR (Distributed Artificial Intelligence Research) Institute (The DAIR Institute, n.d.), to name a few.

Perpetual economic growth – like perpetual data growth, perpetual oil extraction, or perpetual military action – cannot survive on a dying planet, or even a flourishing one. For libraries, our interventions in these conversations may appear to be narrow but, when considered holistically and intentionally, I believe they will be deeply impactful and significant. In the following section, I look closely at existing work in libraries and archives concerned with climate change while cementing the importance for our field to embrace both critical refusal and degrowth as they relate to technological choices, the Cloud, and a livable planetary future.

Not an End, a Beginning

Technological advances, glorious structures, or excellent systems will be useless in a collapsing world. Libraries will be hit just as hard by the changes and crises affecting the planet and its inhabitants as any other institution and any other collective body or human group.

– Civallero & Plaza, 2016, p. 34

As evidenced by recent peer-reviewed articles, conference presentations, professional development coursework, and organizational meetings, many timely climate change conversations have taken place across and within libraries, archives, and information work more broadly.[7] And yet, on a field-wide level, little is being done by our professional organizations, leaders, or administrators to take any form of definitive action in response to the active and expanding consequences of environmental collapse. Select workers have led vigorous efforts to consider the future of libraries and archives on a warming planet, encouraging adaptation and transformation (Edwards, 2017; Finn et

---

7   These conversations have been present at the 2021 Digital Library Forum (DLF, 2021), in the Journal of Critical Library and Information Studies issue on Libraries and Archives in the Anthropocene (select articles from the issue are cited throughout this chapter), through professional groups like the Sustainability Roundtable (Sustainability Round Table, 2013) from the American Libraries Association (ALA) and the Climate Justice Interest Group of the California Library Association (California Library Association, n.d.), the Sustainable Libraries Initiative (Sustainable Libraries Initiative, n.d.), internationally across the Digital Preservation Coalition's extensive work (Digital Preservation Coalition, 2014), and in a recent course offering from Eira Tansey at the 2022 California Rare Book School (CalRBS) on Archives and Climate Change (Tansey, 2022), to name a few.

al., 2020; Nowviskie, 2014; Pendergrass et al., 2019; Tansey, 2015; Winn, 2020). Others have questioned our individual carbon footprints as well as the footprints of what we study (Baillot et al., 2021). However, within the day-to-day operations of many libraries and archives, we workers are expected to align our practices with the status quo. Countless library and archival institutions engage in efforts to maintain normality despite the environmental and material extremes present in our own realities as well as the realities of our patrons (Sax, 2021). The 2021-2024 Strategic Plan for ALA's Sustainability Roundtable, for example, largely focuses on creating carbon-neutral conferences, developing internal resolutions in support of sustainability, providing reading lists, or encouraging individuals to make sustainability pledges (Sustainability Round Table, 2021). Other eco-initiatives within libraries focus on how we can transform our physical spaces to be "greener," lessen our energy usage through equipment choices, or direct our programming resources towards environmental topics (Baillot et al., 2021; Civallero & Plaza, 2016; Lawton, 2020; Sauli, 2021).

Though any strategy that results in a carbon decrease is essential, existing climate-related work in libraries and archives heavily centers on what *we* can do as individuals to adapt rather than what *pressure* we can apply to advance change at a higher level, especially related to our societal, professional, or organizational dependence on fossil fuels, whether direct or indirect. Thus far, the bulk of our *institutional* responses have echoed the greenwashing and virtue signaling that I have already demonstrated as being persistent in Big Tech and Big Oil. In the following section, then, I address these gaps in existing LIS practice and literature, highlighting the necessity for work beyond individual or incremental solutions, while also incorporating numerous examples from domains beyond libraries and archives. I argue for institutions and workers to act collectively in response to climate change by embracing an ethos of critical refusal and degrowth – and further, integrating that ethos into how we approach the adoption of new cloud-based technology, define innovation for ourselves, and reimagine our professional futures.

Critical Refusal

Engaging in critical refusal is not merely saying no as an act of lessening one's workload. Rather, critical refusal is a conscious attempt to opt-out of systems that reproduce or facilitate harm and oppression.

As defined by data and archival scholars Marika Cifor, Patricia Garcia, T.L. Cowan, Jasmine Rault, Tonia Sutherland, Anita Say Chan, Jennifer Rode, Anna Lauren Hoffman, Niloufar Salehi, and Lisa Nakamura (2019) in their "Feminist Data Manifest-NO," this kind of "refusal is work, one that – at its best – can help different feminisms recognize interlocking struggles across domains, across contexts and cultures… [which then] enables us to work in solidarity to prop up and build resilience with one another – to generate mutually reinforcing refusals" (Why Refusal section, para. 2). Within the "Feminist Data Manifest-NO," Cifor et al. embrace the work of "Latinx, Black, queer, trans- and Indigenous feminist thinkers who have mobilized critical refusal as a powerful tool to open up and insist on radical and alternate futures" (Why Refusal section, para. 2). They, in turn, make "a declaration of refusal and commitment" (Cifor et al., 2019) regarding harmful data practices in the academy and corporate world. They refuse various ways that data is manipulated and utilized – especially by extractive, hegemonic methods – and make direct commitments to act generatively and to co-construct better data worlds for the many rather than the few. Since critical refusal lends itself towards collective action and away from ideologies that center individual solutions or saviors, embracing the practice of developing "mutually reinforcing refusals" is necessary as we imagine more sustainable futures for the field of LIS. Academic librarian and scholar Lydia Zvyagintseva (2021) affirms and expands on this notion, stating that, "refusal cannot be understood at an individual level but must be seen as a collective effort" (p. 5).

The work of the Boycott, Divestment, and Sanctions (BDS) Movement utilizes critical refusal as an immediate and powerful tactic against the Israeli State's ongoing occupation of Palestine. A Palestinian-led movement, BDS gains inspiration from "the South African anti-apartheid movement, [and] urges action to pressure Israel to comply with international [human rights] law" (BDS Movement, 2016, April 25). Through encouraging refusal – including refusing the purchase of goods manufactured by the State of Israel or within occupied territories, as well as divesting from technology companies that support or facilitate the regime and occupation – BDS highlights the extent of human rights abuses taking place against Palestinians and champions allied divestment as a tool for socio-political, economic, and material change. For example, boycotting and divesting from Hewlett Packard (HP), which provides technology to the Israeli army as well as the exclusive use of their servers for a state-run biometric ID system, is formally endorsed by BDS (BDS Movement, 2016, July 16).[8] This specific form of critical refusal directly aligns with recent community calls to disassociate from library-centered data firms that contract with Immigration and Customs Enforcement (ICE) in the United States and, consequently, facilitate deportations. Critical refusal vis á vis intentional divestment is a clearly defined form of economic action that can support collective, life-centered, and justice-oriented goals.

In the pivotal essay, "Librarianship at the Crossroads of ICE Surveillance," librarian and law professor Sarah Lamdan (2019) documents how large publishing companies like RELX Group (Reed Elsevier), Thomson Reuters, and LexisNexis fuel big data policing and provide data that allows for, "tracking immigrants and conducting raids at peoples' homes and workplaces" (para. 6). Lamdan (2019) asserts that, "our data is being collected by library vendors and sold to the police, including immigration enforcement officers, for millions of dollars" (para. 1). For libraries and library workers that oppose these developments, a vital response strategy is critical refusal. As evidenced in Lamdan's work, we can refuse by supporting campaigns that call for publishers to break their ICE contracts – like End the Contract and #NoTechForICE initiatives that are led by law school students and immigrant rights organizations – or through canceling our own agreements directly and refusing to work with vendors engaged in this kind of data extraction and violence (*End The Contract Coallition*, n.d.; Mijente, n.d.; Moody, 2021). Consequently, many leading issues in our profession, including how we enable carceral systems, engage in damaging data practices, or fail to adequately support our communities through the climate crisis, all require multiple modes of critical refusal to build a culture that embraces change, takes definitive action, and centers planetary survival.

Degrowth

As acutely demonstrated over the last several decades and heightened by the interlocking crises of the COVID-19 pandemic and the

---

8 While working on this chapter, popular news outlets reported that Google and Amazon shareholders are showing signs of dissent over proposed company involvement with a new Israeli-state cloud endeavor, Project Nimbus, which would centralize Israeli servers within the state and "insulate Israel's computing needs from threats of international boycotts" (Biddle, 2022). The future of this dissent is, as of publication, unknown but demonstrates a new, wider recognition of the ethical implications present in the Cloud.

racial reckoning of 2020, library and archival workers are expected to perform social service duties beyond their professional ones, reach high levels of productivity regardless of whatever current events may be impacting them personally, as well as onboard new projects without adequate funds necessary for labor or maintenance. Our field, our responsibilities, and our collections cannot continue to grow in this manner under such perpetual duress. Further, rhetoric around initiatives like collection-wide mass-digitization or the eternal maintenance of digital objects (whether they be Digital Humanities projects or born-digital records) ignore the material realities bubbling underneath each administrative request or grant-funded project. While cloud adoption has eased many aspects of our work by providing accessible cataloging software, collaborative editing tools, or third-party preservation platforms, its promise of endless capacity has also allowed our field, especially those at the top, to invest uncritically in new and "innovative" products or technological tools that often increase our workloads rather than streamline them. Media and ecology scholar Sy Taffel links ideas of material agnostic growth, like that which occurs in libraries, with the cognitive dissonance of this cultural moment. He states that "the fantasy that digital technology is somehow immaterial – that data is the ultimate renewable resource – allows the imagined continuation of the infinite economic growth that is required for current capitalist economic models to avoid collapse" (Taffel, 2021, p. 13). Infinite growth is not possible; therefore, embracing degrowth as a necessary framework and tactic – where we produce less and consume less – is essential for an ecologically-sound and life-centered future.

Though degrowth has been a theoretical concept discussed across numerous academic fields – most notably economics – since the 1970s, sustainability-minded political, scientific, and social movements started to embrace the term in the late 20th century (Paulson, 2017, p. 427). In "Libraries, Sustainability, and Degrowth," authors Edgardo Civallero and Sara Plaza (2016) establish degrowth as "a social movement anchored in ecologism, anti-capitalism and anti-consumerism" (p. 29). They argue that the ideology of degrowth "proposes that there are biophysical limits to growth that have already been exceeded... and it is therefore necessary to drastically reduce the levels of production and consumption – these levels being the main causes of all environmental problems (climate change, pollution, threats to biodiversity) and of many social inequalities" (Civallero & Plaza, 2016, p.

29). Throughout the article, Civallero and Plaza (2016) discuss existing environmental sustainability work within LIS as well as the necessity for libraries to become intentional activist spaces in favor of degrowth – encouraging workers to leverage collection-based resources and "critically assess the use and diffusion of particular technologies and the support they give them" (p. 35). In a direct reminder to the profession, Civallero and Plaza (2016) state that, "degrowth is no longer an option: the option is how to reach it" (p. 35).

For libraries, archives, and information work, degrowth offers us a critical lens with which to critique our administrative inner-workings – our budgets, vendor-agreements, technology selection, and service priorities. Anthropologist Susan Paulson (2017) argues that the "ideals of degrowth call us to shift value and desire away from productivist achievements and consumption-based identities toward visions of good life variously characterized by health, harmony, pleasure, and vitality among humans and ecosystems" (p. 426). As I have argued throughout this chapter, cloud-based technology has become ubiquitous within the realms of our work and our daily lives by providing us with an illusion of eco-friendly ease of use that is fully divorced from the waste, material constraints, and physical footprints that exist just outside our doors. The tools we choose to utilize, the projects we take on, and the protocols we follow are not apolitical or without power; thus, we must collectively prioritize new ways of thinking, working, and approaching climate change in our institutions and workplaces moving forward. In *Post-Growth Living: For an Alternative Hedonism*, Kate Soper (2020) embodies this call, stating that, "environmental crisis cannot be resolved by purely technical means, but will require richer societies substantially to change their way of living, working, and consuming" (p. 12). For libraries, archives, and other realms of information work – especially those who live in the Global North or otherwise emissions-heavy nations – responding to the crisis of climate change should not be about adopting new technology, buying up faulty carbon credits, attaching ourselves to the next "green" innovation, or appeasing our superiors through unachievable growth-based ideals of success. Rather, we should embody degrowth and critical refusal by scaling back our technological investments (including our use of the Cloud), restructuring how we work, as well as reprioritizing maintenance and repair in services and operations.

Moving Forward

Resistance to environmental degradation is scripted, expected. Actively pursuing environmental interventions is less so.

– Buck, 2019, p. 164

Throughout their 2021 book, *Pollution is Colonialism*, scholar and scientist Max Liboiron elucidates the intrinsic connections between settler colonialism, pollution, and the global rise in plastic production, while sharing practical recommendations for doing anti-colonial science. In speaking about their intentional methods-centric work with the Civic Laboratory for Environmental Action Research (CLEAR), Liboiron (2021) offers that, "sometimes protocols are prescriptive, and sometimes they are about the maintenance of everyday life, but they are always orienting you toward a particular horizon and away from others. They are reproductive technologies" (p. 124). Much of Liboiron's work with CLEAR highlights the power of praxis, and in libraries, archives, and across information work, we must see that the work we do is forever building upon itself. As libraries and archives are not ahistorical institutions, the future practices of our field have yet to be defined. Therefore, we can make different choices, refuse to perform tasks that are harmful, and decrease what projects we take on in a way that aligns better with what we need to do to support our planet, thereby supporting our communities and ourselves. Simply, our current path is not viable, and we need to shift our mindsets and actions towards the already arrived storm of climate change.

Engaging with critical refusal and degrowth at a state or national level, then, functions as a method of both institutional response as well as call to action. Through legislative lobbying by city, state, or national professional organizations, libraries and archives could reject the specific oil contracts, usage of non-renewable energy, and clandestine water rights given to data centers in our local areas. The potential for such organizations to successfully lobby against new oil and gas drilling contracts state-by-state would be extremely challenging but narrowing our focus to specific, active vendor relationships is possible and, in fact, reasonable. One vendor causing environmental havoc, in addition to being known for their predatory financial and data sharing behaviors (Buranyi, 2017; Lamdan, 2019; Resnick & Belluz, 2019), is RELX

Group (Reed Elsevier). Just as current cloud technology ensures the future of oil and gas, Elsevier has, "for more than a decade ... supported the energy industry's efforts to optimize oil and gas extraction" as the top publisher for books aimed at expanding fossil fuel production (Westervelt, 2022). Could or should our field refute the holdings of academic publishing magnates? If so, what transformations within our field would be needed to generate this kind of collective, critical refusal? Lastly, for the public employees among us, we could lean on the same tactics of critical refusal to pressure our pension fund managers to take concrete action: first to divest from fossil fuels; then to divest from any corporation that utilizes their Cloud to boost new oil discovery. From my perspective, these questions and suggested actions call attention to the urgent necessity of transforming our professional practice in the face of the ongoing climate crisis.

Looking ever more closely at critical refusal and degrowth, I believe that workers within libraries and archives should also look toward our collective professional future(s) by examining the environmental viability of our initiatives, programs, and processes. To me, such internal assessments of information services extend beyond the performativity of reusable straws or eco-wellness programs, as they are instead grounded in the material realities of our work and provide space for broad *collective* – not individual – action. For instance, cloud-based digital archives and continued preservation are deeply energy-intensive and require constant attention – will there be a point at which we collectively sunset such activities (Pendergrass et al., 2019)? Or should we focus less on the relatively small energy footprint of digital collections and re-evaluate the ways in which our institutional practices ignore the ecological impact of the technologies we use? Can we restructure the "make-and-dispose approach" (Finn et al., 2020, p. 23) of entrepreneurial-driven makerspaces to those that center maintenance and repair instead? In eliminating some of our cloud-based and waste-heavy commitments, I believe that our field-wide definitions surrounding success, innovation, and progress will also need to evolve. For example, what does technological innovation look like after growth? Will institutional ideals of innovation in libraries ever mean reuse and repair? Though we cannot reject all cloud-based library technology since our dependence on these systems is too vast, as professionals, we must question how we select these tools, the terms on which we provide them to our communities, and what climate change discourse we maintain with our users.

Conclusion

Hope is a discipline.[9]

– Mariame Kaba

For decades, we have been intentionally deceived about the realities of climate change by powerful corporations and failed by our governments in finding viable solutions as carbon emissions have continued to grow. Regardless, we still have more control over our future than those in power often lead us to believe. In echoing the words of Audre Lorde, taking informed action is the only path forward to meet this "approaching storm" (Lorde, 2012, p. 130). Though I have written specifically on the Cloud, the core of this theoretical framework applies to other areas of librarianship and archives work. Critical refusal offers those of us who labor in the information domain the possibility to reject collectively, or at least reduce our reliance on, technologies that perpetuate harm to our planet, our communities, and ourselves. Degrowth, then, allows for a collective release of unnecessary responsibilities and expectations, helping us create space for stronger alignment and deeper engagement around relevant, region-specific climate solutions.[10] Future examination of the questions raised here would benefit from an analysis of the influence of settler colonialism on libraries and computing technology, the characteristics of white supremacy culture (specifically the notion of urgency) in institutional responses to change (Okun, 2021), crisis epistemologies and the impact of entrenched power in institutional decision making (Whyte, 2020), as well as knowledge production in the time of climate change, among others. Rather than focusing on individual fixes that may have a marginal impact on carbon decline, we can direct our collective mental, physical, and emotional energy towards the structures that are both causing and benefiting from these numerous, intersecting disasters.

---

9   See Kaba (2022) – Mariame Kaba's personal website – for an introduction to Kaba's profound abolitionist work as well as a list of her numerous publications and interviews.

10   See Brunvand (2020) for a deeper examination of sustainability-minded and place-based librarianship.

References

AI Now Institute. (n.d.). Retrieved January 31, 2022, from https://ainowinstitute.org/

Amazon. (n.d.). *Water stewardship*. AWS sustainability. Retrieved May 20, 2022, from https://sustainability.aboutamazon.com/environment/the-cloud/water-stewardship

Ambrose, J. (2019, September 20). Google signs up to $2bn wind and solar investment. *The Guardian*. https://www.theguardian.com/technology/2019/sep/20/google-says-its-energy-deals-will-lead-to-2bn-wind-and-solar-investment

Amoore, L. (2018). Cloud geographies: Computing, data, sovereignty. *Progress in Human Geography*, 42(1), 4–24. https://doi.org/10.1177/0309132516662147

Baillot, A., Baker, J., Choksi, M. Z., Gil, A., Lam, A., Peaker, A., Scholger, W., Roeder, T., & Walton, J. L. (2021). *Digital humanities and the climate crisis*. https://dhc-barnard.github.io/dhclimate/

BDS Movement. (2016, July 16). *Boycott HP*. https://bdsmovement.net/boycott-hp

BDS Movement. (2016, April 25). *What is BDS?* https://bdsmovement.net/what-is-bds

Biddle, S. (2022, May 18). Google and Amazon face shareholder revolt over Israeli defense work. *The Intercept*. https://theintercept.com/2022/05/18/google-amazon-israel-military-nimbus/

Bowker, G. C., Timmermans, S., Clarke, A. E., & Balka, E. (2016). The ethnography of infrastructure. In *Boundary objects and beyond: Working with Leigh Star* (pp. 473–488). MIT Press. http://ieeexplore.ieee.org/document/7580150

Brunvand, A. (2020). Re-Localizing the library: Considerations for the Anthropocene. *Journal of Critical Library and Information Studies*, 3(1), Article 1. https://doi.org/10.24242/jclis.v3i1.94

Buck, H. J. (2019). *After geoengineering: Climate tragedy, repair, and restoration*. Verso.

Buck, H. J. (2022, March 27). Decarbonization as a service. *Logic Magazine*. https://logicmag.io/clouds/decarbonization-as-a-service/

Buranyi, S. (2017, June 27). Is the staggeringly profitable business of scientific publishing bad for science? *The Guardian*. https://www.theguardian.com/science/2017/jun/27/profitable-business-scientific-publishing-bad-for-science

Burrington, I. (2015, December 16). The environmental toll of a Netflix binge. *The Atlantic*. https://www.theatlantic.com/technology/archive/2015/12/there-are-no-clean-clouds/420744/

Burrington, I. (2016, January 8). Why Amazon's data centers are hidden in spy country. *The Atlantic*. https://www.theatlantic.com/technology/archive/2016/01/amazon-web-services-data-center/423147/

California Library Association. (n.d.). *Climate justice*. Retrieved June 3, 2022, from https://www.cla-net.org/page/1191

Carruth, A. (2014). The digital cloud and the micropolitics of energy. *Public Culture, 26*(2), 339–364. https://doi.org/10.1215/08992363-2392093

Cifor, M., Garcia, P., Cowan, T. L., Rault, J., Sutherland, T., Chan, A., Rode, J., Hoffmann, A. L., Salehi, N., & Nakamura, L. (2019). *Feminist data manifest-no*. https://www.manifestno.com/

Civallero, E., & Plaza, S. (2016). Libraries, sustainability and degrowth. *Progressive Librarian, 25*, 20–45.

Department of Defense. (2018). *Deputy Secretary of Defense memorandum: DoDcloud strategy*. https://media.defense.gov/2019/Feb/04/2002085866/-1/-1/1/DOD-CLOUD-STRATEGY.PDF

Digital Preservation Coalition. (2014, November 9). *The DPC aims to achieve 'A political and institutional climate responsive to the need for digital preservation.'* https://www.dpconline.org/news/the-digital-preservation-coalition-dpc-aims-to-achieve-a-political-and-institutional-climate-responsive-to-the-need-for-digital-preservation

DLF. (2021). *2021 DLF forum: Online*. https://www.diglib.org/dlf-events/2021-dlf-forum/

Donaghy, T., Henderson, C., & Jardim, E. (2020, May 19). *Oil in the cloud*. Greenpeace USA. https://www.greenpeace.org/usa/reports/oil-in-the-cloud/

Edwards, P. N. (2017). Knowledge infrastructures for the Anthropocene. *The Anthropocene Review, 4*(1), 34–43. https://doi.org/10.1177/2053019616679854

Elgin, B., & Mider, Z. (2020, December 17). The real trees delivering fake corporate climate progress. *Bloomberg*. https://www.bloomberg.com/news/features/2020-12-17/the-real-trees-delivering-fake-climate-progress-for-corporate-america

Emanuel, Kerry. (2019). *Climate science, risk & solutions*. MIT. https://climateprimer.mit.edu

End The Contract Coalition. (n.d.). *End the contract*. Retrieved December 16, 2021, from https://endthecontract.wixsite.com/home

Ensmenger, N. (2018). The environmental history of computing. *Technology and Culture, 59*(4S), S7–S33. https://doi.org/10.1353/tech.2018.0148

Finn, M., Rosner, D. K., Black, S., Cunningham, N., Dew, K. N., Hoy, J., McCraney, K., & Morgan, C. (2020). Troubled worlds: A course syllabus about information work and the Anthropocene. *Journal of Critical Library and Information Studies, 3*(1), Article 1. https://doi.org/10.24242/jclis.v3i1.137

Fountain, H. (2022, February 14). How bad is the Western drought? Worst in 12 centuries, study finds. *The New York Times*. https://www.nytimes.com/2022/02/14/climate/western-drought-megadrought.html

Garcia, P., Sutherland, T., Cifor, M., Chan, A. S., Klein, L., D'Ignazio, C., & Salehi, N. (2020). No: Critical refusal as feminist data practice. *Conference Companion Publication of the 2020 on Computer Supported*

Cooperative Work and Social Computing, 199–202. https://doi.org/10.1145/3406865.3419014

Gonzalez Monserrate, S. (2022, March 1). The staggering ecological impacts of computation and the cloud. *Scientific American*. https://www.scientificamerican.com/article/the-staggering-ecological-impacts-of-computation-and-the-cloud/

Google. (n.d.). *Cloud sustainability*. Retrieved May 20, 2022, from https://cloud.google.com/sustainability

Greenfield, P. (2021, May 4). Carbon offsets used by major airlines based on flawed system, warn experts. *The Guardian*. https://www.theguardian.com/environment/2021/may/04/carbon-offsets-used-by-major-airlines-based-on-flawed-system-warn-experts

Hogan, M. (2015a). Facebook data storage centers as the archive's underbelly. *Television & New Media*, *16*(1), 3–18. https://doi.org/10.1177/1527476413509415

Hogan, M. (2015b). Data flows and water woes: The Utah Data Center. *Big Data & Society*, *2*(2), 1–12. https://doi.org/10.1177/2053951715592429

Hu, T.-H. (2015). *A prehistory of the cloud*. The MIT Press.

Ida B. Wells Just Data Lab. (2021). *Welcome to the lab*. https://www.thejustdatalab.com

Irfan, U. (2021a, February 18). Scientists are divided over whether climate change is fueling extreme cold events. *Vox*. https://www.vox.com/22287295/texas-uri-climate-change-cold-polar-vortex-arctic

Irfan, U., & Leber, R. (2021b, August 9). "There's no going back": The UN's dire new climate report, explained. *Vox*. https://www.vox.com/22613027/un-ipcc-climate-change-report-ar6-disaster

Johnson, A. (2019). Emplacing data within imperial histories: Imagining Iceland as data centers' 'natural' home. *Culture Machine*, *18*, 12.

Kaba, M. (2022). About me. *Being MK – My personal website*. http://mariamekaba.com/

Lamdan, S. (2019). Librarianship at the crossroads of ICE surveillance. *In the Library with the Lead Pipe*. https://www.inthelibrarywiththeleadpipe.org/2019/ice-surveillance/

Lawton, M. (2020, September 1). Ready for action. *American Libraries Magazine*. https://americanlibrariesmagazine.org/2020/09/01/ready-for-action-climate-action-plans/

Leahy, S. (2021, July 31). If the hardiest species are boiled alive, what happens to humans? *The Atlantic*. https://www.theatlantic.com/ideas/archive/2021/07/billions-victims-heat-dome/619604/

Lewis, S. L., Wheeler, C. E., Mitchard, E. T. A., & Koch, A. (2019). Restoring natural forests is the best way to remove atmospheric carbon. *Nature*, *568*(7750), 25–28. https://doi.org/10.1038/d41586-019-01026-8

Liboiron, M. (2018, November 1). Waste colonialism. *Discard Studies.* https://discardstudies.com/2018/11/01/waste-colonialism/

Liboiron, M. (2021). *Pollution is colonialism.* Duke University Press.

Lorde, A. (2012). *Sister outsider: Essays and speeches.* Crossing Press.

Markman, J. (2021, February 9). Why the cloud is Amazon's future. *Forbes.* https://www.forbes.com/sites/jonmarkman/2021/02/09/why-the-cloud-is-amazons-future/

Mattern, S. (2017). The big data of ice, rocks, soils, and sediments. *Places Journal.* https://doi.org/10.22269/171107

Microsoft. (n.d.). Green cloud computing. *Microsoft Research.* Retrieved May 20, 2022, from https://www.microsoft.com/en-us/research/project/green-cloud-computing/

Mijente. (n.d.). *#NoTechForICE.* Retrieved February 16, 2022, from https://notechforice.com/lawletter/

Miller, S. (2021, December 8). The millions of tons of carbon emissions that don't officially exist. *The New Yorker.* https://www.newyorker.com/news/annals-of-a-warming-planet/the-millions-of-tons-of-carbon-emissions-that-dont-officially-exist

Moody, J. (2021, December 6). *Law students protest research database contracts with ICE.* Inside Higher Ed. https://www.insidehighered.com/news/2021/12/06/law-students-protest-lexisnexis-westlaw-contracts-ice

Munn, L. (2021). Data and the new oil: Cloud computing's lubrication of the petrotechnical. *Journal of Environmental Media, 2*(2), 211–227. https://doi.org/10.1386/jem_00063_1

Nowviskie, B. (2014, July 10). *Digital humanities in the Anthropocene.* http://nowviskie.org/2014/anthropocene/

Okun, T. (2021). Urgency. *White supremacy culture.* https://www.whitesupremacyculture.info/urgency.html

Parks, B. W. (2021, November 9). The Dalles approves controversial water deal with Google. *OPB.* https://www.opb.org/article/2021/11/09/google-the-dalles-water-data-center/

Pasek, A. (2019). Managing carbon and data flows: Fungible forms of mediation in the Cloud. *Culture Machine, 18,* 1–15.

Paulson, S. (2017). Degrowth: Culture, power and change. *Journal of Political Ecology, 24*(1). https://doi.org/10.2458/v24i1.20882

Pendergrass, K. L., Sampson, W., Walsh, T., & Alagna, L. (2019). Toward environmentally sustainable digital preservation. *The American Archivist, 82*(1), 165–206. https://doi.org/10.17723/0360-9081-82.1.165

Resnick, B., & Belluz, J. (2019, July 10). The war to free science. *Vox.* https://www.vox.com/the-highlight/2019/6/3/18271538/open-access-elsevier-california-sci-hub-academic-paywalls

Riofrancos, T. (2019, December 7). What green costs. *Logic Magazine*. https://logic-mag.io/nature/what-green-costs/

Sauli, A. (2021, February 25). Study measured the carbon footprint of Finnish public libraries. *Libraries.fi*. https://www.libraries.fi/news/study-measured-the-carbon-footprint-of-finnish-public-libraries?language_content_entity=en

Sax, S. (2021, September 13). Why investing in libraries is a climate justice issue. *High Country News*. https://www.hcn.org/articles/north-social-justice-why-investing-in-libraries-is-a-climate-justice-issue

Solon, O. (2021, June 19). Drought-stricken communities push back against data centers. *NBC News*. https://www.nbcnews.com/tech/internet/drought-stricken-communities-push-back-against-data-centers-n1271344

Song, L. (2019, May 22). An (even more) inconvenient truth: Why carbon credits for forest preservation may be worse than nothing. *ProPublica*. https://features.propublica.org/brazil-carbon-offsets/inconvenient-truth-carbon-credits-dont-work-deforestation-redd-acre-cambodia/

Soper, K. (2020). *Post-growth living: For an alternative hedonism*. Verso.

Starosielski, N. (2015). *The undersea network*. Duke University Press.

Suchman, L. (2020, January 11). Patterns of life: AI and "actionable data" in warfare. *BLARB*. http://blog.lareviewofbooks.org/provocations/patterns-life-ai-translates-human-activities-actionable-data-war/

Sustainability Round Table. (2013, May 8). *Sustainability Round Table*. ALA Round Tables. https://www.ala.org/rt/sustainrt

Sustainable Libraries Initiative. (n.d.). *About us*. Retrieved June 9, 2022, from https://sustainablelibrariesinitiative.org/about-us

Sustainability Round Table. (2021, May 15). *SustainRT strategic plan 2021-2024*. https://docs.google.com/document/d/17208EvSLmVGblRSlc6iVgOZv9F2HhaowOO6uU3ySKH4/

Taffel, S. (2021). Data and oil: Metaphor, materiality and metabolic rifts. *New Media & Society*, 1–19. https://doi.org/10.1177/14614448211017887

Tansey, E. (2015). Archival adaptation to climate change. *Sustainability: Science, Practice and Policy*, *11*(2), 45–56. https://doi.org/10.1080/15487733.2015.11908146

Tansey, E. (2022). Archives and climate change. *UCLA California Rare Book School*. https://www.calrbs.org/program/courses/archives-and-climate-change/

Taylor, A. R. E. (2019). The data center as technological wilderness. *Culture Machine*, *18*, 30.

The DAIR Institute. (n.d.). Retrieved June 9, 2022, from https://www.dair-institute.org

United Nations. (2021, August 9). IPCC report: 'Code red' for human driven global heating, warns UN chief. *UN News*. https://news.un.org/en/story/2021/08/1097362

Very Like a Whale. (2022, March 27). *Logic Magazine*. https://logicmag.io/clouds/very-like-a-whale/

Vonderau, A. (2019). Storing data, infrastructuring the air: Thermocultures of the cloud. *Culture Machine, 18*, 12.

Westervelt, A. (2022, February 24). Revealed: Leading climate research publisher helps fuel oil and gas drilling. *The Guardian*. https://www.theguardian.com/environment/2022/feb/24/elsevier-publishing-climate-science-fossil-fuels

Whyte, K. (2020). Against crisis epistemology. In B. Hokowhitu, A. Moreton-Robinson, L. Tuhiwai-Smith, C. Andersen, & S. Larkin (Eds.), *Routledge handbook of critical Indigenous studies* (1st ed., pp. 52–64). Routledge. https://doi.org/10.4324/9780429440229-6

Winn, S. R. (2020). Dying well in the Anthropocene: On the end of archivists. *Journal of Critical Library and Information Studies*, 3(1), Article 1. https://doi.org/10.24242/jclis.v3i1.107

Zero Cool. (2019, December 7). Oil is the new data. *Logic Magazine*. https://logicmag.io/nature/oil-is-the-new-data/

Zvyagintseva, L. (2021). Articulating our very unfreedom: The impossibility of refusal in the contemporary academy. *Canadian Journal of Academic Librarianship, 7*, 1–24. https://doi.org/10.33137/cjalrcbu.v7.36367

About the Contributors

Danielle Marie Bitz of mixed Métis and German-Ukrainian descent and has familial ties to both Métis and settler communities across the prairies. Danielle was born and raised in Mohkinstsis-Calgary and currently resides in central Winnipeg in an apartment that overlooks the historic trade route that is the Assiniboine river. Danielle holds a Master of Library and Information Studies (University of Alberta, 2020) and a professional position as the Indigenous Engagement Librarian at the University of Winnipeg.

Jedidiah Crook has spent much of his career working at the intersection of social justice and education. He worked internationally with Protestant and Catholic youth from Northern Ireland as well as locally to his home state of New Hampshire as the Assistant Supervisor and Resource Educator of the Adolescent Boys unit at the Nashua Children's Home. He studied the role of colonialism in K-12 science education at Keene State College where he worked in the Office for Multicultural Student Support and Success. He currently works with the Organization of Refugee and Immigrant Success in their New American Farmers Program that empowers refugees and new Americans through food sovereignty and small-scale agricultural entrepreneurship.

Ashley Edwards has Métis, Dutch, and Scottish heritage, and is a citizen of Métis Nation British Columbia. She was raised in Stó:lō territory, in British Columbia, without connection to her Métis roots. Her parents instilled a sense of pride about her Indigenous heritage as a child, and learning about her Indigenity has been a journey of personal discovery, without Elders to guide her. She is grateful for the connections being made within the MNBC community. Ashley has a Library Technician diploma (2009), and a BA in Adult

Education (2015) from the University of the Fraser Valley, and a MLIS degree from the University of Alberta (2020).

Mary Greenshields is a settler librarian and doctoral student from the lands of the Stoney, Očhéthi Šakówiŋ, Niitsitapii, Cree, and Métis. Her research interests exist at the intersections of feminism, love studies, critical pedagogy and librarianship, and settler-Indigenous relations. She lives and works in Florence, Italy.

Ariel Hahn is an information worker, writer, and artist. Ariel has an MLIS from UCLA and identifies as a white, queer, working class settler with Jewish immigrant and colonial era-ancestry. Ariel grew up in Southern Arizona on the traditional homelands of the O'odham people and, at present, lives on unceded Tongva/Gabrieliño land in what is now known as Los Angeles.

Truc Ho is a graduate from the Master of Library and Information Science program at the University of Washington and a 2021-2022 ALA Spectrum Scholar. Currently a data analyst, Truc has previously worked in academic libraries supporting and leading data assessment and visualization projects. Additionally, Truc has a background in nonprofit, focuses on database management and community engagement.

Laura Marie Judge currently works at the Chelmsford Public Library as the Head of Reference and Technology Services Department. Besides working in public libraries, Laura has also been a research assistant at Harvard, a lecturer at Keene State College, a teacher, audio-visual archivist, and has spent time on the lecture circuit in Hungary. She holds a BA in Film Critical Studies, an MA in Film Theory, and a forthcoming degree MS in Library and Information Science. Her research interests include race, gender, and social justice in LIS, technofeminism, and disability studies.

Dr. Julia Lane is a white settler with British, Irish, and Scottish ancestry. Her parents met in Clearwater, Florida (where her mother, Dawn, was raised), Lands of the Tocobaga people. They returned to the territory where her father, Steve, was from, married, and raised their children on the Lands of the Anishnaabe, Haudenosaunee, Mississaugas of the Credit, and Wendat Peoples (near what is colonially known as Toronto, Ontario). Julia's first memories of learning about Indigenous Peoples, cultures, art, languages, and Lands came when her mother returned to school to pursue a BEd and BFA at York University. There, she took Indigenous studies courses and brought what she was learning home to her family.

Julia was privileged to continue this learning through her own education, including during her BA in theatre studies at York University, but especially with her MA in Canadian Studies and Indigenous Studies at Trent University, and her Phd in Arts Education at SFU. Through her studies and her work, Julia has met and learned from many Elders, Knowledge Keepers, and Indigenous artists and scholars and she carries them all with gratitude in her heart as she strives to walk in a good way on Indigenous Lands.

Courtney S. Nomiyama is a recent graduate of the Master of Library and Information Science program at the University of Washington and a 2019-2020 ALA Spectrum Scholar. She currently works as a librarian at a community college, where she provides reference and instruction services. Her interests include critical librarianship, digital humanities, and community engagement.

Dr. Alix Shield is a white settler of English and Scottish ancestry; she was born and raised in Vancouver on the ancestral, traditional, and unceded territories of the xʷməθkʷəy̓əm (Musqueam), Skwxwú7mesh (Squamish), and Səl̓ílwətaʔ/Selilwitulh (Tsleil-Waututh) Nations. Alix completed her MA in English at Dalhousie University on unceded Mi'kmaq territory, where she took a course on Indigenous Literatures that opened her eyes, mind, and heart to Indigenous perspectives (particularly through the work of Kanien'kehá:ka writer E. Pauline Johnson). Upon returning to Vancouver, Alix completed her PhD at SFU, focusing on the Canadian publishing industry and its historical marginalization of Indigenous women's writing and literary agency. Alix is deeply grateful to the Indigenous faculty, mentors, and community members that she has developed relationships with and has learned from (and continues to learn from) over the years. Alix is privileged to live and work on the traditional territories of the Hul'qumi'num-speaking Snuneymuxw First Nation (Nanaimo, Vancouver Island).

Daljit (Dal) Sohal is South Asian of Indian ancestry. She was born in England and moved to what is colonially known as British Columbia at the age of two with her parents. Like many immigrants from countries that have felt the enduring impact of colonial rule (like her parents from India), they moved to Canada in search of a "better life." Dal was raised on the territories of the Semiahmoo, Katzie,

Kwikwetlem, Kwantlen, Qayqayt, and Tsawwassen Nations. Dal extends gratitude to the Coast Salish Peoples who have walked gently on these territories since time immemorial and strives to be a good relative, honouring past and present caretakers. Dal has a MA in Leadership and Training from Royal Roads University and a BA from Simon Fraser University.

Andrew Weymouth is an archivist, exhibit designer and writer working in Tacoma, WA. He is the recipient of the 2021 Visual Resources Association Foundation grant, the University of Oregon's Vollstedt Internship program and the University of Washington's Storytelling Fellows. He has created digital exhibits for faculty concerning Indigenous higher education reform, digital scholarship curricular toolkits and a Middle Eastern graphic novel database for The Evergreen State College, The University of Oregon and The University of Washington respectively. Previous writing concerning displacement, immigration and oral history have been published in the Society of American Archivists' *Archival Outlook* and *The Serials Librarian*.

Gregory Whistance-Smith holds graduate degrees in Architecture and Digital Humanities, and his research explores the relationship between design, technology, and culture in the built environment. He has a long interest in how library architecture can meaningfully serve its communities, and his recent book *Expressive Space* explores the semiotics of video game environments. Gregory practices architecture and design in Edmonton, Canada.

Lydia Zvyagintseva is the Head of Digital Scholarship Services at the University of Alberta. She holds graduate degrees in French Language and Literature, Digital Humanities, and Library and Information Studies, and has published on open data, digital exhibits, labour, and refusal. She has worked in public and academic libraries, including the University of Toronto Scarborough Campus and the Edmonton Public Library. An immigrant from Kharkiv, Ukraine who has lived primarily on Treaty 6 territory, she is currently interested in epistemology and violence.

Index

Abenakis, 7-8, 64-68, 70, 75, 76, 83-85, 87
academic libraries. *See* libraries, academic
ACRL. *See* Association of College and Research Libraries
Akers, W. J., 22
ALA. *See* American Library Association
alienation, 5
American Library Association, 15, 30, 81, 146, 173
Ancient Order of Vikings. *See* Gamle Vikingers Forbund
Association of College and Research Libraries, 100-101
Astoria Public Library, 13, 28
Atelier TAG, 50
Atherton, Gertrude, 21, 28
autoethnography, 9

Bancroft, H. H., 16, 22, 31
Batoche, 155-156, 159-161
BDS Movement. *See* Boycott, Divestment, and Sanctions Movement
Bibliothèque Sainte-Geneviève, 37
Bitz, Danielle Marie, 5-6, 9, 147-150, 157-162, 187
Boise, R. P., 26
Boycott, Divestment, and Sanctions Movement, 174-175
Brayboy, Bryan McKinley Jones, 68
Briarpatch, 4

Canadian Federation of Library Associations' Indigenous Matters Committee, 123
Canadian Reading Camp Association, 18, 25, 28
carbon footprint, 168
Carnegie, Andrew, 14, 28, 31, 38, 47
CFLAIMC/FCAB. *See* Canadian Federation of Library Associations' Indigenous Matters Committee
Chautauquas, 14, 24-26
Chemawa Indian School, 24
Civic Laboratory for Environmental Action Research, 178
CLEAR. *See* Civic Laboratory for Environmental Action Research
climate change, 2, 4, 9, 168, 180
cloud-based technologies, 9, 167-170, 180
colonialism, 1, 5, 7, 14, 15, 64, 95, 96
conceptual metaphor, 7, 39, 45-48, 59

critical refusal, 173-175, 178-180
critical regionalism, 39, 42-44, 59-60
Croatian Fraternal Union of America, 19
Crocker, Charles, 16-17
Crook, Jedidiah, 5-6, 7-8, 187
Cushman Indian School, 24

Dashaway Society, 19
Daughters of the Nile, 26
decolonization, 2, 8, 9, 65, 97-100, 107-108, 110-112, 139, 149
DEI efforts. *See* Diversity, Equality, and Inclusion efforts
degrowth, 9, 175-177, 178-180
Dencke, E. A., 21
Dewey, Melville, 28
Diversity, Equality, and Inclusion efforts, 8, 95, 98-100, 104, 106-108, 110, 112-113
Doheny, Edward L., 16

Edmonton Public Library system
  Calder branch, 7, 39-40, 48-54, 59-60
  Capilano branch, 7, 39-40, 48-49, 54-60
  Central branch, 2
Edwards, Ashley, 5-6, 8-9, 187-188
Eells, Edwin, 23
Eells, Myron, 23-24
embodied cognition, 44
enactive perception, 7, 39, 45-48, 59

First Archivists Circle, 81-82
Fish Creek, 155
Fitzpatrick, Alfred, 17-18, 25
Frampton, Kenneth, 42-44
fraternal organizations, 14, 19-20
Freemasons, 19-20
Funambulist, 4

Gabriel's Crossing, 144
Gamle Vikingers Forbund, 19
gas extraction, 9, 14, 64, 167-168, 179
genus loci, 39, 40-42, 44, 46-48, 59-60
Grange, 20-21, 30
grange libraries. *See* libraries, grange
Greenpeace, 170-171
Greenshields, Mary, 188
Group2, 54

Haabet Literary Society, 19
Hague Ferry, 143

Hahn, Ariel, 9, 188
Ho, Truc, 5, 8, 188
Holbrook, Josiah, 24
Hopkins, Mark, 16-17
Huntington, Collins P., 16-17

ICR. *See* Indigenous content requirement
identification (aspect of dwelling), 41, 46-47
Indian boarding school movement, 23-24
Indigenous content requirement, 99-100
Indigenous knowledge, 6, 64-65, 67-68, 78, 84-85, 97-99, 110-111, 121, 138, 149
Indigenous naming practices, 127
information work, 2, 5, 9, 168
intersectionality, 132-133
Italian Cacciatori D'Africa Society, 19

Jones, William Arthur, 23
Judge, Laura Marie, 5-6, 7-8, 188

Kansas City Public Library, 43
Kelly, Oliver H., 20
Knights of Labor, 22

Labor Library, 22, 25, 30-31
Lady Bountiful, 29-30
land acknowledgements
  examples of, 63-64, 124, 126, 133-134
  importance of positionality to, 125-126, 132-133
  lack of, 103
  purpose of, 124-125, 138-139
  reflective process in, 125, 129-130
  relationship to Diversity, Equality and Inclusion efforts, 95
  vocabulary choice, 124, 134-137
  workshops about, 8-9, 129-130
land-based education, 8, 95, 97-100, 105-106
land grabs, 14, 17-18, 64, 73
land in archives, 3, 5
land in learning, 9
land in libraries, 1-2, 6-9, 14
land in museums, 3
Lane, Julia, 5, 8-9, 188-189
learning organizations, 1, 2, 7
Leupp, Francis E., 24
libraries, academic
  colonialism in, 5
  decolonization of, 8, 95
  in Canada, 2
  in the United States, 2, 8, 95-96, 101
  Indigenous spaces, 2
  research commons, 8
  social media, 101-102
  websites, 101-102
libraries, grange, 14, 20-21, 30

libraries, public
  closed stack system, 13
  history of, 7, 13-14, 28-30, 37
  in Canada, 2
  in the United States, 2, 7-8, 13-15, 30, 37, 66, 68
  Indigenous spaces, 2
  service models, 7, 13-14
libraries, research, 8
library and information science, 5, 6, 15, 65, 81
library architecture, 2, 7, 38, 47-48
Library Association of Portland, 13
library design
  history of, 37-39
  inclusion of Indigenous spaces, 2
  relation to place, 2, 7, 38-40, 60
library neutrality, 5, 14-15, 19, 65, 137, 146
library research commons, 8, 95-98, 100-113
LIS. *See* library and information science
local history collections, 7-8, 66, 69-87, 92
lyceums, 14, 24-26

Marc Boutin Architectural Collaborative, 50
Maynard, Catherine, 28
MBAC. *See* Marc Boutin Architectural Collaborative
Mechanics' Institute, 21-22
memory institutions, 1-2
Métis, 6, 9, 143-149, 187
mining, 14, 16
Mission Santa Barbara, 16
Montgomery, Catherine, 29
Moore, Grace R., 28
Morrow, Lena, 26

national identity, 30, 64, 65
New Hampshire Library Association, 81, 86
New Hampshire Public Library system, 7-8, 64, 66, 68-70, 92-93
New Whatcom State Normal School, 29
Nomiyama, Courtney S., 5, 8, 189
Norberg-Schulz, Christian, 39-42, 44, 46-48, 59-60

off-reservation Indian boarding schools, 14, 22-24, 137-138
oil extraction, 9, 14, 16, 64, 167-168, 179
Oregon Federation of Women's Clubs, 29
orientation (aspect of dwelling), 41

paddling as method of inquiry, 9, 143, 150-152, 155-157, 162, 164
Patkau Architects, 54
Petite Ville, 143-144, 164
positionality, 5, 8, 29, 125-126, 132-133
Positionality and Land Acknowledgement Writing Workshop, 8-9, 129-130

Pratt, Richard Henry, 23
Pride Toronto, 124, 128
Progressive Literary and Fraternal Club, 29
public libraries. *See* libraries, public

Quimby, Lida W., 24

recognition, 5
relationality, 5, 125
research commons. *See* library research commons
research libraries. *See* libraries, research

Sacramento Lyceum, 25
San Francisco Mercantile Library, 22, 28
Seattle Central Library, 38
Seattle Federation of Women's Clubs, 29
settler colonialism, 7, 29-30, 64-65, 69, 76, 86, 92, 95-96, 180
SFU ARC. *See* Simon Fraser University's Aboriginal Reconciliation Council
Shield, Alix, 5, 8-9, 189
Simon Fraser University, 127
Simon Fraser University's Aboriginal Reconciliation Council, 123, 129
Simon Fraser University's Decolonizing the Library Interest Group, 8-9, 128-130
silver extraction, 16
Sohal, Daljit, 5, 8-9, 189-190
South Saskatchewan River, 9
Spanish California Missions, 15-16
St. Laurent Ferry, 162
Stanford, Leland, 16-17
suffrage groups, 27-28
Sutro, Adolph, 16
Switzer, Lucy, 18
Sydney Opera House, 46

temperance groups, 14, 18-19, 28
TribalCrit. *See* tribal critical race theory
tribal critical race theory, 68
Troutdale Woman's Club, 28
Tulalip Reservation school, 22-23

University of Washington Libraries, 95
UW Libraries. *See* University of Washington Libraries

Wade, C.B., 29
walking as method of inquiry, 9, 150-151
Walla Walla Lyceum and Library Association, 25
WCLU. *See* Western Central Labor Union
Western Central Labor Union, 22
Western Washington University, 29
Weymouth, Andrew, 2, 5, 7, 190
Whitstance-Smith, Gregory, 2, 7, 190
Wilkinson, Melville Cary, 23
Willamette Valley Chautauqua Association, 26
Woman's Christian Temperance Unions, 18, 19, 22, 30
women's clubs, 14, 26-30
Women's Crusade, 18
WTCU. *See* Woman's Christian Temperance Unions

YMCA. *See* Young Men's Christian Association
Young Men's Christian Association, 19, 26

Zvyagintseva, Lydia, 190

www.ingramcontent.com/pod-product-compliance
Lightning Source LLC
Chambersburg PA
CBHW041439300426
44114CB00026B/2943